UNLOCKING WRITING

A Guide for Teachers

Edited by

Mary Williams

David Fulton Publishers

David Fulton Publishers Ltd
The Chiswick Centre, 414 Chiswick High Road, London W4 5TF

www.fultonpublishers.co.uk

First published in Great Britain in 2002 by David Fulton Publishers

Note: The right of Mary Williams to be identified as the editor of this work has been asserted by her in accordance with the Copyright, Designs and Patents Act 1988.

Copyright © Mary Williams 2002

British Library Cataloguing in Publication Data
A catalogue record for this book is available from the British Library

ISBN 1–85346–850–9

Typeset by FiSH Books, London
Printed and bound in Great Britain by Bell and Bain Ltd, Glasgow

Contents

Acknowledgements

We would like to thank the many teachers, student teachers and children in west London schools whose work has informed our research and, in particular, the final year BA (QTS) students for the year 2002 who have shared many useful perspectives on the teaching of writing with us.

My thanks go to David for his steadfast patience and support and to all of my colleagues who put up with my nagging and gave unstintingly of their time. Also, to the students in the Department of Education at Brunel without whom much of this would have been impossible.

We are grateful for permission to include the following published extract: Mike Lindley 'Emind Map Detective story'.

Every effort has been made to obtain permission to include copyright material in this book. In case of failure to obtain permission the editor and publishers undertake to make good any omissions in future printings.

Notes on the contributors

Rebecca Bunting is Dean of Education at Anglia Polytechnic University. Her research interests include teacher development, literacy and educational linguistics. She is co-editor of the journal *Education through Partnership* and author of *Teaching about Language in the Primary Years 2000* (David Fulton Publishers).

Robert Catt has taught English within 11–18 comprehensive schools. His interests in language and learning have involved research in both the UK and USA. He has also worked with teachers and teacher educators abroad, most recently in Poland and Uzbekistan. He is now Education staff tutor with The Open University in the South working within the Centre for Language and Communication.

Martin Cortazzi has taught in primary and secondary schools in Britain and has taught and worked with teachers in Britain, Iran, Turkey, Lebanon, Malaysia, Singapore, China and elsewhere. His published work includes research on primary education, narrative and discourse, vocabulary and literacy. He is Head of the Education Department at Brunel University and continues to research links between language, culture and learning.

Robert Fisher taught in London and overseas including Ethiopia and Hong Kong, and was a primary head teacher for five years. He has published more than 20 books on aspects of teaching and learning including the *Stories for Thinking* series, *Teaching Thinking: Philosophical Enquiry in the Classroom* and *Head Start: How to Develop our Child's Mind*. He runs the Centre for Research in Teaching Thinking at Brunel and development projects for schools and LEAs developing literacy, thinking and learning.

John Garvey taught for nine years in primary classrooms in London, and was head teacher of a primary school in Richmond upon Thames. He now teaches in the Department of Education at Brunel University, across ITT courses specialising in Design and Technology and Information and Communication Technology (ICT). He is currently award leader for the PGCE Primary course. His research interests include teaching numeracy and literacy through ICT. He is co-author of Investigating Technology (Simon and Schuster) and has contributed to other books on ICT-related themes.

Lixian Jin taught in schools in China and trained English teachers there, before researching and teaching in Britain. She lectures in linguistics at De Montfort

University, teaching sociolinguistics, syntax and clinical linguistics but is currently seconded to lecture in English at the Chinese University of Hong Kong. Her research interests include children's language, second language development, intercultural communication and cultures of learning. She has also trained teachers in Turkey and Britain.

Colleen Johnson spent several years as an actor in Canada and the UK, working mainly in theatre in education, co-founding two theatre companies. She has a wide range of teaching experience, specialising in drama, voice production and lecturing skills. She teaches drama in education at Brunel University and has published in this area. Her research interests include the development of the teacher as communicative expert.

Deborah Jones has been a primary teacher, a LEA advisory teacher and has worked on the LINC project. She is now a lecturer in the Department of Education at Brunel University and teaches on undergraduate, postgraduate and masters programmes. Her research interests include literacy and gender in education. She has co-authored with Pam Hodson *Teaching Children to Write* 2001 (David Fulton Publishers).

Lizann O'Conor trained as an actor and graduated with MA (hons). She studied for a PCGE at Brunel University in 1995/6 and is currently literacy coordinator in an inner London primary school and a leading literacy teacher for the London borough of Hammersmith and Fulham.

Lynne Thorogood taught in primary schools in London and Surrey for 12 years and was a head teacher in Surrey. She now teaches on both the undergraduate and postgraduate primary ITT courses and contributes to in-service training. Her subject specialisms are in English and Creative Arts, and her research interests include the development of transcription skills, including handwriting and spelling, and curriculum development. She has recently been an adviser on curriculum reform in Poland and on resource-based learning in Lithuania.

Mary Williams taught for 20 years as a primary school teacher, the last nine as head teacher of a nursery/infant school. She is subject leader for English at Brunel University and has research interests that include literacy learning and raising standards in literacy at Key Stages 1 and 2, metacognition and the literacy needs of able pupils. She teaches on undergraduate, postgraduate, MA and doctoral programmes. She co-edited Unlocking Literacy with Robert Fisher 2000 (David Fulton Publishers).

Introduction

This book draws on ongoing research, the Brunel Research Into Literacy (BRIL) project,[1] carried out in west London schools, and offers a guide for those engaged in teaching writing in our schools. It aims to help improve the quality of writing for 5–14-year-olds (Key Stages 1–3 in the National Curriculum for England and Wales) by showing how the teaching of writing, both within and outside the Literacy Hour, can be creative and imaginative. It acknowledges that underpinning all work in literacy is children's ability to speak and to listen while engaging in writing and reading tasks across the curriculum.

The book is based on a number of underlying beliefs about the benefits that being literate brings, which underpin the contributors' work with students and teachers. Being literate provides readers with an invaluable means of thinking about the world around them. Being able to read enables readers to learn from people they cannot possibly know. Written language can be communicated through space and time. It allows writers to record their thoughts at a particular moment in time and for these to be given permanency.

Reading and writing are inextricably linked as dual aspects of literacy. Being literate supports critical and creative thinking and the ability to solve problems. Writing and reading are not just mechanical skills but important functions of thinking. Writing down thoughts enables the writer to sustain and order thinking. It encourages reflection on what is being said and offers the opportunity for systematic and sustained ways of recording what has been said and agreed. The ability to write is essential for extending learning and thinking and in communicating with others. If words form part of the thinking process[2] then teaching children to be literate is an essential part of thinking, as from this they will learn about the world around them.

Children need to learn the conventions of writing but also the context of writing. This means that they need to learn about the social uses of language as well as the structure of words, sentences and texts. Literacy teaching should start from what they already know, based on their implicit knowledge about language and their need to strive to make sense of the world. The teacher is the mediator of their learning, helping them to make what they know intuitively, explicit. The book shows how the development of metacognition is an integral part of the learning process. This involves helping children to become aware of the processes involved in learning so they can gain conscious control over their thinking[3] through the right kind of teaching support.

Children need to be employed in meaningful writing activities both in English lessons and in other subjects across the school curriculum. These activities need to be structured, but also creative, so that learning to write is seen by children to have real purpose. Creative ideas for writing themes and approaches can be made to fit within the structured framework of the Literacy Hour. The principles that underpin the effective teaching of writing outlined in this book include:

- giving children as much ownership over the process as possible;
- direct teaching including 'modelling' of the writing process by the teacher;
- pupils being taught to match their writing style to audience and purpose;
- exposing children to a range of written genres, e.g. narrative, exposition and argument;
- giving pupils time to craft their writing;
- teaching pupils how to spell using investigative approaches;
- teaching handwriting and presentation skills in a rigorous and systematic manner;
- assessing what pupils are able to achieve thoroughly and systematically and setting targets with them for the future; and
- introducing children to a metalanguage to talk about their writing and how they are learning to write.

Children are still experiencing problems with writing. School inspectors have discovered two fundamental issues common to both Key Stage 1 and 2 pupils. These are that:

- the use of full stops and capital letters is not sufficiently secure and there is some evidence of a decline in the accurate use of sentence boundary markers, with increased use of the comma splice in Key Stages 2 and 3; and
- stories begin well but do not offer credible resolutions (QCA 2001b).[5]

However, there is evidence to suggest that children are paying more attention to the structure of non-fiction writing. It is against the background of such concerns – expressed by teachers and HMI – that this exploration of approaches to the teaching of writing will take place. Creative approaches to learning and teaching writing are offered in this book which have been informed by published research and current initiatives in this country and abroad. In particular, our own research suggests that metacognitive awareness will have an important part to play in raising levels of understanding of the writing process, as shown below (Figure 1).

This book aims to show how pupils can be empowered by learning to write effectively. In Chapter 1 Robert Fisher and I consider what knowledge skills and understanding children need to acquire in order to become successful writers. How they develop as writers will be discussed alongside consideration of how such learning can be supported at home and at school. The role that metacognition plays in effective learning, particularly in relation to writing, will be examined by drawing on examples from recent research. In Chapter 2, Liann O'Conor and I consider the impact of the National Literacy Strategy and the Literacy Hour on the teaching of writing and show how 'shared writing' can be developed to help children compose and transcribe effectively across a range of genres. Strategies are suggested which support creative approaches to teaching writing, including the importance of helping children to gain

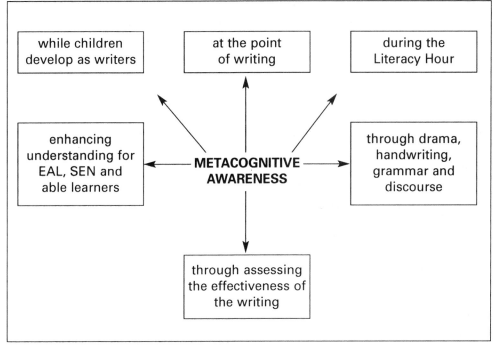

Figure I.1 Elements in unlocking writing

metacognitive awareness of how they are learning. In Chapter 3 Robert Catt asks: what's the worth of writing particularly as it relates to Key Stage 3 pupils, and discusses ways that can be used to motivate Year 7 pupils, at a time when the point of writing as a means of learning across the curriculum needs to be justified in children's minds, as many seem reluctant to write. This chapter also considers whether teachers at Key Stage 3 have anything to learn from colleagues in primary schools, particularly when intervening in children's writing through giving them a sense of audience, purpose and style as a means of increasing their metacognitive awareness.

In Chapter 4 Colleen Johnson explores the power of drama as a motivational force for writing. She demonstrates a variety of ways in which dramatic context both stimulates and enhances the quality of written work. The place of voice and role play in the writing process, and links with reading and enactment, are considered. Metacognitive understanding achieved through reflection on writing, both in and out of role, is also discussed. Lynne Thorogood examines the teaching of handwriting in Chapter 5 and considers how to include it within the Literacy Hour, particularly as Literacy Hour planning sheets seldom make provision for the teaching of this vital skill and few lessons feature handwriting as one of the specified learning intentions. This chapter also shows how links can profitably be made between handwriting and spelling. In Chapter 6 John Garvey considers how ICT can be used to develop writing skills. The role of the computer in developing writing skills within and beyond the Literacy Hour is assessed in the light of recent research into best practice in the classroom. The chapter focuses on how word processors and desktop publishing software aid the development of drafting, editing and publishing skills. Software geared towards developing a range of writing skills is evaluated. The impact of the internet, hypertext and email is discussed in relation to the promotion and development of these new forms of literacy. In Chapter 7 Deborah Jones explores and evaluates different approaches to the assessment of writing and suggests strategies that can be used to assess both the composition and transcription aspects of the process. She considers how assessment can enable pupils to become proficient at writing in different genres and shows how important it is to engage pupils in assessing their own writing. This gives them greater understanding of the learning process.

Ways of supporting learners using English as an Additional Language (EAL) are suggested in Chapter 8 by Martin Cortazzi and Lixian Jin, under the headings of seven 'keys'. The chapter stresses the diversity of EAL learners and illustrates a range of different needs for writing support and applies useful principles through classroom examples. The authors emphasise the need for certain kinds of modelling through interaction and the importance of balancing verbal and visual support. They draw on their own linguistic research with particular learners and stress cultural and metacognitive aspects which are often overlooked. In Chapter 9 Rebecca Bunting considers the difficulties faced by SEN children when it comes to writing and offers practical suggestions to help them overcome these. She considers the importance of raising self-esteem among such pupils and how best to provide them with additional support so that they can achieve appropriately in mainstream classes, particularly during the Literacy Hour. She emphasises the importance of having a suitable range of resources and routines for Special Education Needs (SEN) pupils. Taking up a topical theme, Robert Fisher sets out to show how boys' literacy levels can be boosted in Chapter 10. He offers a comprehensive review of recent research into boys' literacy development and illustrates ways in which teachers can boost boys' motivation and achievement. The chapter explores the extent of the problem of boys' poor performance and provides practical ideas to raise their achievement through the Literacy Hour and beyond. Various contributory factors in boys' underachievement are identified and foundations for forming a whole-school policy on raising boys' achievement are discussed. The chapter concludes with a summary of key strategies for boosting boys' literacy levels, illustrated with examples from recent research in schools. Finally, in Chapter 11, I discuss the challenge teachers face in providing a literacy curriculum for able children. The Literacy Hour is viewed with able children in mind to assess whether their needs are being adequately met within it. Practical examples taken from recent research undertaken with able children in Key Stages 1 and 2 will be used to show how providing appropriate challenges for these children, particularly in terms of writing, can be of benefit to *all* pupils in a class. The importance of giving able children metacognitive awareness of how they are learning is also discussed as this adds an important extra dimension to their learning.

Notes

1. The Brunel Research Into Literacy (BRIL) project involves tutors in the English teaching team and student teachers from Brunel University. It has explored aspects of the implementation of the National Literacy Strategy in a number of west London schools. For further information see Fisher, R. and Williams, M. (2000) *Unlocking Literacy*, London: David Fulton Publishers.
2. Lev Vygotsky (1962) *Thought and Language*. Cambridge, MA: MIT Press.
3. Williams, M. (2000) 'The part which metacognition can play in raising standards in English at Key Stage 2'. *Reading*, 34(1), April.
4. In the Cox Report (DES 1989), 6:18, properly entitled *English for Ages 5–16*, NCC.
5. Evidence from SATs results taken from QCA (2001b) *Implications for Teaching and Learning, Key Stage 1* and *Implications for Teaching and Learning, Key Stage 2*.

Further reading

DES (1989) *English for Ages 5–16*. NCC .

Fisher, R. and Williams, M. (2000) *Unlocking Literacy*. London: David Fulton Publishers.

QCA (2001a) *Implications for Teaching and Learning, Key Stage 1*.

QCA (2001b) *Implications for Teaching and Learning, Key Stage 2*.

Vygotsky, L. (1962) *Thought and Language*. Cambridge, MA: MIT Press.

Williams, M. (2000) 'The part which metacognition can play in raising standards in English at Key Stage 2'. *Reading*, 34(1), April.

CHAPTER 1

Getting the point: how children develop as writers

Mary Williams and Robert Fisher

Well, it's ideas in my head that I show on paper. (Melanie)

Melanie, who was seven years old, offered this definition of what the writing process meant to her. Both aspects of her definition will be pursued in this chapter – 'the getting of ideas' (composition) and how best to show these ideas 'on paper' (transcription). The two can be brought together through *thinking* about what the writing process entails because it is through critical reflection about their own learning that writers can assess whether or not they are putting their message across effectively. To be able to do this, developing writers need knowledge, skills and understanding at text, sentence and word level, as set out in the National Literacy Strategy (1998) (see Chapter 2 of this book), and awareness of how each level interrelates if clarity of meaning is to be given. Much can be learned about how children develop understanding of the writing process from an examination of how they 'emerge' as writers. As they become older they need to be given access to an increasingly wide range of genres including fiction and non-fiction styles and form. They should know how one particular genre, or text type, varies from another according to the purpose it serves. In addition, they need to be aware that some writing requires crafting, and that it may need to pass through several stages, including drafting, editing and redrafting, before it is satisfactorily completed. Therefore, an understanding of how composition and transcription support one another is crucial, with metacognition – thinking about how you are learning – playing an important part in realising this objective.

Developing writing in the early years

Many children have opportunities to put their ideas down on paper from an early age. It is highly desirable that they are given these because it is through these that they begin to understand what writing is about[1] and gain a sense of authorship. Research[2] has shown that children develop a number of principles about the process and experiment with them as they come to terms with the symbolic nature of writing and begin to realise how this relates to the way in which:

- letters recur in variable patterns to form new words;
- text can be generated through knowledge of rules for combining letters and words;

- letters and words are arranged on the page;
- 'signs/symbols' represent objects and ideas in print; and
- print is permanent.

These principles received endorsement in the Early Years documentation issued by the DfEE. For example, in *Curriculum Guidance for the Foundation Stage* (DfEE 2000a),[3] in one of the six areas of learning 'Communication, Language and Literacy' it is suggested that children should have the chance to see adults write and that they should be able to experiment with writing for themselves 'through mark making, personal writing symbols and conventional script'. Also, it is recognised that play is valuable in providing opportunities for young children to use their imagination and to recreate experience. This is further built upon in the reception year of the *National Literacy Strategy* (DfEE 1998) where it is stated that pupils should 'use writing to communicate in a variety of ways, incorporating it into play and everyday classroom life',[1] as, for example, when they pretend to be newspaper reporters (Figure 1.1). These principles are also endorsed in *Developing Early Literacy* (2001) and the *National Literacy Strategy.*

Most importantly these principles do not conflict with widely accepted practices in early years education which emphasise how:

- learning can be achieved through discovery and play; and
- assessment of progress should be based on what children *can do*, rather than what they cannot do.

Young children experiment with the writing process through play[5] and it is through purposeful engagement in this that they make discoveries that increase their knowledge, skills and understanding. Through planning their play children learn to be systematic and this possibly has a direct bearing on how they approach writing (Chapter 11).[6]

Many young children engage in a range of writing activities in the home, including writing present lists, letters or stories. In the past the form of writing that dominated in the early years was that of story. The advantage of beginning with story-writing is that it mirrors more closely the habits of spoken speech, although it should be recognised that written stories are not the same as spoken, as in speech it is possible to convey subtlety of meaning through non-verbal prompts which are much more difficult to achieve in writing. Speech invites immediate feedback so the message can be altered or expanded upon until the meaning has been clearly understood. With writing a response may be offered some time later, if at all! With simultaneous feedback not being the norm, teachers have a key role to play in bridging the gap between reader and writer by challenging children to put their meaning across effectively. Story-writing, derived either from personal experience or from reading exciting books, provides a good starting point for narratives, as children do not have to struggle too much to find ideas to write about. As children's writing ability progresses they need to have access to an increasing number of genres that should include non-fiction forms. These have been somewhat neglected in the past, but since the introduction of the National Literacy Strategy they have been given a much higher focus. The extension of range in writing should start in Key Stage 1 where pupils should be introduced to more than story forms in the context of lessons across the

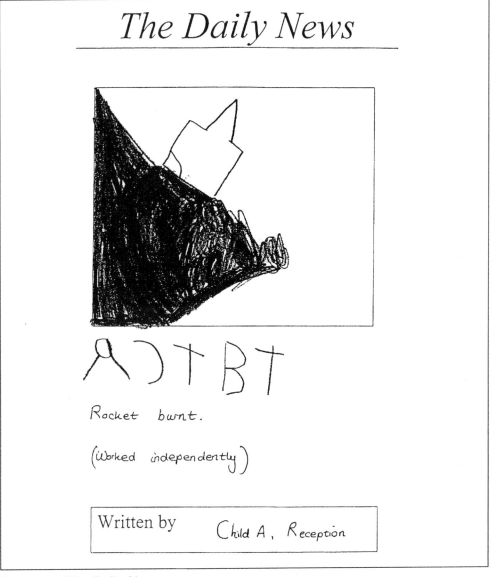

Figure 1.1 *The Daily News*

curriculum, or through cross-curricular themes. Whenever possible they should be encouraged to write:

- signs and posters to publicise events;
- labels and captions to drawings or models;
- lists of what they need to do, or to collect, to undertake certain tasks;
- instructions about how to play a game or how an object can be made to work;
- accounts of events which have happened to them; and
- reports of experiments, or conclusions reached as part of problem-solving activities.

Developing a range of writing as children become older

In Key Stage 2, the range should be developed further to include knowledge and understanding of how to write according to a range of specific genres (see below). Writing – either in a narrative or in non-narrative form – provides children with an intellectual and physical challenge. If the writing is handwritten they have to be able to manipulate the pen or pencil skilfully (Chapter 5), as well as use the appropriate style for their purpose that includes the correct use of grammatical forms, spellings and punctuation. To create clarity in terms of content children need to be able to use a range of cohesive devices so that 'a thread' of meaning runs throughout their writing. With non-fiction writing they have to develop these skills even further, as they need to be able to use precise technical vocabulary, as well as formal and impersonal registers. Non-fiction is organised in a variety of ways – according to the conventions of particular genres – and these have to be learned. The need to consider different aspects of the process, such as purpose, audience, style and form, is vital to an understanding of this.

Purpose

Three broad purposes for writing can be identified as:

- personal – writing for yourself e.g. personal notes, diary, letters;
- imaginative – writing for others e.g. stories, poems, plays; and
- functional – writing for a practical purpose e.g. recipes, instructions, information.

(Fisher and Williams 2000)

Through being read to, and reading for themselves, children become aware of the way style differs according to the purpose of the text. However, they will not just pick this up for themselves and need to have their attention drawn to the differences and similarities between genres, for instance, in 'shared' writing in the Literacy Hour (Chapter 2). Equally, they need to know that a single piece of writing can fulfil a number of separate, but interlinked functions, for example, a letter can be personal, imaginative and functional all at the same time.

Audience

Initially the audience for much of children's writing is likely to be either themselves, or people they know such as their parents/carers, and, at a slightly later date, their teachers. They need to know that writing for unknown audiences makes demands on a writer in terms of establishing the context, explaining terms and spelling out relationships. They should be made aware of the 'reading needs' of their potential audience so that problems in getting meaning across can be avoided. Fundamentally, they need to know that they are writing reading.[7]

Many children do not know, or find it difficult to say for whom they are writing. Melanie, the child in the opening quotation, said that you just write for your teacher and, with a little more prompting, for your mum and dad. However, she was aware that these adults, who were all very influential in her life, had different expectations. Of her dad she said:

> Well, when he looks at it, he can see whether it's neat and tidy, then what spellings I've got wrong. Then I have to learn them.[8]

It is important, therefore, to discuss with children the possible audiences they might be writing for, what expectations different audiences might have, and to give them experience of writing for those who are both known or unknown to them.

Type of audience	Known/unknown
Self	known
Parent	known
Teacher/other pupils/friends	known
Other teachers/classes	partially known
Extended family	partially known
Children in other schools/pen pals/via the internet	unknown
The media/councillors/local businesses/ local community	unknown

Source: Fisher and Williams (2000:72)

Style and form

Children's reading and writing can be broadened through introduction to a range of factual and non-narrative writing forms. Non-fiction genres are highlighted throughout the National Literacy Strategy[9] with their distinctive features, including those shown in Table 1.1.

This inevitably means that children need to have understanding of grammatical functions. It is this that ultimately gives meaning to writing.[10] Knowledge of grammar opens up the range of choices they can make in their writing.

> By structuring and restructuring ideas in writing, children extend their powers of imagination, learn to express increasingly complex, abstract and logical relationships, develop skills of reasoning and critical evaluation.   (DfEE 2000b:8)

Posing a problem can be a useful way to generate non-fiction writing, for example, asking the question 'Why is grass green?' A process of 'think-pair-share' can provide opportunities for important oral groundwork in which prior knowledge is accessed and ideas are shared that form the basis for what is to be written. Children can initially be asked to think about what they know about a particular subject for themselves; then they should discuss this together in pairs. These ideas can be shared with either a group (as in independent work time of the Literacy Hour) or the whole class. Further information can be gathered from relevant books and, finally, the conclusions reached

Table 1.1

Form	Purpose	Distinctive features
recount	retelling of events either to inform or entertain	past tense; cohesive devices such as 'then', 'next', 'after that', chronological order
report	describing the way things are	present tense; cohesive devices such as 'although', 'another', 'finally', non-chronological order
explanation	explaining the processes involved – in a natural occurrence or to explain how something works	simple present tense; connective devices such as 'to begin with', 'after that', 'next', 'then'
instruction	outlining how readers can achieve certain goals	simple present tense or using the imperative; sequential devices such as 'first', 'then', 'next', 'finally'
persuasion	promoting a particular viewpoint in an attempt to get others to agree with it	simple present tense; cohesive devices such as 'although', 'however', 'therefore', 'because'
discussion	presenting a balanced view of different arguments so that an evidence-based conclusion can be reached	simple present tense; connective devices such as 'on the one hand', 'on the other hand', 'because', 'in my opinion', 'therefore', 'however'

Source: adapted from Lewis and Wray 1997[11]

can be recorded in a manner suitable to the particular genre being adopted, possibly making use of computer resources (Chapter 6). Every opportunity should be taken to discuss with children the key features of a broad range of genres. This can take place across the curriculum, as children use information books to extend their knowledge and understanding in a range of curriculum subjects such as in history and science.

An effective strategy to help children in writing either fiction or non-fiction is through the use of 'writing frames'.[12] These provide 'scaffolding' which supports developing writers by giving them starting points through posing key questions that help them to structure their response and require them to fill any gaps in their understanding. (See Figures 1.2(a), 1.2(b), 1.3(a) and 1.3(b).)

Planning a story

What is the title of your story?_____

Who will be in your story?	Where does it begin?
When does it happen – past, present, future?	What happens at the beginning?
Is there an exciting bit?	How will it end?

Figure 1.2(a) Story planning sheet for Key Stage 1 pupils

How composition and transcription should work together

As well as knowing the purpose, audience and style and form, a writer needs to be able to mould a piece of writing together effectively in order to get the meaning across coherently. This is achieved when composition and transcription work closely together so that the writer uses the correct style for the intended purpose and is able to express his/her thoughts and feelings appropriately on a wide variety of subjects. To be able to do this successfully children need to be

- motivated in terms of subject material;
- able to use books and stories as the impetus for finding their own voice in their writing;
- taught to write legibly and to use spelling, grammar and punctuation accurately;
- shown how to plan, draft, revise and edit their writing;

Writing a recipe

To make a _____

Ingredients

- _____
- _____
- _____
- _____
- _____

What you have to do

1. Put the oven on high, medium, low (choose the correct temperature).
2. Collect the ingredients.
3.
4.
5.
6.
7. Cook for
8. Leave to cool for 15 minutes.

Figure 1.2(b) Non-fiction writing frame for Key Stage 1 pupils

- supported in the writing process by a 'response friend', writing group or teacher in order to improve what they have written; and
- encouraged to share, judge and evaluate their writing and the writing of others.[13]

Adopting a 'writer's workshop' approach, focusing on either fiction or non-fiction writing, can be helpful in this respect. Workshop sessions take pupils 'inside' the writing process by getting them to think in depth about the challenges which writers face as they craft their writing. During these workshops (which can easily be incorporated into the Literacy Hour (Chapter 2) the following aspects of the writing process can be explored:

- how various writers have dealt with a theme or issue in writing, through the sharing of pupils' examples;

WHAT TO THINK ABOUT WHEN PLANNING A STORY

Who will read this story? _____

AUDIENCE

What sort of story is it?_____

GENRE

Who will be in it?

1.

2.

3.

CHARACTERS

What are they like?_____

1.

2.

3.

Where does the story happen?_____

When does the story happen? _____

What important action takes place? _____

Think of your title.

Write your title. _____

Write your opening sentence. _____

Figure 1.3(a) Story planning for Key Stage 2 pupils. *Source:* Williams, 2000[14]

- how to share ideas for composition, by asking pupils to compose collaboratively while the teacher scribes what is suggested;
- how to deal with a specific aspect of transcription which has proved challenging for a number of children in the class; and
- how to assess what is good about samples of writing and have the confidence to make suggestions for further improvement.

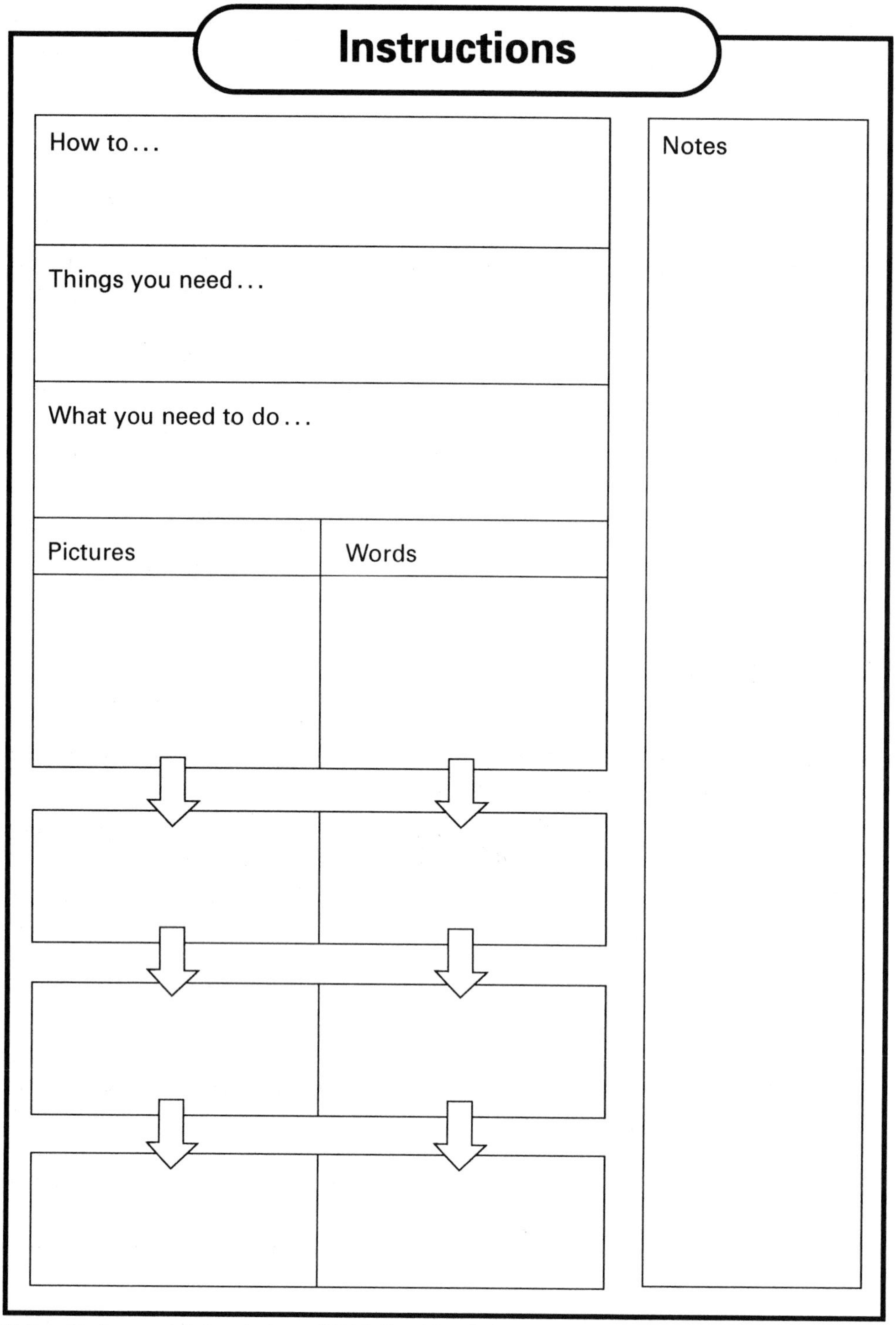

Instructions

How to...		Notes
Things you need...		
What you need to do...		

Pictures	Words

© Pam Hodson and Deborah Jones (2001) *Teaching Children to Write*. London: David Fulton Publishers. (From Figure 4.11, Non-fiction, Instructions 1)

Figure 1.3(b) Non-fiction writing frame for Key Stage 2 pupils

Extracts from the School Experience file of a final year student show how she went about providing such a lesson for a Year 4 class. Her aim was to extend pupils' understanding of the drafting process in order to get them to appreciate that editing should not be concerned with transcription errors alone. She encouraged them to think about the process by:

- modelling the editing process while asking them if she was using the best words possible;
- advocating the use of a response partner to see if the needs of a reader had been met by asking the partner to decide if s/he could understand what had been written;
- challenging pairs to come up with the main themes/ideas in each other's writing;
- getting partners to suggest ideas for improvement in each other's writing; and
- holding a plenary session so that pupils could discuss what was good about the writing they had read and to give evidence from the text for the judgements they had made.

It is through such teaching that children acquire metacognitive understanding about how they are learning to write which deepens their understanding of how they are developing as writers.

What is metacognition?

The following are definitions of metacognition offered by a group of experienced teachers. They thought that metacognition involves:

- 'thinking about thinking and developing the process of solving problems and answering them';
- 'the examination of how we think about how we do things, how we go about finding solutions, how well we can understand and analyse the systems, strategies and techniques we use to think to do things';
- 'an awareness of the process of how an answer is found, what strategies and type of thought has gone on and the previous experiences that have been used';
- 'to *consciously* apply a process, a procedure to a problem or activity and to be aware that the result is satisfactory or otherwise. To be able to "unpick" that strategy/those actions and so improve performance';
- 'awareness of the different processes involved in thinking';
- 'the ability to take out our thinking, and examine it, and put it back, rearranged if necessary'; and
- 'thinking about thinking rather than just remembering facts and recalling events'.[15]

Recently there has been a growing recognition that metacognition, or self-awareness, which includes awareness of ourselves as learners, helps learning to be more effective. The term *metacognition*, first coined by Flavell in 1976,[16] refers to an individual's own awareness and consideration of his or her cognitive processes and strategies. It relates to that uniquely human capacity to be self-reflexive, not just to think and know, but to think about how you think and know. Vygotsky[17] was one of the first to realise that conscious reflective control and deliberate mastery are essential factors in school learning. He suggested there were two factors in the development of knowledge. First its automatic, unconscious acquisition, followed by a gradual increase in active conscious control over that knowledge, which essentially marks a separation between cognitive and metacognitive aspects of performance. He argued that when the process of learning is brought to a conscious level, children can be helped to be more aware of their own thought processes and this helps them to gain control or mastery over the organisation of their learning. This perspective on effective learning is not just about the integration of information into an existing knowledge base, but involves directing the learner's attention to what has been assimilated and understood, and the relationship of this to the processes of learning itself.

Metacognition includes knowledge of self, as thinker and learner, in relation to a task and in relation to a particular environment. It is valuable because it develops the thinking ability of the learner. In terms of writing development it operates at three levels giving knowledge of self in relation to the

- task: what type of writing task is it – its form, audience, and purpose?
- process: what do you need to be able to do – draft, revise, edit, share?
- individual: what kind of writer are you – what helps you to write well?

Some problems in writing can be solved by cognitive methods alone such as applying a spelling rule or editing a text for correct punctuation. To solve such problems the child needs to know how to define the problem and then select an appropriate strategy or rule. However, problems in writing, like life, are ill-structured, complex and made 'messy' by containing many different variables which have no simple solution. What do children do when they do not know what to do? What they need then is not just the application of knowledge but awareness through metacognition that they have a number of learning strategies at their disposal. These strategies develop over time but they also develop through practice, manifesting themselves in different levels of awareness:

Levels of awareness

Tacit use: children make decisions without really thinking about them
Aware use: children become consciously aware of a strategy or decision-making process
Strategic use: children are able to select the best strategies for solving a problem
Reflective use: children can reflect on their thinking, before, during and after the process, evaluate progress and set targets for improvement

How can metacognitive awareness be developed?

Getting children to think about thinking is not an easy task, but is a complex teaching skill that depends on three key factors:

- the writing tasks given to pupils must be worth serious thought;
- the thinking and reasoning of pupils about their writing must be valued; and
- time must be given for review of their writing with others.

One way of teaching for metacognition is to ask metacognitive questions. In doing so the aim is to model the questions children should ask for themselves in terms of their own thinking. To help children 'unpack' their thinking and to reason requires a high proportion of open, or Socratic questions, for example questions that:

- assess awareness of learning (What have you learned? What have you found out? What did you find hard? What did you do well? What do you need to learn/do next?);
- probe attitudes and feelings (What do you like doing/learning? What do you feel good/not good about ... ? What do you feel proud of?);
- encourage target setting (What do you need to do better? What would help you? What are your targets?).

Here a teacher asks questions that probe a ten-year-old child's understanding of the writing process:

TEACHER: What five hints would you give a younger child to help them become a good writer?

CHILD: Well, firstly I would say talk to someone about your ideas, and try to get some ideas from them. Write it in rough first, because you can always change it later. Once you've written it look at the words and change all the boring words into unboring words. How many is that?

TEACHER: That's three I think. Can you think of two more?

CHILD: Always do your writing when it is not too noisy, so you can hear yourself think. And read it through afterwards to try to find your mistakes before the teacher does!

TEACHER: Why is it good for children to learn to write?

CHILD: Well, one reason is to help them get a better job, because if you can't write you can't even apply for a job. I guess that's the best reason.

TEACHER: Are there other reasons?

CHILD: You can write things down to remember them, and you can write stuff for other people. I'd like to be a good writer so I can write stories for my children.

TEACHER: What could you do to improve your writing – to become a better writer?

CHILD: Read it through afterwards to see if it makes sense, and think of some more interesting words. A lot of my writing is quite boring. Sometimes I read it and almost fall asleep! But sometimes my teacher says: 'Very intelligent work'.

(Fisher and Williams 1999)[18]

Children very quickly pick up when they are being offered false praise and when the teacher has not really engaged with the content of their writing (Chapter 7). So it is worth setting time aside for discussion about what is worthwhile. Time is needed for probing questions and for lengthy responses that characterise extended thinking about learning. The skill of the teacher is to help pupils link what they have achieved to other concepts and important ideas about their learning, as well as connecting it to what they have learned in other subjects, and to everyday life. Metacognition is needed if writers are to be helped to engage in their own learning and self-development. Developing one's own voice as a writer is linked to having self-awareness of how you are learning. Therefore, teachers need to understand how children develop as writers – that is, understanding that they need to be given understanding of purpose, audience, style and form – and to appreciate that helping them to think about this and how they are learning about it will be of crucial importance. For their writing to be effective pupils not only need to be helped to gain ideas but need to know how to put them down successfully on paper. This will only be achieved when they clearly understand that composition and transcription must work closely together.

Notes

1. Ferreiro and Teberosky's (1979) research in Argentina showed children's emergent mark making was not haphazard. It was possible to see that they were beginning to make sense of the process for themselves.

2. Marie Clay (1979) showed through research that children did not automatically acquire 'concepts about print' such as directionality, letter and word concepts, book orientation and punctuation and needed to be taught explicitly. Hall (1987) and Browne (1993) have further investigated the principles children adhere to as they emerge as writers.

3. *Curriculum Guidance for the Foundation Stage* (DfEE 2000a) that gave the educational provision for children from the age of three to the end of the reception year its own distinctive identity and set out 'learning and teaching experiences of the highest quality' to underpin their early education and in *Developing Early Literacy* (2001:12), the DfEE acknowledge 'the important tradition of promoting developmental or emergent writing'.

4. In the *National Literacy Strategy* (DfEE 1998:19).

5. Bruce (1991), Nutbrown (1994), David (1998) and Hall and Robinson (2000) have highlighted, through research, the importance of play as a way in which young children learn.

6. Williams, M. and Rask, H. (2000) 'The identification of variables which enable able children in year one to extend and develop their literacy skills'. *Gifted and Talented*, 4(2), November.

7. Barrs, M. and Cork, V. (2001) explore this theme in *The Reader in the Writer*. London: CLPE.

8. Fisher, R. and Williams, M. (2001) Brunel Research Into Literacy (unpublished).

9. For example, in text level work (Years 5 and 6) and in sentence level work (Year 5: term 1 and Year 6: term 3) (*The National Literacy Strategy* (DfEE 1998)).

10. Crystal (1998) in *Grammar for Writing* (2000b), DfEE, published by the National Literacy Strategy to support writing development at Key Stage 2.

11. See Wray, D. and Lewis, M. (1997) *Extending Literacy: Children Reading and Writing Non-Fiction*, Routledge, which draws extensively on the Exeter Extending Literacy

(EXEL) project, which in turn strongly influenced the emphasis on using nonfiction in the National Literacy Strategy (DfEE 1998).

12. Wray and Lewis (1997) offer approaches to 'scaffolding' writing based on the earlier theories of Vygotsky and Bruner.

13. Fisher, R. and Williams, M. (eds) (2000) *Unlocking Literacy: A Guide for Teachers*. London: David Fulton Publishers, Chapter 6 'Is It Write?'.

14. Williams, M. (2000) 'The part which metacognition can play in raising standards in English at Key Stage 2'. *Reading*, 34(1), April, 3–8.

15. Fisher (2001) 'Thinking to Write: Thinking Skills in Literacy Learning'. Paper presented at UKRA international conference, Christ Church, Canterbury, 7 July 2001.

16. Fisher, R. (1978) 'Thinking about thinking: developing metacognition in children. *Early Child Development and Care*, 141, 1–13.

17. Vygotsky, L.S. (1978) Mind in Society. Cambridge, MA: Harvard University Press.

18. Fisher, R. and Williams, M. (1999) Brunel Research Into Literacy (unpublished).

Further reading

Barrs, M. and Cork, V. (2001) *The Reader in the Writer*. London: CLPE.

Beard R. (1999) *National Literacy Strategy: Review of Research and Related Evidence*. London: DfEE.

Browne, A. (1993) *Helping Children to Write*. London: Paul Chapman.

Bruce, T. (1991) *Time to Play*. London: Hodder & Stoughton.

Clay, M. (1979) *Reading: The Patterning of Complex Behaviour*, second edn. London: Heinemann.

David, T. (1998) 'Learning properly! Young children and desirable outcomes'.*Journal of the Professional Association of Early Childhood Educators*, 18(2), Spring.

DfEE (1998) *The National Literacy Strategy*. Sanctuary Buildings, London: HMSO.

DfEE (1999) *The National Curriculum: Handbook for Primary Teachers in England*. London.

DfEE (2000a) *Curriculum Guidance for the Foundation Stage*. London: QCA.

DfEE (2000b) *Grammar for Writing*. London: NLS.

DfEE (2001) *Developing Early Literacy*. London: NLS.

Ferreiro, E. and Teberosky, A. (1979) *Literacy Before Schooling*. London: Heinemann.

Fisher, R. (1998) 'Thinking about thinking: developing metacognition in children'. *Early Child Development and Care*, 141, 1-13.

Fisher, R. and Williams, M. (eds) (2000) *Unlocking Literacy: A Guide for Teachers*. London: David Fulton Publishers.

Hall, N. (1987) *The Emergence of Literacy*. London: Hodder & Stoughton.

Hall, N. and Robinson, A. (2000) 'Play and literacy learning', in Barratt-Pugh, C. and Rohl, M. *Literacy Learning in the Early Years*. Buckingham: Open University Press.

Hodson, P. and Jones, D. (2001) *Teaching Children to Write*. London: David Fulton Publishers.

Lewis, M. and Wray, D. (1995) *Developing Children's Non-fiction Writing*. Leamington

Spa: Scholastic.

Nutbrown, C. (1994) *Threads of Thinking*. London: Paul Chapman.

Vygotsky, L.S. (1978) *Mind in Society*. Cambridge, MA: Harvard University Press.

Williams, M. (1998) 'A Study Which Explores The Impact Of The English National Curriculum (1990) On The Work Of Teachers At Key Stage 2'. PhD thesis (unpublished), Brunel University.

Williams, M. (2000) 'The part which metacognition can play in raising standards in English at Key Stage 2'. *Reading*, 34(1), April, 3–8.

Williams, M. and Rask, H. (2000) 'The identification of variables which enable able children in Year One to extend and develop their literacy skills'. *Gifted and Talented*, 4(2), November.

Wray, D. (1994) *Literacy and Awareness*. London: Hodder & Stoughton/UKRA.

Wray, D. and Lewis, M. (1997) *Extending Literacy: Children Reading and Writing Non-Fiction*. London: Routledge.

CHAPTER 2

Teaching 'write': writing in the Literacy Hour

Mary Williams and Lizann O'Conor

Background

In 1998 teachers were faced with teaching the Literacy Hour for the first time, although in LEAs that had taken part in its forerunner, the National Literacy Project,[1] it was not entirely new. Some training was given before its introduction but, because of limited time, it was rather rushed.[2] Initially, the main impetus for the National Literacy Strategy (NLS) (DfEE 1998) was to raise standards in reading, as there were concerns about the reading standards being achieved by pupils at the end of Key Stage 2. As a result, the training was almost entirely devoted to the shared and guided reading aspects of the Literacy Hour (see below). For many teachers the adoption of the NLS meant that they had to alter the way they taught. Since the implementation of a national curriculum in 1990 they had become used to being told *what* to teach, but for the first time they were being told *how* to teach as well. Consequently, many teachers, who already viewed themselves as successful in teaching English were reluctant to change well-tried-and-tested approaches.

The Literacy Hour

Despite these apprehensions, most teachers are now using the Literacy Hour structure (see Figure 2.1), although those who could prove that they were meeting the required standards already were given the option not to change; but, in fact, very few chose this option.

The 'shared' and 'guided' aspects of the Literacy Hour are now so familiar that they are part of everyday working practice for teachers and, as time has elapsed, the structure is being implemented less rigidly. What was initially advocated for the teaching of writing is shown in Figures 2.2 and 2.3.

The NLS was extended into secondary schools during the academic year 2000/2001[3] and several of the original features of the primary hour were included as part of this. Secondary teachers were recommended to provide English lessons that included the following:

- a short lesson starter (for example, on spelling or vocabulary) lasting from 10 to 15 minutes;

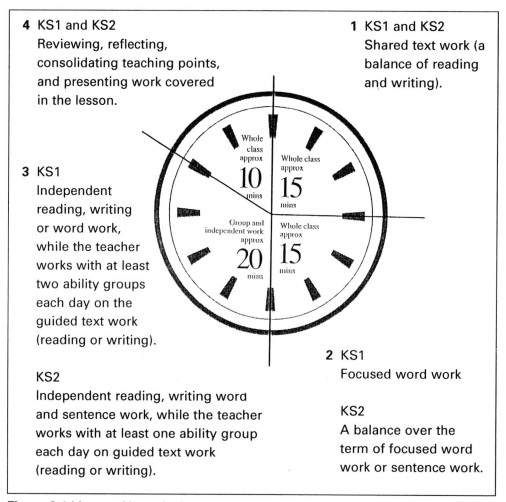

4 KS1 and KS2
Reviewing, reflecting, consolidating teaching points, and presenting work covered in the lesson.

3 KS1
Independent reading, writing or word work, while the teacher works with at least two ability groups each day on the guided text work (reading or writing).

KS2
Independent reading, writing word and sentence work, while the teacher works with at least one ability group each day on guided text work (reading or writing).

Whole class approx **10** mins

Whole class approx **15** mins

Group and independent work approx **20** mins

Whole class approx **15** mins

1 KS1 and KS2
Shared text work (a balance of reading and writing).

2 KS1
Focused word work

KS2
A balance over the term of focused word work or sentence work.

Figure 2.1 Literacy Hour clock

- introduction of the main teaching points through teacher exposition and questioning;
- development of the main teaching points through group activities; and
- plenary to consolidate the learning (for example, through feedback and presentation) lasting 5 to 10 minutes.

As a result of this, by the end of Year 9, it is expected that all pupils will be confident writers who are able to:

- write for a variety of purposes and audiences, knowing the conventions and beginning to adapt and develop them;
- write imaginatively, effectively and correctly;
- shape, express, experiment with and manipulate sentences; and
- organise, develop, spell and punctuate writing accurately.

- The teacher and children collaborate to plan or develop a piece of writing that challenges and extends the children's independent writing skills.

- The teacher models aspects of writing using children's contributions, e.g. letter formation, spelling and layout.

- The teaching may focus upon the structure and content of writing features and also revision and improvement.

- Shared Writing is linked to Reading, e.g. using texts as models.

Figure 2.2 Main features of shared writing with the whole class

- Children are placed in small groups according to writing ability.

- The teacher focuses on a specific, challenging aspect of writing, (e.g. writing a letter of complaint, writing traditional stories).

- The children work on individual pieces of writing often linked to their reading using the knowledge they have acquired from word and sentence level work.

- As writing develops the teacher focuses on the children's skills, e.g.
  – planning
  – drafting
  – revising/editing/proof-reading
  – presenting their own writing.

- The teacher gives explicit feedback and points the way forward.

Figure 2.3 Main features of guided writing with a group

These are laudable aims that not only maintain progress between each sector of education but also make English teaching the responsibility of *all* teachers, both primary and secondary. However, secondary teachers have only given it qualified approval. It is welcomed for the clarity and focus that it gives to learning but the number and complexity of the objectives to be covered has meant that many teachers see it as unmanageable and believe that further guidance on priorities is still required (ATL Interim Report, September 2001).

How did teachers view writing in the Literacy Hour during its first two years?

During the second year of the Literacy Hour trainee teachers sensed that all was not well with the teaching of writing in schools;[4] an issue also identified by Ofsted[5] in an evaluation of the first year of its implementation. It was in Key Stage 2 where this was most evident, with pupils frequently not finishing their work or not being given appropriate individual feedback on how a particular piece was progressing (Chapter 7). The main weakness was that there was not enough time for pupils to develop their writing whilst attending to each aspect of the process appropriately. To 'plan, draft, edit, revise, proof read, present, discuss and evaluate' (DfEE 1999:28) was simply too much to cover within an hour. Schools who were primarily motivated to increase their end of Key Stage test results – not surprising as league tables are published for all to see – offered lessons that concentrated mostly on transcription elements of the process. This is because transcription in the form of grammar, spelling and punctuation is more easily measurable than 'creativity' and 'orginality' in composition. As a result, in the words of one trainee, the hour was in danger of becoming tedious, especially where 'teachers don't breathe some fun into it'.

After two years, based on information from SATs results,[6] it was decided that a higher focus needed to be given to writing in Literacy Hour and, to achieve this, the structure needed to become more flexible. The *Framework* had provided a sound structure on which to base literacy teaching but rigid adherence to it was proving counter-productive. If pupils were to be challenged to produce high-quality work, they should discuss the effectiveness of their writing with their teacher and/or other pupils, with time being made available for this. In particular, extra time for 'extended' writing needed to be found for pupils in Key Stage 2, which may mean that a 'Literacy Hour and a half' is more in line with what is needed.

Concerns about writing

Concerns such as these about standards of writing came to a head in the spring of 2000 when it was recognised that, although standards in reading were improving, there was a problem with writing. John Stannard, Director of the National Literacy Strategy, reviewing the Literacy Hour halfway through its second year of operation, declared that:

> the biggest challenge for us all is . . . writing, which lags behind reading at both Key Stages. At KS1 over half the boys and more than a third of the girls are below Level 2B and, as if to bear this out, similar proportions achieved below level 4 at KS2 . . . Classroom approaches to teaching writing have been slower to change [than for reading]. Traditionally the NC model: plan>draft>edit>revise, gets translated into a linear process. It readily becomes: stimulate ideas>write independently>mark> edit and revise, if time . . .
>
> Much of the solution lies in the improved teaching of shared writing to teach the skills of composition *at the point of writing*.[7]

Shared writing

This put 'shared writing' under the spotlight, as effective whole-class teaching through this was thought to be critical for raising standards in writing. Shared writing is the joint construction of a text by teacher and pupils in which aspects of the process are made explicit through teacher modelling and 'thinking aloud'.[8] In this approach more experienced writers, usually teachers, take pupils inside the learning process through sharing the thoughts and processes they have gone through when writing in a particular form for themselves (Chapter 11). For example, one teacher modelled writing a poem from a picture she had discussed with her Year 5 class. The picture was *Ophelia* by Sir John Everett Millais. She wrote a poem on the whiteboard that she had drafted, using a simple structure of three words per line:

> Petals torn hopelessly
> 'He loves me
> Loves me not
> (Loves me not)'
>
> Soft girlish tone
> Young in despair
> Singing sweet adieus
>
> Hair fanned wide
> Veil turning shroud
> Sodden skirts heavy
> Fingers trace goodbye

After this she shared the strategies she had used to overcome problems in finding suitable words and images, including using all five senses to help brainstorm what was happening in the picture and using a thesaurus to improve vocabulary. This example supported the children when they came to draft poems from their chosen pictures and gave them greater insight into, and understanding of, the thinking which goes into creating a text. Through such means pupils are made aware of what the writing process involves and are encouraged to review their own writing in terms of this knowledge and their reflection upon it (Bereiter and Scardamalia 1987).[9]

'Shared writing' flourishes in an atmosphere where it is recognised that pupils need frequent opportunities to practise the craft of writing, in settings that are conducive to learning. This can be achieved through adopting a workshop approach in which children are given a sense of ownership over their writing, i.e. they are taught how to draft, revise and eventually publish their work. As part of such a workshop they need to receive regular individual input from their teacher who will frequently model relevant aspects of the process to the whole class (Graves 1983).[10] The Literacy Hour can usefully be adapted to provide this, starting with the process of planning a piece of writing. For instance, the teacher might demonstrate how each image in a picture storyboard will become one paragraph in the finished story. It can also be helpful if pupils are provided with aide-memoires that help them to remember what has been discussed in previous 'shared writing' sessions, so that useful strategies can be easily recalled and used, where appropriate, in subsequent writing sessions.[11]

'Shared writing' can be used to model and discuss various aspects of the writing process (Chapter 1). It can be used to help 'match style to audience and purpose'.[12] Through 'shared writing', pupils of all ages can gain understanding of how style is dictated by audience and purpose. To this end they need to know how genres – fiction and non-fiction – differ from one another, so that the field (what the writer is concerned with), the mode (the way the content is to be communicated) and the tenor (the relationship between the reader and writer) (Halliday and Hasan 1985)[13] can be considered appropriately. Inevitably, this means that transcription issues will be brought into play at the point of composition, as part of getting an effective message across (Chapter 1). This makes the process more cyclical and recursive and avoids the linear approach criticised by John Stannard above. Similarly, in the early days of the Literacy Hour, the various levels of shared writing – text, sentence and word level – were often taught separately from one another. For example, lessons were often effective in promoting text level objectives but offered word and text level input that had little relationship to the overall aim of the lesson: a more cohesive approach is needed. For example, a Year 3 teacher will look at the use of dialogue in shared reading of texts, link this with the teaching of how to use speech marks and then investigate ways of using direct speech in shared writing.

Teachers' views about 'shared writing'

Teachers have warmed to many aspects of 'shared writing'.[14] They can see that it provides:

- a structure that helps pupils to appreciate the importance of the editing process;
- modelling which gives pupils the opportunity to see how a good writer composes and transcribes whilst injecting pace into the process;
- collaboration between pupils who support and challenge one another in a non-threatening manner;
- opportunities for ideas to 'spark off' from one pupil to another; and
- a climate in which mutual assessment by peers enhances confidence through knowing that everyone is capable of making mistakes and that this forms part of the learning process.

However, they still have a number of concerns relating to keeping interest alive and making sure that text level objectives do not predominate. They find it difficult to ensure that all children in the class contribute to discussions about the writing equally, especially those pupils who experience difficulties in expressing themselves cogently and concisely. Differentiation is difficult to achieve for children at both ends of the ability spectrum who may be challenged inappropriately, or offered a pace of learning that is either too slow or too fast for them (Chapters 9 and 11). There are dangers that 'shared writing' could become too prescriptive, allowing pupils little opportunity to think individually, or to be creative, as strict adherence to the 'termly objectives' does not encourage the investigation of alternative perspectives or further elaboration of poorly understood concepts. There is insufficient time in the proposed half an hour for older pupils to explore ideas whereas, conversely, younger children find it difficult to concentrate for that length of time. Consequently, these teachers hoped that there would be more flexibility in the future. They wanted to be able to alter the timing to suit the needs of their pupils. They wanted more control over the pace of lessons so that misunderstandings could be ironed out before moving on to the next learning objective. Above all, they wanted older children to be given the opportunity to write for extended periods of time.

In addition, many teachers, aware of the benefits of ICT, would like children to have greater access to laptops so that they can take notes, and use editing devices and writing frames to enhance their understanding of the writing process (Chapter 6). Overhead projectors have potential in terms of modelling but are still sadly missing from many classrooms. Most of these issues relate to funding and need to be resolved quickly, or valuable opportunities will be lost.

Similarly, Ofsted, in its evaluation of the second year of the NLS,[15] echoed some of these views and gave the 'green light' for more flexibility in future teaching. It was concluded that the best shared writing was in lessons where there was:

- careful adaptation of the structure of the Literacy Hour, especially in Years 5 and 6, to give more time to meeting the objectives for writing;
- incorporation of word and sentence level teaching into the broader teaching of writing, so that grammatical knowledge was an intrinsic part of the lesson;
- clarification of audience and purpose at the beginning of the lesson and reference to these during the course of composition;
- making of occasional deliberate errors to encourage pupils' alertness and deal with common mistakes or misconceptions; and
- oral composition of individual sentences combined with frequent re-reading to check for accuracy and maintain the flow of the whole text.

This has given teachers the confidence to adapt the structure of the Literacy Hour so that it can more readily meet the needs of particular pupils, for example, in integrating text, sentence and word level so that they work in harmony to convey meaning. Above all, it highlighted the importance of the Programme of Study for 'speaking and listening' of the English National Curriculum. 'Speaking and listening' has always struggled to maintain equal status with reading and writing but 'oral composition' has now been acknowledged as a vital part of the writing process. In particular, opportunities to practise verbal forms of non-fiction genre are particularly valuable. Marshalling arguments, making explanations, issuing instructions can all be rehearsed orally and the characteristics of each discussed before the shared task of writing them begins.

Guided writing

'Guided writing' provides the opportunity for the teacher to work with groups of children of similar ability on a single focus relevant to their needs. Children feel less daunted working in smaller groups like these and can be encouraged to voice their opinions and misconceptions with each other freely. They respond well to the level of help they receive from the teacher and to supporting one other. This builds up their confidence and motivation for writing. Above all, 'guided writing' gives teachers a valuable opportunity to assess progress, although for this to be really purposeful, each child's 'unique' independent writing needs to be assessed in order to show what s/he can achieve without the support of anyone else.

Teachers have not found 'guided writing' as problematic to introduce as 'shared writing'. It was mostly organisational problems that got in the way of its successful implementation at the beginning. However, it only works well if teachers' knowledge of the writing process is secure and they have a metalanguage to share with their pupils. This enables them to hold meaningful discussions about features of the writing under production.[16] Some teachers are worried that there is insufficient time during 'guided writing' for work to be completed, made more difficult when there are frequent interruptions by the rest of the class who are supposed to be working independently. Some teachers fear that if children always work in a group, they may come to rely on others too much and this might result in an inability to write imaginatively on their own. Therefore, grouping needs to be monitored carefully to ensure that individual members are being challenged appropriately and not becoming too dependent on each other.

These views are endorsed by Ofsted in its second year evaluation report, where the best teaching of guided writing was seen to occur if:

- teachers had good subject knowledge, understood the purpose of guided writing and how to teach it and knew the requirements of the NLS framework well;
- pupils were seated comfortably in an atmosphere which was conducive to writing and where teacher and pupils could hear one another well;
- teachers chose appropriate texts to use as models for pupils' writing;
- writing tasks were often linked directly to a specific genre or skill that had been focused upon in shared writing;
- connections were made between word and sentence level work and composition, i.e. that composition and transcription was worked upon together; and
- teachers occasionally extended a writing activity over several lessons and planned accordingly.[17]

Teachers' own subject knowledge has come under scrutiny recently and is now part of the required standards for entry to the profession,[18] making this a realistic and necessary goal if standards are to rise. Closer linking of learning objectives between 'shared' and 'guided' writing is essential if the teaching of writing is to result in improved standards in writing.

A more flexible approach

Problems about the effectiveness of shared and guided writing within the Literacy Hour suggest that a more flexible approach may be needed in the future. To enable this to occur several issues require further consideration. These include:

- Key Stage specific issues
- differentiation
- the use of response partners
- the use of ICT
- thinking skills and gaining metacognition.

Issues specific to Key Stage 1

Pressure for over-formalisation of the 'early years' curriculum has needed to be resisted and rightly so. Teachers of young children must be imaginative in their teaching in order to make the Literacy Hour fun, as young children gain from learning through play (Chapter 1). However, play needs to be challenging, which is not always the case when children are left to their own devices.[19] Adults – teachers, nursery nurses or classroom assistants – should play alongside children in order to model aspects of the writing process, for example, being a waitress who writes down the order for food in a café. The home corner can often be set up to reflect the theme of a book being used for shared reading. Frequently a stimulus for writing can also be found from this. For example, a thank you letter from *The Tiger Who Came To Tea*, a poster to warn visitors that a monster is about, inspired by *Not Now, Bernard* or a letter from the Three Bears about the upheaval caused in their home by Goldilocks. Here is an example of a first draft of a letter to the 'Three Bears' letter written by a Year 1 able child who managed to find an appropriate voice.

Dear Mr and Mrs Gold

I am sory about this but something has to bee done about your horibale dourter

I would not bee surprised if she was exspeeld form school I think its discraceful not stating to the parth etatting Baby bears priig braeking baby Bers chir and sleeping in his bed whithout sating sory.

Yous senserly
the Bears

Including play themes in a reception class home corner provides a meaningful context for writing which can centre around a multitude of themes for example, shops, jungles, post offices, castles, buses, the beach and boat, to name but a few. The writing produced from such stimuli can include:

- lists
- telephone messages
- advertisements
- bills

- notices
- Letters
- orders
- forms
- bookings
- menus
- recipes
- tickets
- price lists.

Above all, through play children will be given a sense of purpose and audience for their writing as play is their world at the time. It is essential that shared sessions in reading and writing retain the interest of the child so they need to vary in format in order not to become boring. Children need to hear stories read from beginning to end in order to fully experience 'being taken into other worlds' (Meek 1991). This is problematic in the Literacy Hour, if only extracts are ever read. Without time being given to this, children are unlikely to find their own 'voice' in writing. Equally, teachers need to model writing across a broad range of genres (see above), for example, daily plans, shopping lists or written instructions, to increase and broaden children's understanding of the range of writing. A flexible approach to the Literacy Hour should be adopted that includes using several texts relating to a single theme during the course of each week. From these it will be possible to develop understanding and skills in writing at word, sentence and text level, as advocated in the termly objectives for a particular age group. For example, in the final term of Year 2, one class looked at *Five Minutes' Peace* and *Peace at Last* by Jill Murphy and considered why the first has so many questions while the second has only one. They also found out about the author and speculated as to why the search for peace was such a feature of her writing. They then wrote letters to her asking questions about her own family life and recommending ways of finding a little peace and quiet.

Issues specific to Key Stage 2

The 'shared' aspect of the Literacy Hour provides an ideal opportunity for teachers to model aspects of the writing process and there are several ways that this can be achieved. The first is modelling in which the teacher discusses, as part of shared reading, the purposes and features of the genre of a text being read, or where she composes in front of them, in order to reveal the sorts of questions that skilled writers ask themselves as they write, for example:

Features	*Questions to consider*
Purpose	Why am I writing this? What other reasons are there for writing?
Audience	Who am I writing this for? Who else might read it?
Style and form	What kind of writing is this? Should any other style or form be considered? (*Source:* adapted from Fisher and Williams 2000)[20]

Another strategy could involve the joint creation of a written text, with teacher and children composing together, based on a genre or a theme from a text used during shared reading. Additionally, with pupils' permission, examples of their 'work in progress' can be discussed which may have been drafted previously during guided or independent writing time. During future guided group or independent time children can go on to construct new texts in the same genre as the one discussed, either alone or in consultation with a response partner; or they could work on further editing of drafts started in previous lessons. A workshop approach to this can be very useful as it encourages pupils to attend to various aspects of the writing process systematically, i.e. drafting, editing, review and publishing, whilst ensuring that they maintain ownership over what they write (Chapter 1). This may necessitate flexibility in terms of timing and in the emphasis given to either 'shared', 'guided' or independent writing in a particular Literacy Hour lesson.

Providing differentiation

Many teachers found it very difficult to provide appropriate differentiation during the first year of the NLS but have now begun to experiment with better ways of providing this. A range of writing frames, the use of ICT including tape recorders, paired writing and extra support can all help. In schools, where there is more than one form entry, some form of setting has been introduced with pupils across the year group being 'set' according to ability, although this means that children may work with a teacher who is not their class teacher, which can make the practice of non-fiction writing in other curriculum areas problematic. For example, in a Year 2 lower ability set observed recently, each group had a learning assistant allocated to it which greatly helped at the oral composition stage: something much needed by these children. To counter claims that each class teacher should be involved in this vital aspect of her pupils' learning development, the class stayed together for two mornings a week. This allowed more able pupils to challenge and support the less able: one of the benefits of shared work.[21] In schools where setting is not possible, it is essential that the grouping for 'guided' work is assessed and re-assessed regularly.

Response partner/paired writing

Response partners
Acting as 'response partners' (sometimes known as 'friend' or 'buddy') will help children to gain greater awareness of the writing process through discussing features of composition and transcription as part of helping each other to improve on pieces of writing. Whilst acting as a 'response partner', children need to share an appropriate metalanguage to discuss features of composition and transcription effectively. In order to respond thoughtfully, they should engage with a fundamental question that is often a challenge for teachers, 'How do you help someone to improve their writing?' (Chapter 1).

How to be a good 'response partner'

1   Listen carefully to your partner read his/her work.
2. Tell your partner what you liked about the writing.
3. Think how it might be improved –   Will the audience understand it?
                                       Will they find it interesting?
                                       Is there anything missing?
                                       Can you suggest any words or changes?
                                       Is it the right length?
4. Suggest how the writing might be improved.

(Fisher and Williams 2000)[22]

This engages them in thinking metacognitively about the processes involved (see below).

Paired writing

Rather than responding to each other's written efforts at various stages of the process, children can sometimes benefit from being part of a writing partnership where tasks are shared from the outset. Often children who are held back by secretarial difficulties are freed to compose when working with a carefully chosen partner. Children who are not keen on the task of writing can be extremely enthusiastic and hard-working when allowed to share the job with a friend of their own choosing. Different pairings can lead to different advantages. Of course the aim is that eventually each will be a better writer when working alone.

ICT and the Literacy Hour

Word-processing can greatly aid the process of editing. However, problems are still being encountered in many schools where access to word-processing is limited. This makes it difficult to integrate ICT into Literacy Hour writing lessons properly but whenever this is achieved, planning and composing (through story planning sheets and writing frames) is made easier. Equally, the editing process, both in terms of content and transcription, can be undertaken quickly and effectively through use of various editing facilities such as 'cut and paste', spellcheck or grammar check, although the last two have to be introduced with caution. Using a 'track changes' facility can lead to a valuable record of the redrafting and editing process, providing both assessment material and copy for future lessons. The 'shared' element of Literacy Hour lessons can be enhanced through laptop to screen links which allow teachers to model approaches in front of children, and the immediacy of this provides pupils with the opportunity to get involved in the process for themselves (Chapter 6).

Thinking skills and gaining metacognitive understanding during the Literacy Hour

Learning to write involves learning how to communicate thoughts and ideas in a permanent form and it is through thinking about the writing process that children learn to convey their meaning effectively.

Learning to write is a thinking process and, therefore, an awareness of what one is doing, no matter how contextually embedded that may be, is an essential component of the process.   (Wray 1994:56)[23]

The National Curriculum (NC) identifies five thinking skills that it is claimed will underpin learning and performance in school.[24] They focus attention on 'knowing how' as well as 'knowing what' in any subject of the curriculum. The five skills are linked to key questions and features of dialogue, as follows:

Thinking skills (NC)	Characteristic questions	Features of dialogue
Information-processing	What is it about?	Relevant information is shared
Reasoning	What does it mean?	Reasons are expected
Enquiry	What do we need to know?	Questions are asked
Creative thinking	What can we add to it?	Ideas are developed
Evaluation	What do we think about it?	Judgements are made

(Fisher 2001)[25]

There are links here with the higher order thinking advocated for more able pupils (Chapter 10). Information-processing is at the core of thinking. Therefore, in shared writing, opportunities should be provided for children to reflect on and evaluate the writing of either a published author of a text, or their teacher or other pupils. Information-processing can sometimes offer a low level of challenge, for example when children are asked to reproduce information already given, but through higher levels of thinking their cognitive challenge can be increased considerably. This involves them in making judgements, in selecting relevant information and in classifying what has been learned. Critical thinking such as this depends on reasoning, inference and deduction. For example, pupils might be asked to consider Mr Tom's character after reading the opening page of *Goodnight Mr Tom* (see Chapter 4 for further ideas for using this book), basing this on evidence from the text of what he is like. To challenge the thinking of children of all abilities teachers need to plan for, and promote thinking including higher order thinking that is at an analytical and conceptual level.

For example, in relation to poetry, questions can be asked which range across the five key thinking skills above:

- What is poetry? (information-processing)
- What is rhyme? (information-processing)
- What is a syllable? (information-processing)
- Why do poets sometimes choose to use rhyme and other times not? (enquiry/reasoning)
- What are the similarities and differences between my favourite poems? (enquiry/reasoning)
- What poets do I like, and why? (creative thinking/evaluation)

(Fisher and Williams 2001)[26]

Challenging children to think involves engaging them in higher order thinking (Bloom 1956)[27] which can be attained through working collaboratively, as well as individually. In any lesson, good teachers will move backwards and forwards between levels of thinking to provide appropriate differentiation for all. Lesson plans and schemes of work should be devised to ensure that children's thinking is being engaged at all levels.

Some cognitive challenge is posed by any writing task, although children can easily pick up the message that it is only the transcription of the piece that really matters unless care is taken to avoid this. Also, without being given an appropriate challenge they may rely on what they already know, as in the writing of 'news' on Monday mornings that often resulted in young children repeating each week something as banal, as:

Went up my nans. Ate chips. Came home and watched television. Went to bed.

Children need to be stimulated by new, motivating topics and through being taught how to write in accordance with the conventions of a range of genres.

Initially they can be supported in learning a new genre through using writing frames which help them to think about the structure of their writing through a series of supporting questions and cohesive ties (Wray and Lewis 1997). These can help in identifying critical aspects of a particular genre (Chapter 1).

Thinking in the Literacy Hour

One of the main areas where children can be encouraged to think during the Literacy Hour is as part of shared writing where the teacher models the writing process in order to reveal how a writer copes with the challenges involved in creating meaningful and well-written texts. Once a form has been modelled children should discuss it as a means of thinking about it and deepening their understanding before trying to write in it for themselves. The teacher needs to step back a little while they are drafting but should offer support to a particular group during guided or independent writing. In addition, pupils can be encouraged to support one another, but this will only be effective when they are challenged to think deeply about the writing process by their teachers. Children can write collaboratively but should be given frequent opportunities to write on their own. This process should be supported by review, either with the teacher or a response partner, or in the plenary session where they can think about the effectiveness of their own writing compared to that of others, including published authors.

Conclusion

A critical element in improving children's literacy levels is likely to be their metacognitive understanding of how they are learning to become readers and writers. This empowers them and paves the way for successful learning in other contexts (Chapter 1). Shared reading and textual analysis of samples of writing with children can enhance understanding of the process of writing and what it means to be a good writer. Discussion of writing between a child and a teacher in the form of a conference, or with a group of children as in the 'guided' aspect of the Literacy Hour, will aid the development of a shared vocabulary, or metalanguage, for discussing writing. Such discussions should help children become familiar with the technical language of English. This includes the correct use of grammatical terms as well as important textual features such as cohesion, voice or style including the use of imagery, as in this example where a class of Year 5 inner-city pupils discussed the figurative language used in the poem 'A Moon-witch' by Ted Hughes. After this they were asked to make use of metaphor and simile in their own writing to express more than simple description. One pupil tried to combine her feelings of cosiness and awe at the scale of the universe:

a

shower

of stars glow

in the night sky

that's dark like a navy blanket

of velvet tucking up the universe

their beams shine into the

spaces between

the light

years

Notes

1. The National Literacy Project (1997) that was set up in 18 LEAs, where children's levels of literacy were low, in an attempt to raise standards of literacy.
2. The DfEE (1998) National Literacy Strategy Literacy Training Pack which was used for training purposes in LEAs but, as it operated on a 'cascade' model of dissemination was more effective in some schools than others.
3. 'Framework for Teaching English, Years 7–9' to be found on the DfEE Standards website where it is stated that the introduction of this initiative will be accompanied by a professional development programme aimed at raising standards in English across all subjects of the secondary school curriculum.
4. Williams, M. (2001) 'Trainee teachers' perceptions of the effectiveness of the Literacy Hour in primary schools in England'. *Early Child Development and Care*, 2001, 166, 53–61.
5. Ofsted (1999) *The National Literacy Strategy: An Evaluation of the First Year of the National Literacy Strategy*. London: Ofsted.
6. Although there have been improvements in overall standards of literacy in recent years (QCA 2001) with the proportion of eleven-year-olds reaching Level 4 or above rising to 75 per cent (2000), writing continues to lag behind reading, with 78 per cent achieving Level 4 in reading whilst it is only 54 per cent in writing. The gap between girls and boys is even more worrying (Chapter 10).
7. John Stannard, Director of the National Literacy Strategy, writing a foreword to

an edition of Language and Literacy', the United Kingdom Reading Association newsletter, Spring 2000, setting out his concerns about the teaching of writing.

8. Williams, M. (2000) 'The part which metacognition can play in raising standards in English at Key Stage 2'. *Reading*, 34(1), April.

9. Bereiter, C. and Scardamalia, M. (1987) *The Psychology of Written Composition.* Hillsdale, NJ: Lawrence Erlbaum Associates.

10. Donald Graves's process approach to writing shaped the way that it is taught in the United States today and influenced many teachers in the UK throughout the '80s and '90s.

11. Williams, M. (2000) 'The part which metacognition can play in raising standards in English at Key Stage 2'. *Reading*, 34(1), April.

12. A useful phrase from the Cox Report (DES (1988) *English for Ages 5 to 11*, London: HMSO) which succinctly encapsulated what children need to know as they learn to write across a range of genres.

13. Halliday, M. and Hasan, R. (1985) *Language. Context & Text: Aspects of Language in a Social Semiotic Perspective*. Oxford: Oxford University Press.

14. Fisher, R. and Williams, M. (2001) Brunel Research Into Literacy (BRIL), unpublished.

15. Ofsted (2000) *The National Literacy Strategy: The Second Year.* London: Ofsted.

16. Wray, D. (1994) *Literacy and Awareness.* London: Hodder & Stoughton/UKRA.

17. Ofsted (2000) *The National Literacy Strategy: The Second Year.* London: Ofsted.

18. DfEE (April, 1998) *Teaching: High Status, High Standards.* Circular 4/98. London: HMSO. Here the subject knowledge needed for English is set out.

19. Meadows, C. and Cashdan, A. (1988) *Helping Children Learn.* London: David Fulton Publishers.

20. Adapted from Fisher, R. and Williams M. (eds) (2000) *Unlocking Literacy: A Guide for Teachers.* London: David Fulton Publishers, Chapter 6, 'Is it write?'.

21. Ofsted (1999) *The National Literacy Strategy: An Evaluation of the First Year of the National Literacy Strategy.* London: Ofsted.

22. Fisher, R. and Williams M. (eds) (2000) *Unlocking Literacy: A Guide for Teachers.* London: David Fulton Publishers, Chapter 6, 'Is it write?'.

23. Wray, D. (1994) *Literacy and Awareness.* London: Hodder & Stoughton/UKRA.

24. DfEE (1999) *The National Curriculum: Handbook for Primary Teachers in England.* London: DfEE.

25. Fisher, R. (2001) 'Thinking to Write: Thinking Skills in Literacy Learning', Paper presented at the UKRA International Conference, Christ Church, Canterbury, 7 July, 2001.

26. Fisher, R. and Williams, M. (2001) Brunel Research Into Literacy (BRIL), unpublished.

27. Bloom's taxonomy (1956) in which six levels of thinking are proposed. These work through from knowledge, comprehension, application, analysis, synthesis to evaluation, with the three higher levels posing the greatest cognitive challenge.

Further reading

Beard R. (1999) *National Literacy Strategy: Review of Research and Related Evidence.* London: DfEE.

Bereiter, C. and Scardamalia, M. (1987) *The Psychology of Written Composition.* Hillsdale, NJ: Lawrence Erlbaum Associates.

Bloom, B.S. (195G) *Taxonomy of Educational Objectives*, Volume I. London: Longman.

Brown, M., Furlong, T. and Venkatakrishnan, H. September 2001, *Key Stage 3 National Strategy: An Evaluation of the English and Mathematics Strategies*, ATL Interim Report.

Browne, A. (1996) *Developing Language and Literacy.* London: Paul Chapman.

Bruce, T. (1991) *Time to Play.* London: Hodder & Stoughton.

Clay, M. (1979) *Reading: The Patterning of Complex Behaviour*, (second edn). London: Heinemann.

David, T (1998) 'Learning properly! Young children and desirable outcomes' *Journal of the Professional Association of Early Childhood Educators*, 18(2), Spring.

DES (1988) *English for Ages 5 to 11.* London: HMSO.

DfEE (April, 1998) *Teaching: High Status High Standards*, Circular 4/98, London: HMSO.

DfEE (1998) *The National Literacy Strategy.* Sanctuary Buildings, London: HMSO.

DfEE (1999) *The National Curriculum: Handbook for Primary Teachers in England.* London.

DfEE (2000) *Curriculum Guidance for the Foundation Stage.* London, QCA.

Fisher, R. (1995) *Teaching Children to Think.* Cheltenham: Stanley Thornes.

Fisher, R. (1995) *Teaching Children to Learn.* Cheltenham: Stanley Thornes.

Fisher, R. (1998) *Teaching Thinking: Philosophical Enquiry in the Classroom.* London: Cassell.

Fisher, R. (1998) 'Thinking about thinking: developing metacognition in children'. *Early Child Development and Care*, 141, 1–13.

Fisher, R. and Williams, M. (eds) (2000) *Unlocking Literacy: A Guide for Teachers.* London: David Fulton Publishers.

Graves, D. (1983) *Writing: Teachers & Children at Work.* Portsmouth, NH: Heinemann.

Halliday, M. and Hasan, R. (1985) *Language, Context & Text: Aspects of Language in a Social Semiotic Perspective.* Oxford: Oxford University Press.

Meadows, C. and Cashdan, A. (1988) *Helping Children Learn.* London: David Fulton Publishers.

Meek, M. (1991) *On Being Literate.* London: Bodley Head.

Nutbrown, C. (1994) *Threads of Thinking.* London: Paul Chapman.

Ofsted (1999) *The National Literacy Strategy: An Evaluation of the First Year of the National Literacy Strategy.* London: Ofsted.

Ofsted (2000) *The National Literacy Strategy: The Second Year.* London: Ofsted.

QCA (2001) *Standards at Key Stage 2: English, Mathematics and Science.* London, www.qca.org.uk

Stannard, J. (2000) 'Language and literacy'. *UKRA News*, Spring.

Vygotsky, L.S. (1978) *Mind in Society.* Cambridge, MA: Harvard University Press.

Wray, D. (1994) *Literacy and Awareness.* London: Hodder & Stoughton/UKRA.

Wray, D. and Lewis, M. (1997) *Extending literacy: children reading and writing non-fiction.* London: Routledge.

Children's Literature

Hughes, Ted (1970) 'A Moon-witch', *Moon Bells*. London: Chatto & Windus.
Kerr, Judith (1973) *The Tiger Who Came To Tea*. London: Collins Picture Lions.
McKee, David (1987) *Not Now, Bernard*. A Beaver Book.
Murphy, Jill (1980) *Peace At Last* London: Macmillan.
Murphy, Jill (1986) *Five Minutes' Peace*. London: Walker Books.

CHAPTER 3

'What's the worth?': thinking about writing at Key Stages 2 and 3

Robert Catt

Introduction: writing is difficult

Writing is difficult for most of us Academic writing – whether in the academy of the Key Stage 3 classroom or in the university – is particularly difficult There is a difference – a difference of text and a difference in texture – between the writing we undertake for immediate and instrumental purposes – the scribbled shopping list, the hurried note (don't forget your PE kit!!!!) left on the kitchen table – and the writing undertaken for academic purposes – writing up our history homework, a discursive exercise for English, an examination paper or, indeed, a chapter like this.

When undertaking academic writing, we tend to dither; we tend towards displacement activities. I've just snatched at the opportunity to hang out a line of washing and now I wonder if it's time to make more coffee.

Remember, too, those monochrome 'B movies' in pre-word-processor days where a tough, usually smoking, crime reporter sits tapping at 'a typewriter against a backgrounded Manhattan auralscape of police sirens. He rips the paper from the typewriter – remember that satisfying 'zzziiiiiiip'? – and hurls it towards a wastebin. Fade down; fade up to bin now full to overflowing with balls of paper. Cut to writer: head in hands, full ashtray, empty whisky bottle. Vygotsky characterised writing as high on abstraction and 'like speech without an interlocutor, addressed to absent or imaginary persons or to no-one in particular' (1986:181) and this, no doubt, explains something of its difficult nature.

Reluctant writers

I am observing a trainee English teacher in a demanding 'inner-city' secondary classroom. He is working with a class of quite rowdy Year 7 boys. They have been reading Ian Serraillier's *The Silver Sword*. 'Not my choice,' complains the trainee. 'It was in the stock cupboard and I was told to use it.' And it is tough going for this class. That said, while the trainee reads from the text – and he reads well – the boys are attentive. They also seem to listen when he suspends the reading to provide contextual information. This is a story set in Poland during World War Two and the trainee has been appalled by the boys' lack of knowledge of the period. He feels, he tells me, that he has 'to keep giving a history lesson'.

Things, in general, are going well until the trainee introduces 'the writing'. He explains the task clearly, asking the boys to write a 'diary entry' for the protagonist who is fleeing from the Nazis. He talks about diaries, the need for a date, and the kind of information that is likely to be recorded.

It doesn't work. The boys grumble and find it difficult to get started. There's a good deal of muddle: elaborate 'business' with exercise books, pencils and pens; some minor squabbles erupt over the ownership of rulers and rubbers. It is seized upon by the whole class as a welcome distraction. Still the trainee does well. He quells and encourages, cajoles and threatens; he writes starter sentences on the board and promises more reading towards the end of the lesson. But these boys are reluctant writers. And then it starts. Almost, at first, a whisper from one child, then taken up by another and then another. And louder. 'What's the worth?' It begins as a question but, soon, is a chant from the whole class as they condemn the task to futility: 'What's the worth... What's the worth... What's the worth!'. The trainee looks towards me...

It's not a rebellion. These Year 7 youngsters are mischievous rather than malevolent. The trainee gets the lesson back on the rails and – and here's the paradox – once settled to the task, the boys soon 'get into' the writing.

In the lesson debrief we talk about that strange chant. Where's it from? Is it soap opera – *EastEnders*? Is it East London vernacular? Whatever its origins, the complaint is direct and clear: What's the point of this? What's in it for me?

National Literacy Strategy: Evaluation

That cameo exemplifies a key finding from the first DfEE evaluation of the National Literacy Strategy in primary schools (DfEE 2000b). While standards of reading have shown improvement, there is still concern about the quality of writing and from boys, in particular. This concern informs the rationale for the Key Stage 3 National Strategy and is given some immediate attention in, for example, the English Department Training Materials:

> Writing standards are lower than reading at the end of Key Stage 2 and boys' writing is a particular issue. Many pupils transferring with an overall Level 4 for English are still writing at Level 3. These differences tend to remain in Key Stage 3 (DfEE 2001a:2).

The Key Stage 3 National Strategy Framework for teaching English: Years 7, 8 and 9 provides a broad model of literacy and sets out a commendable series of 'sophisticated literacy skills' expected of pupils 'by the end of Year 9' (DfEE 2001b:10). The complementary Key Stage 3 National Strategy English (NSE) Department training materials draw upon the *QCA Qualitative Report on 2000* English results,[1] to identify rather more technical priorities for the development of writing in the secondary school:

- Develop spelling strategies to improve accuracy.
- Punctuate accurately both at the boundaries and within sentences.
- More developed use of sentences to include more subordination and expanded noun phrases.
- Use and secure use of paragraphs to structure writing and improve coherence, including layout of direct speech.
- Structure non-narrative writing more effectively, linking sentences and paragraphs logically by use of appropriate conjuncts and adverbials.

(DfEE 2001a: 4)

Few teachers would disagree with this list of priorities. As Myhill points out:

> ...a concern for improving children's writing is axiomatic, a fundamental part of the very stuff of being an English teacher, and all English teachers know the frustration of the child who can say more than he or she can express in writing...
>
> (Myhill 2001:13)

But what's the worth? Those priorities need what might be called a 'situated' context. PGCE English trainees, for example, are enthusiastic about children's writing but often find it tough to teach in classrooms where 'the worth' – the point and purpose of writing – can seem elusive, even obscure. When, in seminar discussion, trainees examine literacy practices it seems evident that writing is fairly peripheral to many people's lives. The 'worth' question is, frankly understandable.

In discussing school experience, pre-qualified teachers of English tend to echo Myhill's continuing concern that:

> Recent debate about writing...has often failed to consider the needs of learners or the practical realities of many classrooms. The time is ripe for a reconceptualisation of how we teach and how students learn writing. (2001:13–14)

In this chapter I want to discuss the teaching and learning of writing and, following the theme of this book, draw attention to the importance of *thinking about writing*. In doing so, I shall be drawing upon my own work as a teacher of English, my work with PGCE Secondary English trainees and observations of classroom practice at Key Stage 3. To return to that paradox, above, much 'happy writing'[2] demonstrably does take place in schools. There is ample evidence of quality and enjoyment. My trainee's class of reluctant writers did settle to the task and here I am now, line of washing neglected, coffee cold in the cup, settling to mine.

The National Writing Project (NWP)

In the current atmosphere of curriculum and initiative overload a glance back to the National Writing Project (NWP)[3] is informative rather than merely sentimental and nostalgic. The materials themselves had a different texture: nothing like the slick typography and glossiness of the NSE folders. The emphatic difference, however, is in the NWP's emphasis upon purpose in writing and the sharing between teachers across the country of classroom ideas and practice. The Project had a welcome 'bottom-up' approach. There is, in contrast, a concern that the NSE – which is certainly rich in materials and ideas – places more emphasis upon linguistic features, perhaps at the expense of purpose and relish, and that it feels top-down, prescriptive and authoritarian.

The interim evaluation of the pilot phase of the Key Stage 3 National Strategy, commissioned by the Association of Teachers and Lecturers, is positive about aspects of the NSE materials and recommended teaching structures. The report, however, also reflects the unease of teachers:

> Much more emphasis on writing technique: much less on creativity, sensitivity, personal response, development of opinions, etc. Teaching is now a largely technical impersonal operation...

> These things can be wonderful or useless, but they are always introduced immediately with very little preparation and staff are given little time to train, digest, plan and evaluate the effects of what they are doing.
>
> (Furlong *et al.* 2001:10,18)

Although, in this chapter, I shall acknowledge the value of the literacy materials now available at Key Stages 2 and 3, I shall also remind readers of the important emphasis upon literacy practices – an understanding of the relationship between writers, task, audience and purpose – and the concomitant working lives of busy teachers, which was a significant strength of the National Writing Project.

Thinking about writing

Fetch me a pen, I need to think. (attributed to Voltaire)

When I think about writing I also find myself thinking about not writing. Let me explain. Like most of us I am dependent upon writing. Lecture notes, evaluations, policy documents, letters, memos, emails and now 'texting' are essential sites in my work. But I also write to think; I work things out in writing; nascent ideas are realised as I write; the blurred image begins to achieve clarity in the developing tray of words. It's happening now. But, perhaps like many of us (and particularly when I become immersed in the production of so many documents for so many inspections (as one teacher put it: 'the "fabrications" of "evidence" and near-truths' – which are now such a familiar feature of educational practice), I often wonder if something has been lost in our technological reliance upon writing. The idea, perhaps, that my word is my bond, that I am as good as my word, has been denigrated. Faced with yet another 'action plan' my colleague at the desk opposite wearily complains: 'Why can't I just say I do it? Why do I have to write it down?'

In the 1950s my wife's parents bought their first house. They had borrowed money from the bank but still didn't have enough to complete the purchase. So the seller of the house simply suggested that they owe him the balance and pay him back each week. And they shook hands on the deal. At the end of each week – and this went on for a period of years – my father-in-law would walk two or three miles to where the seller now lived and paid over some cash. Try that with your local bank or building society: 'I'd like to borrow some money. You have my word that it'll be re-paid'!

But that idea – that somehow, something, an integrity, has been lost with the advance of literacy – is, surely, a merely romantic lament. We now live in a literate culture and we don't have to think far about writing before recognising its value in sustaining and developing ideas – its transformative qualities – and in communicating those ideas across space and time. Through the remarkable symbolic system of writing, we can open windows on other worlds.

'Tabby' Bramble, undertaking the wild adventure of a cross-country journey in 1771 – a mere outing in these modern times – worries, like us all, about the security of the home she has left behind. But, thanks to the technology of literacy, her anxieties are accessible to us today in the letter written to her housekeeper, Mrs Gwilym:

Glostar, April 2

Mrs. Gwyllim,

When this cums to hand, be sure to pack up in the trunk male that stands in my closet, to be sent to me in the Bristol wagon without loss of time, the following articles, viz. my rose collard neglejay, with green robins, my yellow damask, and my black velvet suit, with the short hoop; my bloo quilted petticoat, my green mantel, my laced apron, my French commode, Macklin head and lappets, and the litel box with my jowls. Williams may bring over my bum-daffee, and the viol with the easings of Dr. Hill's dock-water, and Chowder's lacksitif. The poor creature has been terribly consturpated ever since we left huom. Pray take particular care of the house while the family is absent. Let there be a fire constantly kept in my brother's chamber and mine. The maids, having nothing to do, may be set a spinning. I desire you'll clap a pad-luck on the wind-seller, and let none of the men have excess to the strong bear. Don't forget to have the gate shit every evening before dark. The gardnir and the hind may lie below in the landry, to partake the house, with the blunderbuss and the great dog; and I hope you'll have a watchfull eye over the maids. I know that hussy, Mary Jones, loves to be rumping with the men. Let me know if Alderney's calf be sould yet, and what he fought; if the ould goose be sitting; and if the cobbler has cut Dicky, and how the pore anemil bore the operation. No more at present, but rests,

Yours,
Tabitha Bramble

Delightful here is the compression – a cameo – of a social history. The writing 'opens a window' on a world now gone. It illuminates Tabby's rather dominant and interfering character and it reveals some fascinating domestic information. I like that concern about the security of the house 'the gardnir and the hind . . . with the blunderbuss and the great dog' and the behaviour of the servants – 'that hussy, Mary Jones . . .'. I notice, however, that the 'spellchecker' on my word processor is quite busy with this piece. A text of this kind presents obvious opportunities for language work at word, sentence and text level: how English changes over time, for example (note 'robins' for 'ribbons';

'fought' for 'fetched'; and 'shit' for 'shut'); the complex syntax of the opening sentence; and the cohesive textual and contextual demands which will be made upon the reader – and which might direct them to a dictionary or glossary – including the identity of 'the poor creature' (Tabby's dog) and 'Dicky' (a horse).[4]

Language work aside, a piece like this presents reflective opportunities in which, I feel, the teaching of writing should be rooted including, as I've suggested, the nature and power of literacy.

But then there's another reflective level. This isn't a genuine letter. It's from Tobias Smollett's epistolary novel *The Expedition of Humphry Clinker*. There's an author behind the letter taking on the persona of a middle-aged countrywoman and having some fun. This, of course, is one of the other great assets of writing. It allows us to play with text – to adopt or adapt an identity. We're back to purpose.

Classroom practice: thinking and talking about writing

Figure 3.1 is an example of a boy in Year 7 undertaking – in some small way – something of Smollett's task. He has written a letter of complaint. Unlike Smollett, his purpose isn't satirical; and his orthographical 'gaffes' are unintentional. But, in writing, he's adopted a particular persona perhaps because he feels it lends authority – 'gravitas' – to his complaint. I do much the same myself – and I bet you do, too – when writing a formal letter. It's the equivalent of the suit we put on for the interview or the telephone voice we adopt on formal occasions.

There's a good deal of thinking to be done about this text. A Year 7 English teacher recently used a copy of this novice letter – photocopied from the original handwritten draft – as an effective example to air some thinking about writing: 'why' and 'how' we write.

On first reading, the piece was fairly scornfully dismissed by youngsters as 'scruffy' (and, interestingly, some girls immediately identified it as 'boys' work' because of 'the awful writing') with 'bad spelling' and 'bad grammar'. There were also negative comments about layout – 'the address is wrong...his address should be here and their address should be there' – and formal conventions – 'Mr TV Programme is stupid...You start with their name or "Dear Sir" or something and he hasn't finished it properly with "Yours sincerely"...'.

This gave the teacher an excellent opportunity to discuss various conventions and, usefully, she introduced some metalinguistic terms: addressor, addressee, salutation and subscription. But she suggested helpfully, 'If, like me, you find those words a bit stuffy then you can call them "my address", "their address", "the greeting" and "farewell"'. She then talked about herself as a writer and how, despite the availability of electronic media she still liked to write letters – to her friends, her aunt in Canada and, especially, letters of complaint. There was motivated interest when she talked about writing to complain about a 'mouldy bar of chocolate' and how the company had sent her a whole box of free bars.

As the discussion progressed, youngsters began to see more merit in the letter and the ways in which the writer had tried to 'use some difficult words' and to 'sound like

Mr T.V. Programme
BBC TV
1 London

Dear Mr TV Programme,

I am write to complain about the vilonce I sore last night on last nights bill. Their were lots of times when I felt the need to turn over as lots of times I felt sickend. I am a great lover of the programme and look forward to watching it however, last night the programme portrayed the police in an unessassary light. I used to be a policeman myself and the force that P.C. Quinnon was seen to use on that drug dealer was to explicit. Young people today have a very bad view of the police and this programme did not help their image. If my young granddaughter had seen the programme what would she have thought.

I hope you will note my complain and continue to make the bill in the fashion I have come acustome to.

Figure 3.1 Year 7 boy's letter of complaint

a grown up'. But, it was agreed, the recipient of the letter would be unimpressed by such poor spelling and presentation.

This skilful teacher was now able to guide the class in their thinking about writing. What impressed me was the way she repeatedly 'modelled' by using her own experience. The reasons for using salutations and subscriptions, for example, promoted some excited discussion. The teacher was amusing when explaining that she could never understand why she was expected to write 'Dear...' even when writing to someone she didn't much like or had never met: 'I had to write to my bank manager...and she's a woman, by the way...and I called her "Dear Ms X" but I've never even seen her.' And, 'I've often written "yours faithfully" or "yours truly" or "yours sincerely" and I haven't been feeling at all faithful or sincere.'

This was warmly echoed by a number of children who said they 'felt silly' writing 'Dear...' and who, even, gave this as a reason for not writing letters. The discussion, however, produced counter examples: 'My mum never does it when she writes to school if I'm away. She just goes "Mr (X), Janine was off school with flu...".' Youngsters were also aware of the way the salutation could be exploited by advertisers (a technique which linguists call 'synthetic personalisation'):[5] 'My brother gets these letters and they say "Dear Darren (B) you have won a million pounds" and he just throws them away and I say he's mad but he says it's just junk mail done by a computer.'

Salutations, ventured the class teacher, were, perhaps, 'a way of being polite' and 'an important convention...We all have to do it'.

But do we? Is it important to know how to write a letter? This also generated a good deal of thinking and discussion. Although there were some dissenters – 'You can text them...' – the consensus was evident. Letters were important 'for jobs...for complaining'. Consumer interest was very evident here. If you didn't write and complain you wouldn't 'get things back' and if you didn't write 'thank you' letters for gifts you wouldn't 'get anything next time' (although the class teacher and I were disappointed that very few of this Year 7 class seemed ever to have written letters of thanks). It was also loosely agreed that the conventions – spelling, layout, address, greeting and farewell – did, indeed, matter or 'you won't be taken seriously'. Although the electronic lobby remained, generally, unconvinced of the power of the formal letter, there was some thoughtful discussion about and a general acknowledgement of the status of writing. It would, the majority of youngsters felt, be better to write than to phone or complain in person: 'they can see you're only twelve or whatever but if you're writing they don't know...you could be anyone...you could be like...your mum...like grown up'. Discussion, here, was edging towards a sophisticated debate on language, power and the status of standard English: 'If you're on the phone or you go up there...and you speak...well if you speak like (laughter)...not proper(ly)...but in a letter...if it's all neat and spelled right...they can't...how do they know who you are...that you're not posh?'

There was some passion in this discussion with some obvious and early recognition of the relationship between language and social identity. Many youngsters had a grievance as consumers, particularly when complaining about mobile phones and there was a feeling that they weren't taken seriously by retailers or when phoning service help lines: 'they know you're only a teenager...'. Interestingly, in this respect, it was felt that the word-processed letter of complaint would have more credibility because 'with handwriting they can tell who you are'. Again, at this point, the class teacher was explicit about her own literacy practices: she would 'use the computer for some letters' but she was 'proud' of her handwriting and would always 'handwrite letters to my friends and family (because) I think they'd be offended if they had something printed and impersonal'.

Unflagging class discussion of the value and purpose of writing was, on this occasion, easily sustained for 25 minutes and my colleague told me of her subsequent plans to show the class a wider range of examples including 'history facsimiles' and edited extracts from letters from a friend abroad 'who puts these terrific drawings and comic characters in the margin'. As already indicated, however, it was the class teacher's impressive modelling and reference to personal literacy practice which encouraged youngsters to participate in the session. She told the class about the miserly uncle whose Christmas letters used to end: 'I was going to put a five pound note in with this letter but I'd already sealed the envelope before I remembered, so I'll send it next year'; and the friend who usually began: 'I'm writing this slowly because I know you can't read quickly'. Readers will, of course, recognise these examples as corny apocrypha but this was nonsense which delighted and motivated these Year 7 youngsters.

The session also worked as a pre-writing activity. Youngsters were subsequently expected to write letters expressing their views on a local road improvement scheme.

The writing task would have a real audience – the letters would be posted to the local council and would also form part of a display for parents – and some urgency of purpose as this was a 'hot' local topic. Discussion of the exemplar letter also facilitated some understanding of the genre and allowed the teacher to be explicit about success criteria: the essential features of a formal letter.

Teaching writing

My extensive and varied classroom observations at both Key Stage 2 and 3 would suggest that this kind of thinking about writing, enlivened by discussion of example and anecdote, is not a typical feature of classroom practice. Further, rather than teaching writing, many teachers tend merely to set writing tasks. Myhill complains that often, in classrooms

> attention is devoted to the 'what' of writing, the content, whilst the 'how' is often ignored

and, she continues,

> It is worth considering how regularly writing is taught, in a context that devotes explicit attention to the writing itself (2001:14).

Significant research into the teaching of writing has been undertaken in the USA by Scardemalia and Bereiter (1985). They examine a familiar tension between substantive ideas and the rhetorical demands of a particular genre (1985:299). This often comes out in the classroom – and the university – as 'I know what I want to say but I can't get it down on paper.' Scardemalia and Bereiter suggest, however, that this tension can be productive. The familiar distinction in writing between 'knowledge telling' and 'knowledge transformation' can be illuminated through more attention to 'reflective thought during composition' (1985:307). A characteristic academic difficulty is the writer's struggle with the conventions of an unfamiliar genre: recount, exposition, argument etc. (Chapter 1). That struggle can, however, stimulate the change, development and transformation of knowledge as ideas have to be reworked, examined in detail and recast.

Myhill's critical view is certainly shared by the National Literacy Strategy. The very useful DfEE guidance *Grammar for Writing* also echoes her concern and illustrates the difficulties of novice writers:

> faced with too many hard things to do at once. They have to plan what they will write, think of which words and sentences to write, work out the spellings and transcribe it all onto the page. Often, most of their attention is taken up by spelling and scribing, leaving little mental space to think about the compositional aspects of their writing. Repeated experiences of this kind are likely to reinforce, rather than overcome, children's problems, making them increasingly reluctant writers in the process.
>
> (DfEE 2000a:12)

Teaching at the point of writing

The Key Stage 3 National Strategy materials provide a wealth of ideas for supporting pupils and for teaching writing. Significant here is the nature and timing of such teaching. As I have indicated, much writing practice in classrooms consists in setting the task, leaving children to write, then 'marking' and commenting on their work – often, briefly: 'Well done!' – sometimes with a grade. The guidance in *Grammar for Writing*, is critical of the 'implicit sequence to this teaching:

> the teacher prepares and stimulates ideas for writing with the class;
> the children write independently;
> the teacher responds, e.g. discusses, marks, etc.

Such a sequence suggests that

> the teaching of writing can easily be reduced to teaching by correction – teaching after the event – instead of teaching *at the point of writing.*
>
> (DfEE 2000a:11)

I find this emphasis upon teaching and intervention in the writing process – rather than intervention post-writing – a welcome feature of some observed classroom practice.

> Teaching at the point of writing focuses on demonstrating and exploring the decisions that writers make in the process of composition.   (DfEE 2000a:12)

This emphasis is complemented by the encouragement of shared writing and a

> focus on particular aspects of the writing process: planning, composing, revising, editing and redrafting...
>
> (DfEE 2000a:13)

Children also work with writing frames and use response partners (McCormick 2001); and it is claimed, the word processor has transformed much of the writing process (Chapter 6).

Medwell *et al.* (2001) consider a number of these strategies for 'teaching the writing process'. Many will be familiar to classroom practitioners and they include a welcome attention to collaborative work. Valuable in this account is the way in which teachers are involved in the writing process by, for example, modelling, scribing, prompting, sharing ideas and drafts and, again, using writing frames.

Metacognition: externalisation of thinking

I particularly support the recent emphasis on modelling because it foregrounds metacognition. It is a technique for thinking about writing, for making explicit and externalising those often taken-for-granted features of the expert writer. Medwell *et al.* are writing within the context of the Key Stage 2 classroom but their suggestions for teacher modelling are equally applicable at Key Stage 3:

- Rehearse a sentence orally before writing it, make changes to it, explaining why you chose certain words and not others, point out mistakes you have made or points on which you can improve
- Show (pupils) what you do in writing when you run out of ideas (reread what you have written, discuss it with another person, brainstorm some ideas, refer back to your plan)
- Show (pupils) what you do when you need to write quickly (write in note form, use abbreviations)
- Show (pupils) what you do when you don't know how a word is spelt (try it several ways to see what looks right, write what you think and mark it to check later, use a similarly meaning word that you can spell!).

(Medwell *et al.* 2001:112)

(I would, however, strongly disagree with this last piece of advice which, surely, encourages avoidance of rather than an engagement with spelling difficulties.)

Modelling by the teacher is a key feature of the metacognitive process. I still remember art lessons in school where, when I was stuck, the art teacher would intervene by drawing a helpful line or by executing a similar sketch herself. Moreover, the art teacher was an artist herself. A similar task, surely, for the English practitioner, is to make visible and explicit structural features of their own often taken-for-granted and habitual writing practices. As Cox, amongst others, has argued: 'Teachers also should write, as they can serve as role models' (Cox 1995:11). I don't think that necessarily means we should all be spending our leisured evenings and weekends writing that novel or re-working that sonnet. There is, however, enormous value in reflection upon our own writing practices; and this reflection can be shared and externalised in selective and appropriate ways as my colleague, above, has done.

This – making our practice visible – is an integral element in thinking about writing. Glaser (1990) pursues a metacognitive theme in discussing 'expertise' and the ways in which this needs to be made accessible to 'novices'. Expertise demands a knowledge of genre with which new writers will initially struggle, often in a way which is too readily dismissed as mere incompetence. ('Undergraduates can't write!' grumbles my colleague in frustration as he reads through a pile of essays. Of course, they can write and what he means is that they have yet to develop expertise in writing academic essays.) 'Novice writers,' suggests Glaser, tend to be 'insufficiently familiar not only with information about specialised topics but also with the specific conventions or techniques'. They tend only to 'work on surface features, using word and punctuation deletion and addition as important strategies' whereas 'experienced writers conceptualise the task as a holistic enterprise'. What, of course, can be frustrating for novice writers is that the practice of 'proficient writers . . . takes on the character of intuitive performance' (Glaser 1990: 94–6).

It is those intuitive features of expertise in writing which teachers need to make explicit and observable – which they need to model. Glaser emphasises the social features of learning and his following significant point will be appreciated by practitioners who already involve learners in shared writing:

A most salient aspect in a social context for learning is the elevation of thinking to an overt observable status.   (Glaser 1990:99)

Bruner (1996), in setting out his core beliefs in education, similarly points to this visibility of thinking in what he refers to as the 'externalisation tenet'. In discussing this, he also emphasises the social and collaborative in learning – the joint effort which, for many of us, is made visible in the classroom display, the dramatic presentation, and the school publication. The value of such externalisation is that the nascent idea is expressed and becomes amenable to response, analysis, discussion (Chapter 11) and that public acknowledgement and approbation so important to the development of self-esteem.

Bruner's point is significant and colleagues interested in thinking about writing would do well to consider the importance of externalisation in the classroom.

> Externalising, in a word, [claims Bruner] rescues cognitive activity from implicitness, making it more public [and] negotiable…At the same time, it makes it more accessible to subsequent reflection and metacognition. Probably the greatest milestone in the history of externalisation was literacy, putting thought and memory 'out there' on clay tablets or paper. Computers and e-mail may represent another step forward. But there are doubtless myriad ways in which jointly negotiated thought can be communally externalised as oeuvres – and many ways in which they can be put to use in schools. (Bruner 1996:164)

Readers might, at this point, care to reflect upon opportunities for their students to externalise ideas. If writing is crafting then its processes as well as its products deserve visibility so that improvements can be made and achievements acknowledged.

So, what's the worth?

Teaching at the point of writing demands technical, analytical, pedagogical skill and a knowledge of genre. Now, more than ever, teachers have some excellent resources to hand in the materials within the National Literacy Strategy and the Key Stage 3 National Strategy for English.

Teaching at the point of writing demands also a revitalised understanding of literacy practices, purposes and audiences. And this understanding needs to be conveyed to young writers themselves. We also need to *think* more about writing and, in this respect, literacy initiatives across the curriculum provide some whole-school opportunities. Yes, we need to teach writing; but writing tasks themselves need to be meaningful, purposeful and, from the viewpoint of young writers, invested with a sense of worth.

Endnote

I have quoted, above, from Smollett's swansong, *The Expedition of Humphry Clinker*, completed in the year of his death, 1771. In his first novel *The Adventures of Roderick Random* (1748) the eponymous orphan hero is sent to the village school at the age of six. He learns quickly and, proud of his achievement, writes letters to the grandfather who has disowned him. This incenses the old and wealthy gentleman who complains to the schoolmaster. Young Roderick describes how this shameful schoolmaster (who clearly has an awareness of audience and purpose in writing!), afraid of an influential patron and in order 'to prevent my future improvement', then:

> caused a board to be made with five holes in it, through which he thrust the fingers and thumb of my right hand, and fastened it by whip-cord to my wrist, in such a manner, that I was effectually debarr'd the use of my pen. (Smollett, 1999edn:5).

What's the worth, indeed?

Notes

1. These, presumably, are an analysis of the results of Key Stage 2 and Key Stage 3 standard assessment tests. However, no further detail is provided in this DfEE training folder.
2. Wason (1980:357) illustrates this as 'a kind of writing, familiar to experienced writers, in which the output is associated with a sense of elation and commitment'.
3. I wonder how many teachers remember or are aware of this national project (1986–1988) directed for the School Curriculum Development Committee by Pam Czerniewska. A 'bottom-up' ethos was in evidence in materials produced and analyses made of the writing process. Examples of this are the documents headed *Teachers of Writing Need a Clearer View of the Writer, of the Classroom, of the (writing) Repertoire and of our own Intervention* and *What We Need when We Write* (John Richmond); *Questions and Practice* (Eve Bearne); and *Responding to Children's Writing* (Jeremy Tafler). Significantly, the last two bear the footnotes: 'based on contributions from project working groups', and 'based on contributions from Project participants', respectively.
4. There are some other interesting glosses of features of this text. That 'French commode' is not what this reader first assumed but, it seems, 'a tall head-dress of silk or lace ('Macklin head' is 'Mechlin lace') supported by a wire frame'; I also thought that 'bum-daffee', like the 'dock-water', was a medicinal drink but it is, (probably plum-) coloured taffeta.
5. Examples of this abound. Advertisements often address the reader directly: 'What would *you* do with a million pounds?'; or suggest a collective effort: 'Working together *we* can improve our roads/railways/communications/public services.' Most common is the junk-mail letter incorporating the recipient's name. Telephone sales now often begin with an informal introduction: 'Hi. My name's Lisa . . .'. Note, too, the way politicians use the repeated informality of the interviewer's forename to express authority and calm: 'Well, Sue, as usual the opposition are making something out of nothing . . .'

Further reading

Bruner, J. (1996) 'Culture, mind and education', in Moon, B. and Murphy, P. (eds) (1999) *Curriculum in Context*. London: Paul Chapman in association with The Open University.

Cox, B. (1995) *Cox on the Battle for the English Curriculum*. London: Hodder & Stoughton.

DfEE (2000a) *The National Literacy Strategy: Grammar for Writing*.

DfEE (2000b) *News* (Press release 6/1/00 Ref. 2/00).

DfEE (2001a) *Key Stage 3 National Strategy*. English Department Training 2001.

DfEE (2001b) *Key Stage 3 National Strategy Framework for Teaching English: Years 7, 8 and 9*.

Furlong, T. *et al*. (2001) *Key Stage 3 National Strategy: An Evaluation Of The Strategies For Literacy And Mathematics – Interim Report*. London: ATL.

Glaser, R. (1990) 'Expert knowledge and processes of thinking', in McCormick, R. and Paechter, C. (eds) (1999) *Learning & Knowledge*. London: Paul Chapman with The Open University.

McCormick, J. (2001) 'Talking About Writing', in Goodwin, P. *The Articulate Classroom: Talking and Learning in the Primary School*. London: David Fulton Publishers.

Medwell, J., Wray, D., Minns, H., Griffiths, V. and Coates, E. (2001) *Primary English: Teaching Theory and Practice*. Exeter: Learning Matters.

Myhill, D. (2001) 'Writing: crafting and creating'. *English in Education*, 35(3), 13–20, Autumn, NATE.

Scardamalia, M. and Bereiter, C. (1985) 'Development of dialectical processes in composition', in Stierer, B. and Maybin, J. (eds) (1994) *Language, Literacy and Learning in Educational Practice*. Clevedon: Multilingual Matters in association with The Open University Press.

Smollett, T. (1965) *The Expedition of Humphry Clinker*. Everyman's Library (rev. edn).

Smollett, T. (1999 edn.) *The Adventures of Roderick Random*. Oxford World's Classics (rev. edn).

Vygotsky, L. (1986) *Thought and Language*. Cambridge, MA: MIT Press (rev. edn).

Wason, P.C. (1980) 'Conformity and commitment in writing'. *Visible Language*, XIV, 4, 351–63.

Children's Literature

Serraillier, Ian (1956) *The Silver Sword*. Harmondsworth: Puffin.

CHAPTER 4

Writing aloud: drama and writing

Colleen Johnson

STUDENT: How does drama help you with your writing?
PIPPA: Because I'm there and I know what it's like!

At a time when drama appears to be making a comeback in primary education, with its heightened status in the National Curriculum (DfEE 1999a), teachers are struggling to find space for it in an already full timetable. With teacher training focusing so heavily on core subjects, expertise in the arts is under threat. In this chapter I hope to redress the balance a little by offering examples of tried-and-tested suggestions for drama activities which will be:

- easily accommodated in the classroom, in short bursts of time;
- accessible to the teacher with little experience of drama; and
- useful in promoting learning outcomes in terms of writing.

I would like to begin by referring to drama's current status in primary education, to acknowledge its motivational force, to explore the myriad contexts for communication which it offers – with specific reference to writing – and finally to consider how involvement in, and reflection on, the dramatic experience offers opportunities for developing children's metacognitive awareness.

Drama's current status

Enthusiasts for drama[1] were not slow to welcome the explicit reference to the subject in both *English in the National Curriculum* (DfEE 1999)[2] and *The National Literacy Strategy* (NLS) (DfEE 1998). Indeed, the NLS was supplemented by the very useful *Opportunities for Drama in the Framework of Objectives* (DfEE 1999b)[3] which highlighted a range of dramatic possibilities to enrich literacy teaching at word, sentence and text level from Reception to Year 6. For the purposes of this chapter I would like to focus specifically on drama's crucial role in fostering children's competence and interest in understanding the writing process. Drama's implicit potential emerges in both the new requirements for fostering group discussion and interaction (DfEE 1999)[4] and the teaching of personal, social, moral and health education (PMSE).[5] Inevitably some of the examples offered here will be cross-curricular both in content and application, showing how drama links curricular areas such as English and humanities, as well as enhancing collaborative learning skills.[6]

Drama's motivational force

Participating

Anyone who has been involved with drama can testify to the range of emotions it stimulates. From the role play corner to the amateur theatrical society stage, its common denominators are enjoyment, motivation and stimulation. Through it, participants are taken 'out of the ordinary' and 'beyond the humdrum'. In the classroom such experiences, introduced to foster learning, reflect the best of group and whole-class teaching (Hertrich 1998).[7] It offers both active and interactive learning in which children of all academic abilities can thrive by working together. For some children, this may be their only chance to excel in school and to feel valued and praised, not just by teachers and other adults, but also by their peers. This is a point I will come back to when discussing drama and metacognition.

Spectating

A great deal of conversation, on any level of society and within any age group, is *about* drama. Adults and children discuss plays, mostly experienced in the form of television drama. We enjoy laughing, sometimes crying, even getting angry in response to drama, and then sharing the experience with others, both at the time of the event and in the discussion following which may be hours, days, weeks, even years later. Successful teachers, recognising the level of armchair-critic expertise which so many children bring into the classroom, will capitalise on this 'social experience' (Hertrich 1998)[8] to generate writing in all forms, from scripting to film reviews; storyboarding to promotional advertising. For these reasons alone, drama merits a place in language and literacy teaching but there is so much more, besides.

Contexts for communication

> Research into language and education has shown the importance of experiences for children which provide meaningful contexts in which to use language for a variety of purposes.
>
> (Heathcote 1980:81)

Drama offers unique opportunities for creating contexts, not just for talk (Johnson 2000) but for other forms of communication, of which writing is a key element. When children talk to each other, to their teacher, to their parents, their 'audience' is before them, whereas they can struggle to envisage the 'hidden' audience required for writing. What follows are a number of examples of how drama has stimulated and enhanced children's writing by generating a 'real' sense of purpose and audience. The writing may well take place in preparation for, during, or following dramatic activity. In some cases it will have occurred in all three.

The volcano with Year 4 children

A common theme to be found in drama, and in much of children's literature, is the community under threat. Drama need not always be about conflict between members of a group. This is one such example. The structure encourages the children to work collaboratively as members of a community, while the threat – in this case, an impending volcanic eruption – comes from outside. From this stimulus the children wrote, in letter and diary form, first person accounts of the events.[9] Drama activities, which helped them to be able to do this, included the following:

Activity 1: Making a map of the island

The children were seated in a circle. The teacher introduced the theme by saying that their drama would begin on an island and that they would be playing the islanders. She asked the children to imagine their island, identifying key factors which would enable the community to be self-sufficient: fresh water, food generation – land for farming, animals and crops, fishing boats, a wood for timber, homes, a hospital, schools, transportation routes.

She told them that before recreating the classroom as the island, they would need to produce a map of the island to guide them around. She placed a large sheet of paper, with some marker pens, on the floor in the middle of the circle. On it she had drawn an outline of the island and a number of children identified where the farm lands, villages and fresh water supplies were to be found. Other children were chosen to help identify and locate other significant features, such as woodland, beaches and a harbour. This activity served a number of purposes:

- it stimulated the children's interest;
- it helped them 'take ownership' of the island and to identify with the community living there;
- it enabled them to bring to the task knowledge and learning from other areas of the curriculum, such as geography and maths;[10]
- it allowed children of all levels of ability to produce symbols to represent key sites, so that those less able in terms of spelling, as well as EAL (English as an Additional Language) children still struggling with written English (Chapter 8), were able to offer valuable contributions to the map; and
- it meant that all information added – including grids, signs and even compass points – had to be clearly understood by all the children, and this put pressure on those responsible for them to represent what each stood for clearly.

After this the teacher said, ' There is one significant feature we haven't put on yet. It's a volcano.' There were gasps. Then she added, reassuringly, 'Oh – but it's inactive.' There were a few sighs of relief at this. The children were already empathising with the community!

Activity 2: Setting out the island

The next task was for the island to be recreated in the classroom, using the map as the guide. The children grouped tables to represent the volcano and the houses. Larger spaces were cleared for farmland. Then the teacher asked the children to choose a job which would be needed on the island and to go to the area where it would be done. There followed discussion between the children as they chose their work. Several went to the farmland; some to the harbour where the fishing boats were; others to the forest to chop wood. Then they were asked to go into role. They imagined that they were real islanders carrying out their day-to-day work. This required them to mime what such work would require. For example, one girl, as a forest worker, mimed chopping down trees, which would be needed to build houses. As they did so, the teacher placed post-it notes and pens around the room. She asked them to pause in their work and introduced thought tracking, a strategy which requires the child to speak out loud the thoughts of the character which she or he is portraying, at any given moment:

> TEACHER: As I go about my work on the island, I am thinking about what I enjoy about life here.

The children were invited to write – in role – statements on the post-it notes and to place them on the floor in front of them (I will come back to the use of post-it notes in drama/writing activities later in the chapter). When these were finished, she asked them to freeze in groups of four. The rest of the children then had the opportunity to see the images of those at work, to guess at the jobs being represented in the freezes, and to read the statements, discussing similarities and contrasts between them: for example, identifying how many islanders claimed to enjoy the weather, and how many commented on the friendliness and safety of living in a small, self-sufficient community.

Activity 3: The Emergency
Next, the teacher announced:

> I have some very bad news. The volcano has become active. We must leave the island.

What followed was a meeting of the islanders to discuss the reliability of the evidence suggesting volcanic activity. The teacher explained that it would not be possible to take animals on any of the escape boats, including domestic animals and pets.

Collaborative group work
In family groups the children had to make lists of what they would need to take on the boats when they left for another island. Each group had to choose a scribe to do the writing.

Part way through the task, the teacher interrupted the children:

> Islanders – we have fewer boats than we thought! We must cut down on what we take. Eliminate at least five items from your lists!

The children argued the merits of 'rope' over 'tents'; 'fresh water' over 'extra clothing'. The tension mounted!

The lists were pinned on the wall. Families were asked to scan each other's lists to see if they could 'double up' on any of the items. Again the children, in role, became the audience for each other's writing. The responses to this writing stimulated yet more drama.

Activity 4: Leaving the island

The teacher announced that the boats were being loaded with supplies and, while they were waiting to get on board, there would be time to write one letter, or even a diary entry. Again, thought tracking is central to this activity, which the teacher introduced by saying:

As I prepare to leave our island, I am thinking to myself...

She moved from one child to another. As she stopped by each, this provided the cue for the character's thoughts to be spoken aloud:

MOLLY: I wonder if we'll ever see this island again?
JAMIL: I feel bad about leaving our cows behind.

Several of these statements gave a sense of shared loss and apprehension and encouraged less confident children to offer their own ideas. The children were asked to choose who would receive the letter they would write. Eric chose to write it to his young son, 'to read when he gets older, so he'll know what it was like here', demonstrating the importance, as Wyse (1998) suggests, of allowing children to decide on 'the most appropriate audience' for their writing.

The children wrote their letters and diary entries quietly and were then asked to read them aloud, or to ask the teacher to do it for them. In this drama ritual the text generated contributed to the performance element. The children were then invited to comment on what they had heard. What was striking was the fact that the length of the pieces produced did not matter – each was listened to with respect, and each contributed to the overall atmosphere of the drama. A less prolific writer experienced her work being given equal status to that of a child who had written at length.

This drama impetus coincided with a similar evacuation of the island of Montserrat. The children were encouraged to bring in newspaper articles about this event and to discuss how their own writing in role compared to statements made by the inhabitants of this real island, and this helped them make connections with real-life events.

This drama starting point afforded a range of opportunities for writing, both individually and collaboratively:

- mapping, including producing grids, symbols and codes,
- inventing captions,
- list-making,
- letters, and
- diary entries.

Throughout, there was a strong sense of purpose and audience for the writing. In addition, the opportunity for reflective writing was exploited, both within and beyond the drama.

The Pied Piper with Year 3 children

A similar starting point was produced through exploration of another community under threat with a class of Year 3 children.[11] This highlighted the importance of oral composition, identified as 'a powerful feature of the best writing sessions.' (Ofsted 1999).[12] In this example, the class teacher wanted to use drama to help the children learn about both the construction of formal letters and to explore elements of persuasive writing, through presenting points of view in letter form.[13]

Activity 1: The letter to the council

The teacher and children, in role as the citizens of Hamelin, wrote to express their anger over the growing rat problem in their town and wanted local councillors to 'do something about it'. The teacher said, 'Let's write the strongest letter we can and then we'll SEE their reaction to it when they read it!' This offered the children a cue that they would eventually, in turn, take on the roles of the councillors responding to the letter. The teacher acted as scribe, modelling the formal style of the letter – encouraging contributions from all of the children, drafting, editing, polishing and reading it over with them – thereby showing them how to focus upon the 'secretarial and presentational skills' of transcription (Wyse 1998:36) and demonstrating these 'at the point of writing' (Ofsted 1999):

> . . . it is vital to feed the writing back into the drama in order to influence and further stimulate the situation that has produced it, because that way the children can see that their writing is serving its purpose, and their investment in it is genuine.
>
> (Nixon 1982:99)

Activity 2: The council reads the letter

The teacher photocopied and enlarged the final draft of the letter and pinned it to the wall for all to see. Then, in role as the mayor and councillors, she and the children re-read the letter from a new perspective. They decided they would need to take the action further, leading to the next activity that involved the teacher acting as scribe.

Scribing

There are several advantages to the teacher acting as the children's scribe, as in the above example:

- the teacher models the writing and shows the correct style;
- the teacher and children compose collaboratively, which helps in the generation of ideas;
- as they refine and edit their writing, the children are having to pay close attention to both the composition and transcription elements of the text;
- the teacher can provide differentiation in a number of ways: for example, by targeting specific children with different questions, reading the text aloud with those who lack confidence, and so on; and
- children who might only manage one or two tortured lines unaided are able to contribute to the whole text.

Most children will feel a sense of achievement from having contributed to the composition of a piece of writing which is of a higher standard of work than would have been possible if they had been working on their own or with a group of peers.[14]

Another significant benefit of this approach is demonstrated in the next drama/writing activity:

Activity 3: The advertisement

Children learn how to scribe effectively when the task is first modelled by the teacher. In this activity, the children were required to work in groups in the role of advertising design teams whose brief was to create a campaign to promote a new rat poison, to be marketed in Hamelin. In each group, a scribe was identified to summarise, collate, take notes and help organise the campaign, freeing others in the group to focus on brainstorming and thinking creatively, rather than being over-concerned with the transcription element of the writing. Some of the children chosen to scribe were less confident in speaking and listening than others. Here, they had a central role in the planning and this served to enhance both their self-esteem and their status within the group. In addition, the teacher had introduced examples of job pages from the local newspaper and during the shared writing aspect of the Literacy Hour had deconstructed two examples, to assist the children in devising their own.

The teacher chose to exploit opportunities for writing across a range of genre. Each group was given a different context for their 'ad' from one of the following:

* newspaper;
* poster;
* television or radio advertisements, requiring the children to script, rehearse then edit, in order to meet the constraints of the time limits of such advertising.[15]

Through such activities it is possible to differentiate in a number of ways, for example:

* identifying roles within a group (Chapter 11), such as scribe;
* setting groups different tasks, requiring varying levels of complex language, such as the poster design which required a mixture of words and pictures to the more challenging scriptwriting; and
* producing writing frames to help children identify the features of an advertising format.[16]

The teacher then widened the children's experience of generating the persuasive language of advertising to that which would reflect personal engagement and empathy with the characters involved in the story.

Activity 4: Pleading with the Pied Piper

The children, in the role of parents/siblings in family groups wrote letters to the Pied Piper, pleading with him to give their children back, giving a sense of purpose to their collaborative writing. In role, they discussed what should go into the letter and, again, a scribe was given the responsibility for transferring the family's thoughts onto paper. The letters were, as can be expected, full of emotive and emotional language reflecting the children's empathy with the plight of the families:

He is our only son. Please let him come home.

Put yourself in our place. How would you like it if a stranger took your child away? Do you have children? Do you know what it's like?

In both of the last two examples offered, drama promotes:

> ...collaborative talk...as well as extending the form and content of children's own writing (Baker and Leak 1993:27),

and the two are mutually beneficial. Such work demonstrates strong links with the NLS in that, by using non-fictional writing in fiction contexts, the children were able to explore elements of persuasive language, and how this language can be used to powerful effect, and for a number of purposes.

Offering a 'short cut' into writing within a drama context is the strategy known as the still image (Woolland 1993; Kitson and Spiby 1997). This tried-and-trusted approach lends itself to a range of writing activity. Through it, groups of children are required to organise themselves into creating a three-dimensional image to represent a dramatic moment or a visual 'summing up' of a situation (Johnson 2000). For example, during the 'island' project, children were working in groups as families, preparing to leave the island. They formed 'photographs' of the families standing before the homes they were about to leave. Using the thought-tracking strategy (see above), they wrote down, instead of speaking aloud, their thoughts at the point of departure.

Using post-its

A Year 5 class had been reading *Goodnight Mister Tom*[17] which is set during World War Two. In drama, they had been improvising a scene in which a group of evacuees – city children who had been sent for safety reasons to the countryside – were waiting in the village hall to be collected by those people who were prepared to take them in. Again, using thought tracking, the teacher said, 'As I stand here, in this cold, damp hall, waiting for a stranger to come for me, I think to myself...' She had placed 'post-it notes' and pencils within easy reach of the children and they were invited to write down their thoughts. Once completed, all these 'thoughts' were collected and placed on a board, together. The teacher, and some of the children, read each aloud, in turn. The children had generated an emotional response to the drama through their writing, and were then able to discuss the range of emotions which were in evidence.

'Post-it notes' have much to offer in drama:[18]

- they are easy to administer;
- in size, they are less daunting than larger, blank sheets of paper, therefore 'requiring less writing';
- children associate them with note-making, where the content is more important than transcription, leaving them free to concentrate on the message itself;
- they can be stuck on walls (as in the above example) and even on people (for example, as inscriptions on statues);
- they can be stuck in books and used to stimulate further writing; and
- they can serve as 'aide-memoires' for future literacy and drama work.

Scriptwriting

When children write down words that are intended to be read aloud, they are already engaged in scriptwriting. This writing activity features throughout the NLS.[19] Children often respond enthusiastically to the challenge of having to produce script for themselves and others. There are a number of reasons for this:

- using a screenplay format is ideal because this is a range of genre familiar to most children;
- scenes and dialogue are usually shorter in television drama than in plays written for the stage;
- adding stage directions and even character descriptions extends children's use of descriptive language;
- children find it easier to write script once they have seen, or taken part in improvisation on which the writing is to be based. Indeed, some of the best professional screenwriters use this approach;[20]
- an effective stimulus can be found through a brief extract of dialogue which children are then required to embed in their own writing. This can be very fruitful if the style of language is unfamiliar to the children, or even archaic;
- initiating the work in shared writing, with the teacher acting as scribe, provides a means of modelling the process; and
- in preparation for performance, for example a school assembly or play for an invited audience, children deliver scripts of their own devising with more conviction, so they have a better chance of remembering the lines!

So far we have seen how drama contributes to children's thinking, their ability to create meaning and how it is possible to exploit this process to fuel writing. However, at the heart of learning both in, and through drama, is reflection, and this makes a valuable contribution to helping children consider how they are learning literacy in general, and writing in particular.

Drama and metacognition

> Experience itself is neither productive nor unproductive; it is how you reflect on it that makes it significant (Heathcote and Bolton 1995:164).

Throughout and beyond the dramatic experience, it is fruitful to exploit opportunities for children to reflect so that they can both discover and articulate what the experience means, or has meant to them. This reflection is equally valid both within and beyond role playing, and teacher questioning is central to the process, as the following will illustrate.

Reflection in drama

Reflection in role can help children analyse their engagement with the writing process. A student had been reading *Charlie and the Chocolate Factory*[21] with a Year 3 class. In role as Mr Wonka, she had welcomed them as visitors to the factory and had given them a guided tour, inviting the children to comment on 'all the wonders you see before you', which they did collaboratively – improvising and thrilling each other with their descriptions of the extraordinary factory taking shape in their classroom! Later, 'Mr Wonka' asked them to write home from the factory to their parents to describe their experiences, exploiting the potential for such work to be extended from speaking and listening into writing. 'He' had produced postcards for this purpose. As the children wrote, 'he' moved among them, still in role, questioning them:

MR WONKA: Ah, I see you are drafting your message before putting it onto the card. Why is that?
JAMIL: Because there isn't much space on the card and I don't want to waste any by crossing bits out. I'm going to get it right first.

The quality and quantity of the descriptive work was greatly enhanced by the drama input. Phoebe wrote, 'When Mr Wonka opened the gate to the chocolate room, I shivered. There was so much teeth-rotting stuff.' Stephen, who had, in previous lessons, complained of having 'nothing to write about', was now, thanks to the drama activity, having a different problem:

MR WONKA: My dear chap, are you finding it hard to start writing?
STEPHEN: Yes, because there is so much to write about!
MR WONKA: Might I suggest a brainstorm?

Stephen took up the suggestion and poured ideas onto a page, from which he chose three on which to focus.

The student, noticing another child busily writing at a furious pace, stopped to question her:

STUDENT: How does drama help you with your writing?
PIPPA: Because I'm there and I know what it's like!

Other reflective writing can take the form of diary entries or a 'day in the life of a character'. Drama allows us to distort time, to ask characters to predict what they think might happen to them next, or to place them a long way ahead in the future, giving them the opportunity to develop 'hindsight'. This can give a child the opportunity to articulate a character's past history. Such work demands great imaginative leaps, with the children projecting themselves first into a role, then imagining that person many years on, or thinking back to when they were young! This is potentially a fruitful approach for stimulating deeply empathetic writing. For example, in the *Charlie and the Chocolate Factory* example, the student asked the children, now in role as 'old people', to think back to the meeting with Mr Wonka, in his factory, 'so many years ago, when you were young'. They were to write down their memories from that visit and to say 'how the visit had changed their lives'.

Reflection beyond drama

Out of role, the subsequent reading aloud of such writing stimulated further discussion, with the student highlighting the children's own metacognitive processes. She identified and used key questions:

STUDENT: Which phrases did you find most moving? Why? What do such phrases tell you about the people who wrote them?

There followed discussion about 'what memories may we be storing up for our own futures?' The children highlighted 'friendships', 'being bitten by a dog', 'being afraid on my first day at school' and 'the day my baby brother was born'. At any level, it is possible to help children make connections between dramatic experience and their own lives and to empathise with others, hence drama makes a significant contribution to personal, social and moral education. Just as in play, children accommodate the 'flip-flopping' between being in and out of role and within this constant shifting lies the gateway to metacognitive experience. It is the teacher's role here to identify and seize opportunities to help children become aware of how their thinking is informed, and how it is challenged by their engagement in the drama process. Again, teacher questioning is central to such an approach.

Moving from classroom drama to performance

Finally, the question arises as to whether the teacher and class should opt to adapt their work in drama in order to create a performance for an audience beyond the classroom, using the children's discussion and selection of significant moments to write a script that communicates their response and understanding to others, and this necessitates a further metacognitive journey.[22] This is enhanced throughout drama work with the teacher's prompting of 'What worked well and why?' The children then become used to, and adept at, reflecting upon key dramatic moments which they have observed and shared. This helps them to select and refine them, with a new audience in mind, using the range of drama tools, e.g. still image, that are familiar to them. Such work makes demands upon the children as armchair television critics. As discerning members of the audience for drama on a daily basis, it is crucial to offer children the opportunity to consider their own responses to performances they see beyond, as well as inside, school. In terms of creating contexts and purpose for writing, there are opportunities here for rehearsal schedules, storyboarding, scripting, adding stage directions, and even supplying programme notes and tickets for the invited audience. The possibilities are endless!

Conclusion

Drama's place in language teaching is 'official' but to exploit it to its maximum potential in enhancing children's learning we need a 'flexible approach to the Literacy Hour' (Fisher and Williams 2000) and we need to acknowledge:

- its gifts of purpose and context;
- its value to the writing process;
- the quality of thinking it is possible to generate through effective teacher questioning in, and beyond, drama;
- its cross-curricular role;

- its potential in terms of PSME and citizenship;
- its timely higher status in initial teacher training; and
- the need for teachers to experience it in action.

The teacher who includes drama in her classroom repertoire is taking children on a truly collaborative adventure; making what is implicit explicit and helping them to acknowledge not just what they know but what they didn't know they knew! Sometimes this self-awareness helps them reflect upon, and even challenge their own perceptions of, themselves as learners. As Beth (aged 9) wrote:

> I didn't think I was good at writing but today it was easy. I learned that drama gets you in the writing mood.

Notes

1. S. Clipson-Boyles (1998) explores drama's contribution to literacy teaching.
2. References to drama feature more prominently than hitherto in *English in the National Curriculum* (DfEE 1999a).
3. Specific references to drama throughout Key Stages 1 and 2 are helpfully provided in the handout *Opportunities for Drama in the Framework of Objectives* (DfEE 1999b).
4. In *English in the National Curriculum* (DfEE 1999a), a new section headed 'Group Discussion and Interaction' shows the heightened status of collaborative work in the classroom.
5. The National Curriculum requirement to deliver personal, social and moral education (PSME) can be met through the careful inclusion of drama, in which relevant issues and themes are explored. See also, Winston, J. and Tandy, M. (2001) *Beginning Drama 4–11*. London: David Fulton Publishers.
6. Drama has a key role in supporting *Literacy Across the Curriculum*, the title of a background briefing paper produced by the NLS for Initial Teacher Training Providers in 2000.
7. Hertrich, J. (1998) *Good Teaching in Art, Dance, Drama and Music*, Ofsted, in which good practice is explored.
8. *ibid.*
9. NLS Framework of Objectives, 1998, Year 4, term 3, text level objective 23: to present a point of view in writing, e.g. in the form of a letter.
10. See Note 6 relating to cross-curricular application.
11. This example was discussed by Johnson, C. (2000) in Fisher, R. and Williams, M. (eds) *Unlocking Literacy*, London: David Fulton Publishers, but here the focus is on writing.
12. Ofsted (1999) reviewing good practice in *The National Literacy Strategy – An Evaluation of the First Year of the National Literacy Strategy*, DfEE.
13. NLS Framework of Objectives, 1998, text level 3 objective 23.
14. See Johnson, C. in Fisher, R. and Williams, M. (eds), *Unlocking Literacy*. David Fulton Publishers, 2000.

15. *ibid.*

16. Jones, D. and Hodson, P. (2000) *Teaching Children to Write*. London: David Fulton Publishers.

17. Magorian, M. (1981) *Goodnight Mister Tom*. London: Puffin.

18. I am indebted to Patrice Baldwin who gave me the idea of using post-it notes during an excellent workshop which she conducted with teachers for 'London Drama' in 1992.

19. *Opportunities for Drama in the Framework of Objectives* (1999) Year 3 term 1 objective 14: to write simple playscripts based on reading and oral work.

20. The British screenwriter Mike Leigh, for example, scripts from actors' improvisation.

21. Dahl, R. (1985) *Charlie and the Chocolate Factory*. London: Allen & Unwin.

22. Bowden, J. and Marton, F. (1998) *The University of Learning*. Hemel Hempstead: Simon & Schuster.

Further reading

Barker, R. and Leak, L. (1993) 'Drama and the National Curriculum for English', in Crimson, J. (ed.) *Move Back the Desks*. Sheffield: NATE.

Bowden, J. and Marton, F. (1998) *The University of Learning*. London: Kogan Page.

Clipson-Boyles, S. (1998) *Drama in Primary English Teaching*. London: David Fulton Publishers.

DfEE (1998) *The National Literacy Strategy: Framework for Teaching*. London: HMSO.

DfEE (1999a) *English in the National Curriculum*. London: HMSO.

DfEE (1999b) *Opportunities for Drama in the Framework of Objectives*. London: HMSO.

Fisher, R. and Williams, M. (2000) *Unlocking Literacy*. London: David Fulton Publishers.

Heathcote, D. and Bolton, G. (1982) *Drama for Learning: Dorothy Heathcote's Mantle of the Expert Approach to Education*. London: Heinemann; Hemel Hempstead: Simon Schuster.

Hendy, L. and Toon, L. (2001) *Supporting Drama and Imaginative Play in the Early Years*. Buckingham: Open University Press.

Hertrich, J. (1998) *Good Teaching in Art, Dance, Drama and Music*. London: Ofsted.

Johnson, C. (2000) 'What did I say' in Fisher, R. and Williams, M. (eds) (2000) *Unlocking Literacy*. London: David Fulton Publishers.

Johnson, L. and O'Neill, C. (1984) *Dorothy Heathcote: Collected Writings*. London: Routledge.

Jones, D. and Hodson, P. (2000) *Teaching Children to Write*. London: David Fulton Publishers.

Kitson, N. and Spiby, I. (1997) *Drama 7–11: Developing Primary Teaching Skills*. London: Routledge.

Nixon, J. (1982) *Drama and the Whole Curriculum*. London: Hutchinson.

Ofsted (1999) *The National Literacy Strategy – An Evaluation of the First Year of the National Literacy Strategy*. DfEE.

Winston, J. (2000) *Drama, Literacy and Moral Education*. London: David Fulton Publishers.

Winston, J. and Tandy, M. (2001) *Beginning Drama 4–11*. London: David Fulton Publishers.

Woolland, B. (1993) *The Teaching of Drama in the Primary School*. Harlow: Longman.

Wyse, D. (1998) *Primary Writing*. Buckingham: Open University Press.

Children's Literature

Dahl, R. (1985) *Charlie and the Chocolate Factory*. London: Allen & Unwin.

Magorian, M. (1981) *Goodnight Mister Tom*. London: Puffin.

CHAPTER 5

Is neatness a virtue?: handwriting in the Literacy Hour

Lynne Thorogood

The role and changing status of handwriting

> The process of writing is not merely a mechanical task, a simple matter of putting speech down on paper. It is an exploration on the use of the graphic potential of a language – a creative process, an act of discovery.
>
> (Crystal 1987:11)[1]

What better way to introduce the art of handwriting, and what better way to encourage children in our schools to move on in their writing? Writing and its teaching has certainly been the subject of radical rethinking in recent years, with first of all the work of Donald Graves[2] and his colleagues having had immense impact on it in the 1980s and then the National Writing Project (1990)[3] acting as a catalyst for change in teaching practices. Hence a shift of focus from content to accuracy in presentation, and back again, has characterised the writing environment in primary classrooms over the last 15 years.

With the introduction of a Literacy Hour in 1998 some teachers believed that handwriting would decline even further in significance since the days when it was given its own status as a separate attainment target in the first version of the National Curriculum (1989). It is now a single part of the word level requirements of the *Framework of Objectives* of the National Literacy Strategy (NLS), but that does not necessarily mean a lessening of importance. Everything that is written must be readable if writing is to be a means of communication. Well-formed and legible handwriting is the way the majority of primary school children will achieve this.

Handwriting is part of the writing process, a skill to be developed in context. Teachers need to become aware of the hidden assumptions that colour their responses to pupils' writing specifically because it is both process and product based. The very fact that there is almost always a tangible end product to the act of writing means that attention concentrates on the features of the 'finished' piece of writing. In the world outside education, writing as product is subjected to all kinds of complex judgements about its aesthetic appearance, legibility, success in communication of meaning and quality as art. Judgements are made about individuals based on their handwriting, and the quality of their children's handwriting is often regarded by parents as an indicator of progress and success at school. The marks children make as beginner writers (Chapter 1) are personal ones, indicative of character, personality, training an culture, and for any individual, becoming literate is a personal, political and cultural watershed. A person's handwriting is a representation of himself or herself on paper; the way they present themselves to the world. Because of this, the pressure that parents put on their children to conform to an outward sign of educational success and maturity is often considerable.

Once we have learned how to do it, handwriting is something that we tend to take for granted. It is something that literate adults do automatically, seldom questioning how they learned to do it or how the system works. Indeed, handwriting does not work properly for the writer until it has become automated, and it is difficult to become analytical about an automated system. As teachers, we recognise that handwriting does not develop 'naturally', but lacking the detailed guidance given for phonics, spelling and grammar in the National Literacy Strategy, we are sometimes less confident in our approach to teaching it. The newly published NLS handbook on Writing at Key Stage 1 *The National Literacy Strategy: Developing Early Writing* (2001) – offers a belated, but useful, set of suggestions about the ways in which handwriting can be included in Literacy Hour work, and this will also be considered in this chapter. Insights into how the system works may help educators to plan their teaching more effectively and ultimately help their pupils to reap benefits in later years.

Learning to write using the Latin alphabet

English, like other western European languages, is written down using the Latin alphabet. The main rules that govern our writing system are outlined by Rosemary Sassoon[4] and can be summarised as follows:

- The direction of writing is left to right.
- There are conventional points of entry and directions for the strokes that make up the letters. This determines the movement of the writing implement through the letters.
- Letters are of different heights, and these heights are consistent in their relation to each other.
- Letters and words are spaced regularly and evenly.
- There are two sets of letters, capital letters and small letters, which are sometimes referred to as upper case and lower case letters.

(Sassoon 1995)

Directionality

Teachers should be aware that for some pupils learning English as an additional language, earlier exposure to a different writing system, such as Arabic or Cantonese, may result in some rules they have learned in relation to these systems having to be 'unlearned' before they can succeed in developing their written English. Directionality is probably the most significant issue here. A coloured strip of paper stuck down the left side of each page and the instruction to 'start at the green edge' can help in the early stages. For some left-handed pupils whose inclination is to start at the right-hand side of the page, this can also be a useful aide-memoire. Similarly, many foundation stage writers benefit from a dot or arrow indicating the starting point at the beginning of a new page.

Letter formation

Correct movement of the writing implement through each letter is important, because once this has been mastered, however quickly the letters are written and whatever personal adaptations are introduced, the writing generally remains legible and the script can be fluently joined. Many adults encourage young children to write by allowing them to produce visual approximations of letters, such as the example shown in the figure.

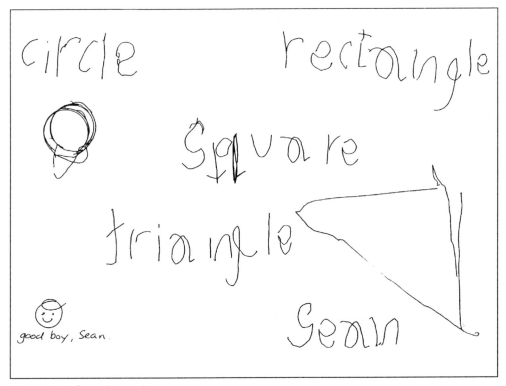

Figure 5.1 Sean's work

Figure 5.1 shows an attempt by a five-year-old which drew praise from a classroom assistant in his Reception class. However, this may have unfortunate consequences later on. He, like many foundation-stage pupils, started school with faults in letter construction firmly embedded. Another common mistake, often made by parents or carers before children start at nursery, is showing them how to write their name in capital letters. Writing is a motor skill, which means that the body learns, then automates the movement of the hand and arm, which, in turn, produces the written trace. Once a movement is automated it is notoriously difficult to alter. Inappropriate letter formation or writing all in capitals is much more difficult to 'unlearn' than to learn in the first place. As retraining of a motor movement is so difficult, it is important that children should be observed when making their first attempts at letter formation so that they can get it right from the start. Scrutiny of the end product is not enough. Children's letter construction should be monitored as they learn to write, and teachers and learning support assistants need to intervene and demonstrate, explaining why one way is correct and another incorrect. This gives children early metacognitive understanding of why they need to learn in a particular way. (For instance, a clockwise 'o' looks remarkably similar to an anti-clockwise one to a four-year-old, but the clockwise formation will not join so easily, and forms an inappropriate foundation for forming letters in the same graphic 'family'.)

Exercises can be developed which both show and help the pupil to feel movement, as well as offering a description of the direction of strokes. For foundation-stage learners pattern work is an important precursor and support strategy for letter formation. The potentially repetitious nature of this can be avoided by linking it with other curriculum areas such as art and craft, or the development of listening skills. The writing patterns shown in Figure 5.2 were produced after dictation followed by modelling by the Reception class teacher, who first read out a line then modelled the particular pattern or stroke:

The sun is a swirly spiral in the sky

The sunbeams shine out in every direction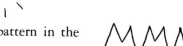

The mountains make an up and down zig-zag pattern in the background

The castle stands in front of the mountains and the battlements make an up and along pattern

A river runs in a wavy line in front of the castle

The fence stops the children from falling in the river

The grass sticks up in tufts in the field

After each instruction the teacher first moved her finger in the appropriate way to indicate movement, encouraging the children to copy her, then she demonstrated on the whiteboard. The children listened and watched before making their own picture-patterns on prepared sheets using coloured pencils. Exercises such as this can help children to practise all the directional strokes necessary to develop competent hand control for letter formation.

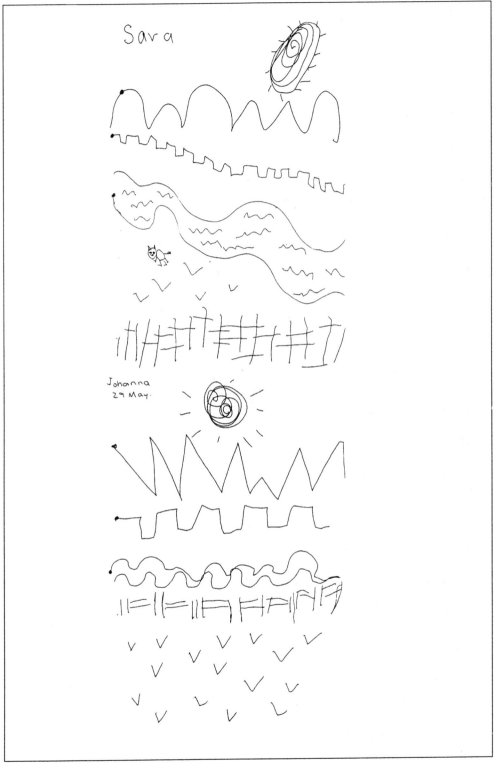

Figure 5.2 Writing patterns produced by Reception class pupils

Height, size and position

The legibility of writing depends upon correct height differences and the correct positioning of the 'tails' on some letters such as 'y'. This is because fluent readers do not always look at the individual letters in a word, but scan the shape of words to gain their meaning. Simply pointing out the need for height adjustment and repositioning may be sufficient for some pupils, such as in Mervyn's writing (Figure 5.3).

Figure 5.3 Mervyn's writing

For some children practice exercises may be necessary. Certainly the provision of a baseline upon which to sit their writing will help, but for some, resorting to the old-fashioned copy books which give four lines to guide the size and position of letters (see Figure 5.4) may be the best solution until the problem is resolved.

Upper and lower case letters – what style?

Lower case

For a child learning to write, the selection of a consistent style for letter formation is important. The model that is learned may depend upon local authority or school

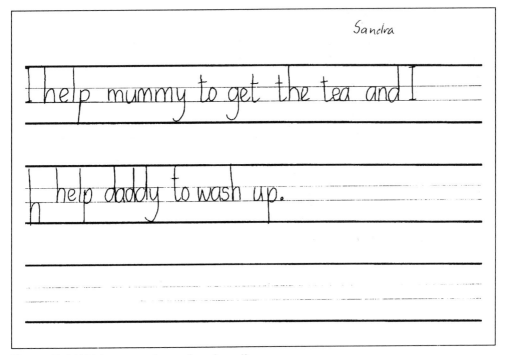

Sandra

I help mummy to get the tea and I

help daddy to wash up.

Figure 5.4 Writing practice using four lines

policy, or (less likely) the personal preference of the teacher, but it may have far-reaching consequences for the learner. Whichever model is adopted it should be one which will lend itself to being written with a variety of writing implements, from a crayon to a fountain pen, and one which is easy for children to modify and 'personalise' as writing fluency develops. Looped and elaborate styles have fallen out of favour in the UK in the last 25 years, and basic modern styles are now favoured by the majority of schools. Many are based on *New Nelson Handwriting* (Smith)[5] or on the Christopher Jarman style[6] which both adopt an oval rather than a round shape for small letters, and is easy for children to adapt to their own personal hand as their writing speeds up.

The 26 small letters are grouped into families determined by the basic movement made to create all the letters in a particular group. This presents teachers with the opportunity to structure their teaching of handwriting so that learning each letter in the group is consolidated as new members of the letter family are introduced and practised. The letter families are as follows:

Family 1 – a c d e g o q   are based on an oval, starting at '1 o'clock'
Family 2 – b h k m n p r   all start with a straight down stroke from the top left point
Family 3 – f i j l t z   are based on vertical or horizontal straight lines
Family 4 – s u v w x y   can be grouped into subsets, depending on the writing style adopted.

In some writing styles, subset 'v, w and y' could be called 'the problem family', as the diagonal strokes they are made up of are the most difficult to form, particularly for a child with poor motor coordination or control. If this prevents an individual child from producing well-formed handwriting, a change to a style which adopts a rounded base for these letters may be helpful. No style should be immovable, and no child should suffer from unbending rules. One useful rule to offer children is that only three letters require the writer to make two pencil strokes, these being 'f, t and x'. All the others can be made with a single pencil stroke in a continuous movement, and should be formed without lifting the pencil off the paper. If you need to lift your pencil off, you are not doing it correctly. In due course, small letters can be joined to each other to form a cursive script. To facilitate this, some handwriting schemes, including Christopher Jarman's, suggest teaching letters with their 'lead ins and lead offs' or joining hooks in place. Some styles, such as the rather outdated Marion Richardson[7] scheme, join every letter to the next, and others join only those which link readily. The majority of children devise their own joining style after practice. Those who revert to print at the upper end of Key Stage 2 usually do so because faults remaining in letter formation from the early years make it impossible to join letters easily.

Capitals

Pupils should know that capital letters belong to different families from the small versions. Knowing what these are can again help teachers to make the most of their teaching time by grouping letters together for practise exercises, and giving children this knowledge makes learning more manageable:

Family 1 – I L V W Z	a single stroke, straight lines
Family 2 – J M N T X Y	two strokes, generally straight lines
Family 3 – A E F H K	three strokes, straight lines
Family 4 – C G O S U	one stroke, generally curved lines
Family 5 – B D P Q R	two strokes, both straight and curved lines

There are no exit hooks. Capital letters are not meant to be joined, although some fluent writers link capitals for the sake of speed later on. Children who begin to do this should not be discouraged, provided the writing remains legible.

Imposed rules which restrict the development of a personal writing style are seldom helpful unless accurate communication is at risk, and no prescribed style is ever as speedy as a personalised one. Once a fluent cursive style has been established, usually in the middle or towards the end of Key Stage 2, there is a decreasing need for rules and the modelling of handwriting. Indeed, some pupils' writing may suffer as a result of the imposition of unbending rules, such as 'you must not lift off your pencil until you have completed each word'. This is apparent in the rather laboured-looking writing of a Year 5 child in Figure 5.5. The s, with its contorted doubling back formation, must restrict this writer's speed, as well as doing nothing to enhance the appearance of the completed script.

This is not to say that handwriting should not continue to be taught in the older Key Stage 2 classes. This is the stage at which an emphasis on presentation and

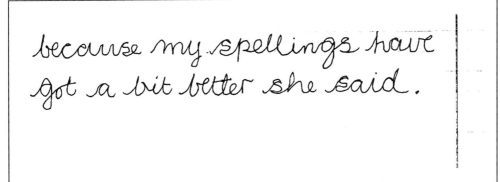

because my spellings have
got a bit better she said.

Figure 5.5 Farida's writing

extension of the range and repertoire for handwriting can replace the pattern work and letter formation of the Foundation Stage and Key Stage 1 handwriting programmes to good effect.

Exploiting links between spelling and handwriting

There are, undoubtedly, links between handwriting and spelling. Currently, there is little research that suggests that the ability to spell accurately is a precursor to neat, well-formed or aesthetically pleasing handwriting, although Klein and Millar (1990) suggest that competence in spelling helps with the fluency of handwriting, and Sassoon (1990) agrees that poor spelling is often combined with untidy-looking handwriting. However, the converse – that those with a more fluent handwriting style often develop into better spellers – has been argued by several researchers. The most notable and influential study was that carried out by Cripps and Cox (1989).[8] They point out that since the development of handwriting involves establishing and habituating a motor trace for each letter, learning to write in a cursive (joined) style from the beginning can help to establish and habituate a motor trace for common letter strings. This, in turn, can support development in spelling, as children attempting to spell new words can more easily draw upon their repertoire of established spelling/writing patterns. This is clearly a sound alternative to making purely phonic-based attempts, which are frequently doomed to failure due to the inconsistency of English orthography. Cripps and Cox advocate the early teaching of cursive script to take advantage of this handwriting/spelling link. However, learning to write in a cursive style right from the start is not necessarily the best way for every child to develop a good handwriting style, particularly those with motor-control difficulties, or those who simply cannot remember the pattern of long letter strings at the early stages. In some countries in continental Europe cursive handwriting has been taught from the first days at school for many years with no negative effects. However, it must be remembered that children in most European systems start formal schooling between their sixth and seventh birthdays, compared with the age of four in the case of many

UK pupils. As the motor capabilities of children who are four years old are significantly different from those of pupils who are approaching the age of seven, it may be better to delay teaching a cursive style until the end of Key Stage 1.

Many foundation-stage pupils who are encouraged to join their script early nevertheless manage to do so successfully after the occasional shaky start. Figure 5.6 shows the early attempts at handwriting made by a Reception class child aged 4 years 9 months, 4 years 11 months and then nine months later at the beginning of Year 1.

One of the difficulties with her earlier attempts was that Anna was unable to decipher and read back her own writing, which continued to look like unravelled knitting for many weeks! For those children for whom the method is successful, greater confidence and accuracy with both handwriting and spelling, and an enhanced awareness of the structure of words can be achieved (Cripps and Cox, 1989). Byers (1963) reports on a study in which eight- and nine-year-old pupils were assessed for spelling accuracy – first on a dictated passage which they were required to write in cursive script, and later a passage containing the same vocabulary which they wrote in print style. Byers concluded that more mistakes were made in both omitting letters and transposing pairs of letters when the pupils were using print. However, the subjects were more likely to omit entire words when using cursive style.

Figure 5.6 Anna's work

The benefits of introducing a cursive script at an earlier stage, rather than leaving it until the beginning of Key Stage 2, are accepted by many teachers. However, if it is the only writing style that is taught in Foundation and Key Stage 1 classes, then teachers must decide when they will introduce printing. After all, their pupils will also need that skill in due course for diagrams, labels and similar purposes. Better, maybe, to start with a simple print at the early stages, quickly introducing joining hooks, and then encouraging those pupils who are ready to join their writing to do so as soon as possible. In this way the possible benefits of improved spelling are available early for the maximum number of children, and those for whom cursive handwriting is a tremendous struggle may take a little more time.

Handwriting in Literacy Hour

Teachers can economise on time by helping children to explore spelling while practising handwriting. This is emphasised in the DfEE publication *The National Literacy Strategy: Developing Early Writing* (2001). In the early stages, letter formation can be reinforced during word level whole-class work. Guided group time can be used for handwriting teaching twice a week. This can be linked with grapho-phonic correspondence. Such group work provides an opportunity for careful individual monitoring, which is difficult to achieve when undertaking whole-class teaching. In the case of older children, practising joins by linking common consonant blends and digraphs supports both the development of spelling and handwriting skills. Similarly, writing words with common letter strings reinforces spelling patterns whilst helping the establishment of a motor trace for fluent handwriting. Issues related to correct joins can be a feature of word level work focused on phonics. Lists and collections of words (thematically grouped, opposites, contractions, words with silent letters) can be discussed and common features identified. Finding and writing others in the same family is a useful handwriting and spelling activity, which can be undertaken during independent work time. Teachers will find many opportunities to introduce or consolidate aspects of phonic and spelling work in a well-structured handwriting programme, to the benefit of writing development overall.

Guided group sessions with handwriting as their main theme should occur in most weeks in Key Stage 1 and the earlier part of Key Stage 2. Handwriting practice can be included as independent group activities in the days following on from when it has been a guided activity. This may include materials taken from the chosen writing scheme. For younger pupils, parents can become involved in handwriting practice by sending home sheets of patterns, mazes and practice letters, together with guidance notes about their use to ensure continuity and consistency of letter formation. For older children, self-help in developing and improving their writing can be effective, and homework tasks can be set dealing with specific aspects of handwriting.

Practical application of handwriting will naturally occur in a variety of contexts for all ages, and across most areas of the curriculum. However, tasks with a specific focus on handwriting can be introduced at all stages within the Literacy Hour lesson. For the younger age group, production of a class or group story or poetry books can be achieved in shared writing sessions, followed by guided redrafting. Letter writing can be introduced in Key Stage 1 and continued in Key Stage 2, with a growing repertoire of purposes and audiences. Children in Key Stage 2 can occasionally be asked to produce work specifically for display purposes, with presentation and handwriting being priority features. Activities and projects in a range of curriculum areas will require a range of handwriting competences, such as making greetings cards, designing posters or book covers (see Figure 5.7), composing sets of instructions for games and making notices.

Figure 5.7 The front and back covers of a home-made book

Towards the end of Key Stage 2 handwriting requirements will include providing headings and labels in block capitals or clear print, and making captions for pictures or models. Issues of accuracy and presentation will arise across a range of subjects in the curriculum.

Conclusion

An important task for teachers at all stages is to take positive steps to ensure that children appreciate the functions of writing. Teachers who make a point of telling their pupils about the writing that they have been doing themselves and about letters and cards they have enjoyed receiving are helping to bring about this awareness of the importance of writing. However, it is also important that the children see the teacher actually writing. Recent publications from the National Literacy Strategy[9] emphasise the significance of shared writing, and this provides an opportunity for teachers to focus on aspects of handwriting in a relevant context and in an unthreatening manner.

At all stages there should be a consistent policy throughout the school. This is not to say that children should be constrained to produce handwriting that conforms to a rigid model. The model should be used to guide letter formation in the initial stages to help children progress smoothly from early letter construction to a fluid cursive style. Pupils and parents should recognise that different levels of handwriting are acceptable for different purposes. Personal notes require less crafting than items that are going to be displayed. Pupils should not, however, see handwriting as something that can be turned on and off – 'Do we have to do joined-up writing for this?' – but should regard it as part of their repertoire of communication skills, and like writing style, adapt it for the purpose and target audience.

Notes

1. Crystal, D. (1987) *Child Language, Learning and Linguistics: An Overview for the Teaching and Therapeutic Profession*. London: Edward Arnold.
2. Graves, D. (1983) *Writing: Teachers and Children at Work*. Portsmouth, NH: Heinemann.
3. *The National Writing Project* (1989, 1990), sponsored by the National Curriculum Council, looked at aspects of children's writing including purpose and audience. (Published by Nelson, Walton-on-Thames.)
4. Sassoon. R. (1995) *The Acquisition of a Second Writing System*. Oxford: Intellect Books.
5. Smith, P. first devised this style in 1984 and many teachers' manuals and copybooks have been developed since then, and continue to be produced and updated.
6. Jarman, C. (1979) *The Development of Handwriting Skills*. Oxford: Blackwell. Many additional books and materials have been produced and developed to support this popular handwriting scheme.
7. A handwriting style that was very popular from about 1940 until the mid-'70s, said to be based on children's natural hand movements. It is still taught in a few schools.
8. Cripps, C. and Cox, R. (1989) *Joining the ABC*. Wisbech: Learning Development Aids.
9. As in the *Shared Writing on School Placement* pack (2001), produced by the NLS to help teachers to work with student trainees.

Further reading

Alston, J. and Taylor, J. (1987) *Handwriting: Theory, Research and Practice*. London: Croom Helm.

Byers, L. (1963) 'The relationship of manuscript and cursive handwriting to accuracy in spelling'. *The Journal of Educational Research*, 57(2).

Cripps, C. and Cox, R. (1989) *Joining the ABC*. Wisbech: Learning Development Aids.

Crystal, D. (1987) *Child Language, Learning and Linguistics: An Overview for the Teaching and Therapeutic Profession*. London: Edward Arnold.

DfEE (2001) *The National Literacy Strategy: Developing Early Writing*. London: HMSO.

Early, G.H. *et al.* (1976) 'Cursive handwriting, reading and spelling achievement'. *Academic Therapy*, 12.

Graves, D. (1983) *Writing: Teachers and Children at Work*. Portsmouth, NH: Heinemann.

Jarman, C. (1979) *The Development of Handwriting Skills*. Oxford: Blackwell.

Klein, C. and Millar, R. (1990) *Unscrambling Spelling*. London: Hodder & Stoughton.

Sassoon, R. (1990) *Handwriting: The Way To Teach It*. London: Stanley Thornes.

Sassoon, R. (1990) *Handwriting: A New Perspective*. London: Stanley Thornes.

Sassoon. R. (1993) *The Art and Science of Handwriting*. Oxford: Intellect Books.

Sassoon. R. (1995) *The Acquisition of a Second Writing System*. Oxford: Intellect Books.

Smith, P. (1993) *New Nelson Handwriting: Teacher's manual*. Walton-on-Thames: Nelson.

CHAPTER 6

Authenticity, modelling and style: writing and ICT

John Garvey

Introduction

Metacognition refers to 'that uniquely human capacity of people, to be self-reflective, not just to think and know, but to think about their thinking and knowing.'[1] Wray[2] has identified metacognition as a key factor in developing reading and writing, drawing upon Vygotsky's[3] argument that bringing the process of learning to a conscious level will enable learners to gain mastery and control over their learning. Central to metacognition are the processes of representing ideas dynamically (to oneself or others), gaining feedback and flexibility in responding to the evaluation of one's own ideas. Such a description mirrors research findings into how literacy teaching can be enhanced by the use of ICT, which can offer the following benefits:

- the capacity to present or represent ideas dynamically or in multiple forms;
- the facility for providing feedback to pupils as they are working; and
- the capacity to present information in easily changed forms. (Moseley *et al.*)[4]

Fisher[5] asserts that writing can help develop the process of metacognition at three levels, with regard to knowledge of self in relation to:

- Task – what is the writing – its form, audience and purpose?
- Process – what do you do – plan, draft, edit, share?
- Oneself – what kind of author are you – what helps you to write well?

ICT can enhance the development of these levels of awareness in the following manner:

In terms of *task*, it is essential that children see the task as *authentic*, with a clearly defined and understood sense of audience and purpose.

With regard to *process*, writers, teachers and peers should act as 'critical friends' in *modelling* and sharing key elements of the writing process.

With respect to *oneself*, a range of software is currently available that can support a variety of *writing styles* and help emerging writers to develop their own style in an effective manner.

This chapter will attempt to address the issue of how the computer can be used as a tool for enhancing children's self-awareness of authenticity, modelling and writing style.

Authenticity: audience and purpose

Authenticity has a central role to play in metacognition. Children's writing should be rooted in authentic contexts that will enable them to develop a keen sense of purpose and audience, thus giving them a reason for writing and thinking about strategies to improve their writing. Knowing that what they are doing is worthwhile can be empowering and emancipatory for children and adults alike. One major advantage of the word processor and desktop publishing software is the manner in which it can enable children to present work of publication quality. Of course, one has to beware of mistaking the 'gloss of technology' for high-quality content, but writing using a computer can be powerfully motivating for children if they are aware of the audience for which the work is intended. Work by Wray and Medwell on providing an authentic context for children's writing through the creation and publication of newspapers concluded that the public nature of work on the computer enabled Year 5 children to develop a more acute awareness of the needs of their intended audience. The effect was enhanced when the work was complemented by the involvement of personnel from local newspapers who introduced them to the various features of newspapers, and through visits to a newspaper office. Their small-scale research indicated that the 'double whammy' of involvement with 'real newspaper people' and a genuine audience for their newspaper enabled children to again a heightened awareness of aspects of the writing process such as drafting, editing and publishing. They concluded that:

> It appears that interaction with a local newspaper office offers children a particular type of authenticity which can develop not only these children's understanding of newspapers but also their understanding about writing.[6]

Email

Email opens up new possibilities for writing (Turrell).[7] It is relatively easy to get to grips with, saves time, enables communication on a global scale, and is very flexible: 'It can be written in any style imaginable and is the perfect medium for children to develop their individual "inner voice" and explore different genres and persona.' Turrell has provided a concise summary of contexts for using email including children finding pen pals in other schools, developing joint projects with schools in other parts of the country/world and developing contacts with experts in their field such as authors, poets, musicians, artists, scientists, designers and other teachers. Careful monitoring of such contacts is needed to ensure that children do not become involved in inappropriate communications and to ensure that projects remain focused. However, the motivational effect of gaining rapid feedback from diverse individuals and cultures is undeniable and can act as a powerful mechanism for children to develop strategies for reflecting upon purpose and audience.

Children designing their own web pages

There has recently been tremendous growth in school websites. Unfortunately, some primary school websites seem to have been written by ICT-literate teachers with the occasional insertion of samples of children's work to serve as exemplars of what is happening within the school. Recent versions of word-processing software such as Word (commonly available in schools) allow a fairly quick and easy route into the insertion of hyperlinks (links to other web pages or websites) that are the key tools needed for creating simple web pages. There is no reason why children at Key Stage 2 should not get to grips with inserting hyperlinks into their own word-processed documents. Such an approach provides a sense of authenticity to children in publishing their own work as knowing that children from across the world are likely to view and respond to their efforts is powerful motivation indeed!

Presentation software

Presentation software has been, to a large extent, neglected at primary level, partly because such applications were perceived originally as being primarily for business use. However, packages such as PowerPoint contain features that are powerful in terms of motivating children to write. A series of slides can be readily produced, accompanied by animated effects, which allow text to appear on screen in a variety of forms and offer exciting sound effects such as glass breaking, gunshots or whooshes. Animated backgrounds can be used to maintain interest. Consider how a pair of Year 6 children constructed the opening of a story, using a sound effect to capture the reader's attention (see Figure 6.1).

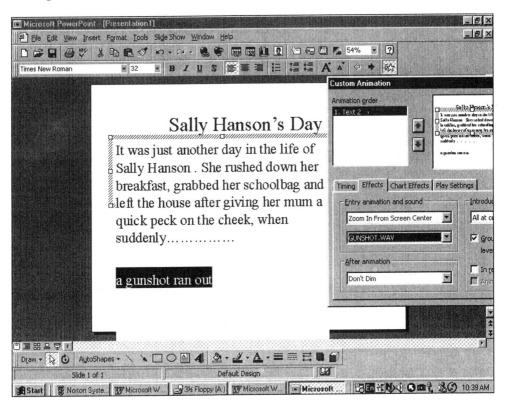

Figure 6.1 Sound effects in PowerPoint

An understanding of purpose and audience is critical for high-quality writing. In order for such writing to develop, children need to be given the opportunity to interact with and learn from others about key elements of the writing process.

Modelling and teacher questioning in the Literacy Hour

Modelling

The powerful role played by newspaper personnel in enhancing children's understanding about writing indicates that the modelling of features of the writing process by knowledgeable others can be very beneficial. Bruner[8] has emphasised the importance of children 'inheriting the structure of disciplines' in their formal education. For example, in relation to learning about history they should act as historians, collecting evidence about the past and evaluating it to try to form a picture of their own and others' heritage. The role of 'experts' is critical – Heathcote[9] in her work in the field of drama, stresses the value of children inheriting the 'mantle of the expert'. The definition of 'expert' might include children learning from established authors, teachers and their own peers who might have particular skills and strategies to offer in developing their potential as writers.

Modelling through websites

One key role played by such experts is that of the demonstration of their expertise through the modelling of features of the writing process. The computer has a powerful role to play here. Nothing can beat the presence of real authors in the classroom who can offer an insight into how they create their stories. As second best, the use of ICT offers genuine promise through authors sharing their thoughts on writing over the World Wide Web. This is exemplified by a recent initiative undertaken by the Poetry Society, in response to the recognition that the teaching and learning of poetry can be problematic for teachers and pupils alike. Sprackland[10] reports the concerns of an experienced primary school teacher, which characterises the feelings of many teachers: 'I just don't know where to start. I know poetry's a good thing. I know I should be doing more of it, but how can I when all I can remember is learning Wordsworth's 'Daffodils' off by heart 25 years ago?'

A collaboration between the Poetry Society and the DfES has led to the creation of the website Poetryclass (www.poetryclass.net). This offers children and teachers a portal into the world of poets, who share their thoughts about writing and the strategies they use for composing poetry. The website is particularly valuable for teachers in that it offers tried-and-tested strategies for approaching poetry in the classroom. It also offers links to other sites such as the Young Writers website (www.mystworld.com/youngwriter/), which offers children the chance to hear the views of established writers such as Anne Fine, Roger McGough, Dick King-Smith, Michael Rosen and Jill Murphy on how they gain the inspiration to write and how they approach different aspects of the writing process. Gaining an insight into how experienced writers go about constructing prose and poetry can give children valuable insights into strategies that might be adopted in developing their own writing. Experienced writers seem to use different strategies from inexperienced ones – most do indeed plan, edit and revise their work. Inexperienced writers do not spontaneously edit their own writing (Monahan).[11] Many children often equate editing and revising their work with 'doing a good copy,' or tidying up their text, graphically described by Donald Graves[12] as 'putting a good manicure on the corpse'. For most children revision means little more than correcting glaring errors in spelling and punctuation. Graves notes that: 'The problem that kids have with writing is that they feel the words they put down are inviolate . . . that when it's down, it's down forever.'

The challenge for the teacher is to enable children to realise that the expression of their ideas can be refined and improved. The provisional nature of text produced on a word processor can be of obvious benefit here. Chandler[13] documents several reasons for the lack of radical revision amongst inexperienced writers. These are:

- state of readiness related to developmental age;
- insufficient awareness of the needs of their readers, so revision may not appear necessary;
- lack of value accorded by the individual to writing or lack of any real urge to undertake a particular piece of writing;
- lack of demonstrations of the usefulness of revision;
- difficulty in juggling the cognitive and memory demands of simultaneous revision and composition;
- lack of any effective diagnostic and remedial strategies for use in revision;
- lack of intervention by another person to encourage revision; and
- a physical disincentive relating to the fact that major revision using traditional tools involves a considerable amount of re-copying.

Modelling during shared writing

Shared writing modelled by the teacher as part of the Literacy Hour, using a word processor and a large screen, can help to overcome many of these barriers to children editing their own work. Teachers can use this tool to move children on from recording ideas drawn from their own existing understanding of the writing process to an awareness of strategies that might help them to refine the expression of their ideas effectively. Witness how the teacher of a Year 3 class intervened during a plenary session in the Literacy Hour, using a child's piece of word-processed work as a starting point for thinking about strategies to enliven non-fiction accounts (see Figure 6.2).

The dynamic nature of such teacher interventions on screen can help children to be more aware of writing conventions, the provisional nature of their writing and the potential of the word processor for editing text in a relatively painless but effective manner. The example in the figure was characterised not only by the teacher's confident use of the word processor but also by an understanding of the value of explicitly modelling processes and strategies that might be of benefit to the emerging writer. It is difficult to distinguish, as is so often the case, the impact of the teacher's interventions and the impact of ICT. However, attitudinal research suggests that:

In their teaching pro-ICT teachers gave significantly more feedback to pupils after correct responses than other teachers did. They also tended to have longer plenary sessions in which the teacher tended to use a question and answer format and . . . model processes for the pupils in English lessons.[14]

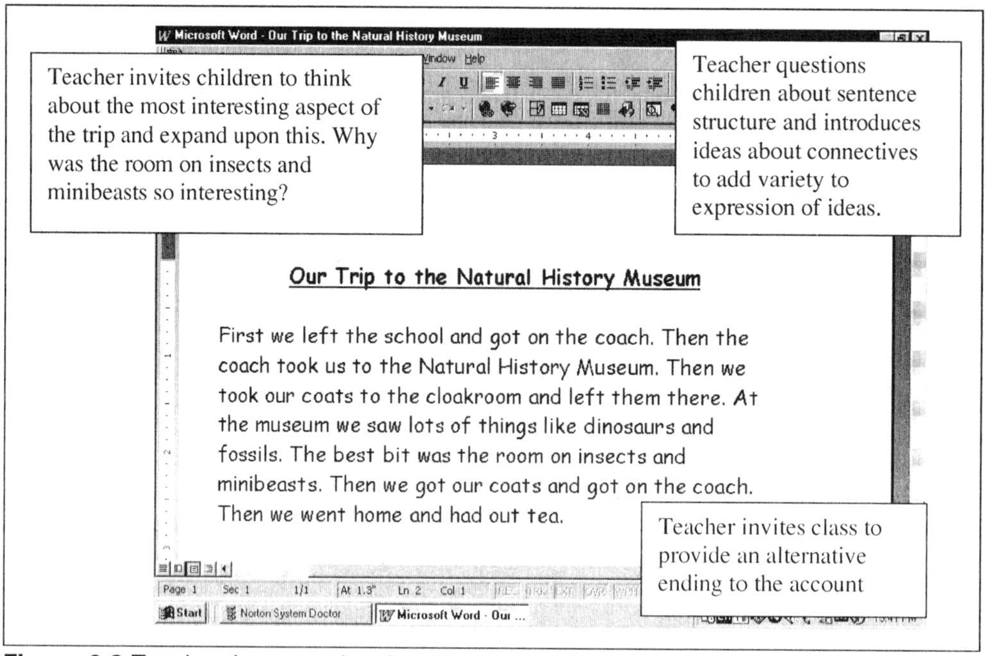

Figure 6.2 Teacher intervention in plenary session of Literacy Hour

Such teacher modelling of the key processes of writing non-fiction can be complemented by the use of on-screen writing frames to demonstrate how different genres may require the use of different structures and conventions (Lewis and Wray[15] and Hodson and Jones[16]). Consider the model in Figure 6.3 of how Year 5 children were guided to analyse a traditional fairy story with a view to thinking about how they might construct their own. Rather than following the long-accepted advice that a story should contain a 'good beginning, middle, and ending', the children are guided towards an analysis of the key elements of plot, which might involve the resolution of a problem or dilemma; a device used in many stories. Such a strategy for analysing a very simple story can enable children to reflect upon problems and dilemmas with a view to including such plot conventions in their own stories. In this case a group of children were Invited to summarise the characters, events and plot of *Goldilocks and the Three Bears* – their work was then shared on a large screen and the teacher invited the whole class to record their collective ideas on the problem, resolution and conclusion to (or moral of) the story. The children's ideas are interesting in that they combine the viewpoints of the main protagonists of the fairy tale.

Modelling through electronic writing frames using hyperlinks
Writing frames usually take the form of off-screen work on hard copy. However, with children's increasing familiarity with the internet, which requires an understanding of the concept of a hyperlink (i.e. a link to another web page or website), there is potential for the design of electronic writing frames which incorporate links to support children in thinking about their own writing strategies. In the example in Figure 6.4, when the

---

Problem
- The three bears shouldn't have left the door of the house open.
- Goldilocks should have gone into the house – it's not hers.
- She's breaking and entering.
- Goldilocks is tired and hungry, so she couldn't help herself.
- She shouldn't have fallen asleep and got caught – she would have been all right otherwise.
- Goldilocks isn't very nice really.

Resolution
- Goldilocks eats the porridge and has a sleep.
- The bears come back and find everything eaten and the chairs broken. They find Goldilocks but she runs away – she was lucky to get away.

Conclusion or Moral of the Story
- Goldilocks goes free but the bears will be upset and angry.
- Never leave your door open.
- Don't go into places where you are not meant to be.
- Don't get lost in the woods – you could end up in big trouble.

Figure 6.3 Analysing *Goldilocks and the Three Bears*

child clicks on one of the underlined phrases they are given guidance on-screen on how to complete each section of the writing frame.

The value of modelling is also clearly evident in a further example based upon a strategy used by a teacher working with Year 6 children included in the CD-ROM NLS resource *ICT in the Literacy Hour: Whole Class Teaching*.[17] The teacher made full use of the capacity of the computer to present an information source (a CD-ROM encyclopaedia) side by side with a word processor.

Through using this technique, the teacher can demonstrate the unique benefits offered by electronic texts and develop an understanding that sentences and paragraphs can be summarised to suit the reader's/writer's purpose. The act of skimming texts in order to identify key words to inform summarising and note taking is a key skill that children need to develop in their reading and writing.

Teacher and pupil questioning

The teacher has a vital role to play in developing metacognition with regard to the writing process. Teachers and children need to develop a shared language, through high-quality teacher and pupil questioning, when talking about aspects of literacy development (Williams).[18] The quality of teacher intervention is critical, whether it be

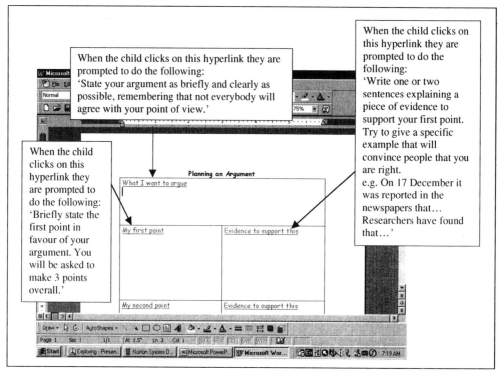

Figure 6.4 Electronic writing frame

through the provision of prompts to enable children to think about how they will structure their writing, on-screen modelling of writing processes or through supportive but probing questioning:

> High levels of questioning by the teacher will encourage children to problem solve, to reconsider decisions they have reached about what they are reading or writing and revise what they have written in order that their knowledge is transformed.

Children themselves can also act as 'critical friends' in the writing process, sharing their expertise with peers. Fisher[19] stresses the desirability of creating a 'writing community' within which ideas can be explored and developed in spoken and written form. Children have a key role to play within that community – more able children can help others through acting as 'response partners' with a view to improving their own and other children's writing. The act of looking critically in a constructive manner at another's work is undoubtedly very challenging, but can help children to develop skills of analysis, communication and self-reflection – key elements of metacognition. If one puts oneself in the position of evaluating another's work then one should be prepared to subject one's own work to critical scrutiny. The creation of a supportive writing community is heavily dependent on the role model set by teachers in their own modelling of the writing process. The classroom 'writing community' needs to be sensitively managed by the teacher and it is helpful if rules for being an effective response partner are established to guide children (Chapter 2 of this book).

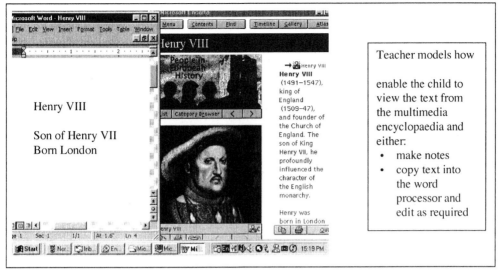

Figure 6.5 On-screen editing of electronic text

ICT has a major role to play in the development of such a community, with its capacity to allow children to edit and revise their work in a relatively painless manner and through its potential for enabling children to publish work for the classroom community and beyond. An added benefit is that using a word processor fosters collaborative talk and, as such, can encourage oral composition at the screen within small groups who are working together.

Writing style

The role of planning

Learning and writing styles differ. Chandler[20] has documented a simple but useful distinction drawn by Stephen Spender[21] of two poles in compositional styles Mozartian and Beethovenian:

> The Mozartians (or serialists) are executors – planning extensively and revising minimally; the Beethovians (or holists) are discoverers, planning minimally and revising extensively. So for Dick Francis, 'My first draft is it,' whilst for Hemingway, 'The first draft of anything is s***'. The Mozartian-Beethovenian model is particularly valuable as a caveat against dispensing standard advice to inexperienced writers.

The National Literacy Strategy requires that from Year 3 onwards children should use different planning formats for their writing such as charting, mapping, flow charts and simple storyboards. ICT can offer excellent support for children with this.

Writing frames suit a linear approach to writing, although the use of hyperlinks can add another dimension. Other linear approaches might draw upon software such as

PowerPoint that allows for the storyboarding of ideas on-screen through the presentation of ideas in slide and note form. Consider the storyboard in Figure 6.6, written by a pair of Year 6 children, based upon slides prepared by the teacher which focus the writers' attention on key elements of plot construction such as the introduction, problem, resolution and conclusion.

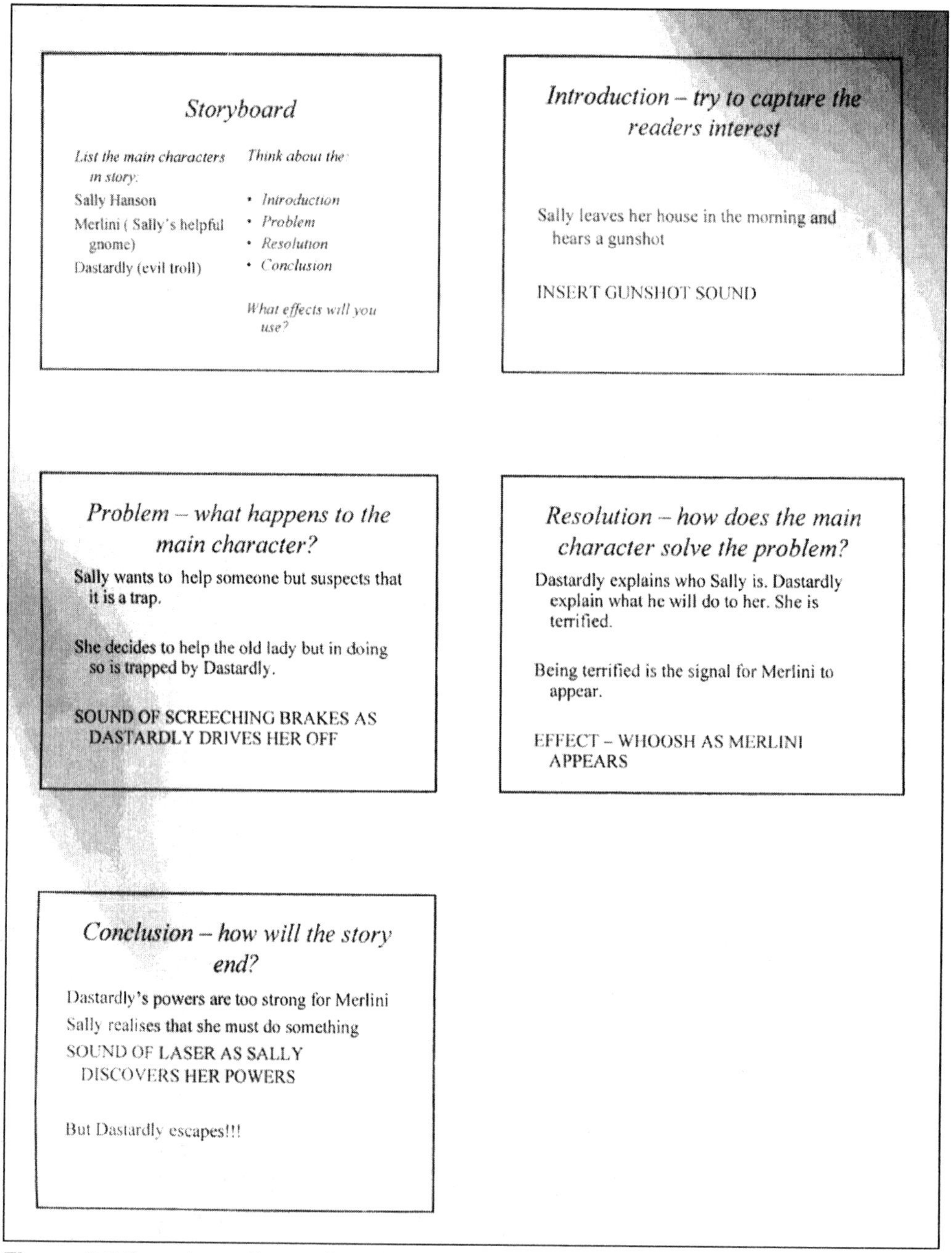

Storyboard

List the main characters in story.

Sally Hanson

Merlini (Sally's helpful gnome)

Dastardly (evil troll)

Think about the:
- *Introduction*
- *Problem*
- *Resolution*
- *Conclusion*

What effects will you use?

Introduction – try to capture the readers interest

Sally leaves her house in the morning and hears a gunshot

INSERT GUNSHOT SOUND

Problem – what happens to the main character?

Sally wants to help someone but suspects that it is a trap.

She decides to help the old lady but in doing so is trapped by Dastardly.

SOUND OF SCREECHING BRAKES AS DASTARDLY DRIVES HER OFF

Resolution – how does the main character solve the problem?

Dastardly explains who Sally is. Dastardly explain what he will do to her. She is terrified.

Being terrified is the signal for Merlini to appear.

EFFECT – WHOOSH AS MERLINI APPEARS

Conclusion – how will the story end?

Dastardly's powers are too strong for Merlini
Sally realises that she must do something
SOUND OF LASER AS SALLY DISCOVERS HER POWERS

But Dastardly escapes!!!

Figure 6.6 Storyboarding using PowerPoint

Planning with Hyperstudio

Hyperstudio is an example of a multimedia authoring package designed for children, based upon the use of hyperlinks to link pages to a central home page, mirroring the design of websites. The use of such software necessitates a highly planned approach to the structuring of ideas away from the computer, before the committal of ideas to the screen. Such an approach can foster the development of oral composition and might be of particular value to those who prefer a 'Mozartian' approach to composition and allow for an insight into children's own writing strategies. Multimedia authoring packages can allow for the insertion of children's own computer-generated drawings, sounds and video to provide for a heightened sense of purpose and audience. The example in Figure 6.7 was produced by a Year 5 child.

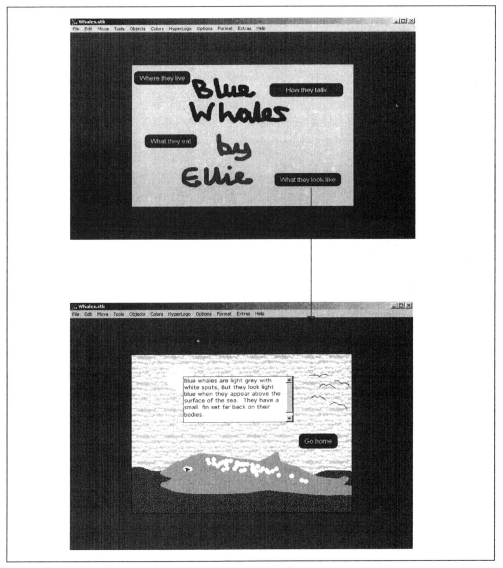

Figure 6.7 Non-fiction writing using Hyperstudio

Planning using EMindMaps

EMindMaps are a recent software development which enables children to plan their work in diagrammatic form (Sparrowhawk[22]). It should be noted that original approaches to the development of software for educational software are few and far between. Most software for educational use tends to fall into the category of 'drill and practice' or child-friendly adaptations of office applications (Seymour Papert's[23] programming language LOGO being an honourable exception). However, EMindMaps seem to offer a genuinely original approach, drawing upon the well-established idea of concept mapping. The software is flexible enough for ideas to be easily edited and rearranged. Any text that is typed into the diagram can be easily re-presented in document format. It demonstrates that writing can be an iterative process. The software lends itself to collaborative work and is a powerful tool to enable children to think about writing conventions and how to construct texts. As Sparrowhawk comments:

> Discussing the relevant elements using a tool like this can enable children to understand the overall process, but also to begin to make judgements about what is important for the particular exercise they are carrying out.

The use of EMindMaps can enable a more flexible approach to structuring ideas than writing frames, which have been criticised for constraining the writer. It also offers potential for children to modify and personalise the framework to adapt their writing style to particular genres. In the example in Figure 6.8, a teacher, Mike Langley,[24] has used the software to prompt children about the key elements of constructing a detective story.

The open-ended nature of EMindMaps means that it can be tailored to suit a variety of writing genres, providing both a support mechanism for children and a vehicle for developing their own ideas.

Conclusion

Given that new technologies are often seen as impersonal, it is interesting that the unifying strand that runs through the use of ICT for developing metacognition through writing is, paradoxically, the potential of the computer to humanise the writing process. Through providing an avenue to develop an understanding of purpose and audience, applications such as word processors and desktop publishers can put emerging writers into contact with others in order to share ideas. This is dramatically illustrated in the capacity of the internet and email to provide a wider audience for communication. Being able to connect with others to model aspects of the writing process through ICT can unlock in the emerging writer an awareness of strategies needed for refining and improving the expression of ideas. The flexibility of software such as Hyperstudio and EMindMapping can enable the writer to personalise the way in which they can explore and present ideas. The use of ICT as a tool for writing is still in its infancy. As yet, we are only scraping the surface of its potential as a medium for enabling children to think about how they approach their own writing. We do not know what is around the corner or what the future will bring, but we can only anticipate it with enthusiasm.

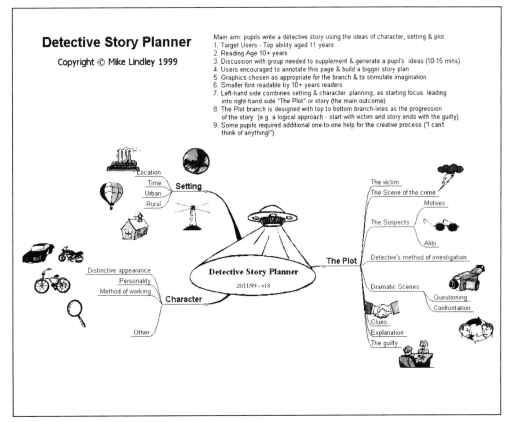

Detective Story Planner

Copyright © Mike Lindley 1999

Main aim: pupils write a detective story using the ideas of character, setting & plot
1. Target Users - Top ability aged 11 years
2. Reading Age 10+ years
3. Discussion with group needed to supplement & generate a pupil's ideas (10-15 mins)
4. Users encouraged to annotate this page & build a bigger story plan
5. Graphics chosen as appropriate for the branch & to stimulate imagination
6. Smaller font readable by 10+ years readers
7. Left-hand side combines setting & character planning, as starting focus leading into right-hand side "The Plot" or story (the main outcome)
8. The Plot branch is designed with top to bottom branch-lines as the progression of the story (e.g. a logical approach - start with victim and story ends with the guilty)
9. Some pupils required additional one-to-one help for the creative process ("I can't think of anything!")

Figure 6.8 Planning a detective story using EMindMap

Notes

1. Fisher, R. (2001:6) 'Thinking to Write: Thinking Skills in Literacy Learning'. Paper delivered at UKRA Conference, Christ Church University, Canterbury, 7 July.
2. Wray, D. (1994) *Literacy and Awareness*. London: Hodder & Stoughton/UKRA.
3. Vygotsky, L.S. (1978) *Mind in Society*. Cambridge, MA: Harvard University Press.
4. Moseley, D., Higgins, S., Bramald, R., Hardman, F., Miller, J., Mroz, M., Tse, H., Newton, D., Thompson, I., Williamson, J., Halligan, J. and Bramald, P. (1999) *Ways forward with ICT: Effective Pedagogy using Information and Communications Technology for Literacy and Numeracy in Primary Schools*. Newcastle: Newcastle University.
5. Fisher, R. (2001) 'Thinking to Write: Thinking Skills in Literacy Learning'. Paper delivered at UKRA Conference, Christ Church University, Canterbury, 7 July.
6. Wray, D. and Medwell, J. (1996) 'Newspapers in education and children's writing'. *Reading*, July, 43–6.
7. Turrell, G. (1999) *Email – Punching Holes in Classroom Walls*. MAPE Focus on

Communications. Birmingham: MAPE Publications, Section C, pp. 1–2.

8.   Bruner, J.S. (1971) *Towards a Theory of Instruction*. Cambridge, MA: Harvard University Press.

9.   Heathcote, D. and Bolton, G. (1995) *Drama for Learning: An Account of Dorothy Heathcote's 'Mantle of the Expert' Approach to Education*. Portsmouth, NH: Heinemann.

10. Sprackland, J. (2001:6) 'Beyond "Daffodils": the poetry class project'. *Reading*, 11.

11. Monahan, B. (1984) 'Revision strategies of basic and competent writers as they write for different audiences'. *Research in the Teaching of English*, **18**, 288–304.

12. Graves, D. (1983:27) *Writing: Teachers and Children at Work*. Exeter, NH: Heinemann.

13. Chandler, D. (1990:3) 'Student Writers and the Word Processor: A Review of Research for the Classroom Teacher'. Paper delivered at the Centre for Applied Research in Education Conference, University of East Anglia, Norwich, July.

14. Moseley, D., Higgins, S., Bramald, R., Hardman, F., Miller, J., Mroz, M., Tse, H., Newton, D., Thompson, I., Williamson, J., Halligan, J. and Bramald, P. (1999:8) *Ways Forward with ICT: Effective Pedagogy using Information and Communications Technology for Literacy and Numeracy in Primary Schools*. Newcastle: Newcastle University.

15. Lewis, M. and Wray, D. (1998) *Writing across the Curriculum: Frames to Support Learning*. Reading: University of Reading.

16. Hodson, P. and Jones, D. (2001) *Teaching Children to Write: The Process Approach to Writing for Literacy*. London: David Fulton Publishers.

17. The National Literacy Strategy (2001) *ICT in the Literacy Hour: Whole Class Teaching*. London: DfES Publications.

18. Williams, M. (2000:5) 'The part which metacognition can play in raising standards in English at Key Stage 2'. *Reading*, 34(1), April.

19. Fisher, R. (2001:6) 'Thinking to Write: Thinking Skills in Literacy Learning'. Paper delivered at UKRA Conference, Christ Church University, Canterbury, 7 July.

20. Chandler, D. (1990) 'Student Writers and the Word Processor: A Review of Research for the Classroom Teacher'. Paper delivered at the Centre for Applied Research in Education Conference, University of East Anglia, Norwich, July.

21. Spender, S., quoted in Chandler, D. (1990:1) 'Student Writers and the Word Processor: A Review of Research for the Classroom Teacher'. Paper delivered at the Centre for Applied Research in Education Conference, University of East Anglia, Norwich, July.

22. Sparrowhawk, A. (2001) 'Will mapping your mind help?' *English 4 to 11*, Spring, 25–6.

23. Papert, S. (1982) *Mindstorms*. New York: Harvester Press.

24. Langley, M. (1999) – refer to the website www.emindmaps.com/

Further reading

Chandler, D. (1990) 'Student Writers and the Word Processor: A Review of Research for the Classroom Teacher'. Paper delivered at the Centre for Applied Research in Education Conference, University of East Anglia, Norwich, July.

Fisher, R. (2001) 'Thinking to Write: Thinking Skills in Literacy Learning'. Paper delivered at UKRA Conference, Christ Church University, Canterbury, 7 July.

Heathcote, D. and Bolton, G. (1995) *Drama for Learning: An Account of Dorothy Heathcote's 'Mantle of the Expert' Approach to Education.* Portsmouth, NH: Heinemann.

Hodson, P. and Jones, D. (2001) *Teaching Children to Write: The Process Approach to Writing for Literacy.* London: David Fulton Publishers.

Lewis, M. and Wray, D. (1998) *Writing across the Curriculum; Frames to Support Learning.* Reading: University of Reading.

Moseley, D., Higgins, S., Bramald, R., Hardman, F., Miller, J., Mroz, M., Tse, H., Newton, D., Thompson, I., Williamson, J., Halligan, J. and Bramald, P. (1999:8) *Ways forward with ICT: Effective Pedagogy using Information and Communications Technology for Literacy and Numeracy in Primary Schools.* Newcastle: Newcastle University.

National Literacy Strategy (2001) *ICT in the Literacy Hour: Whole Class Teaching.* London: DfES Publications.

Sparrowhawk, A. (2001) 'Will mapping your mind help?' *English 4 to 11,* Spring, 25–6.

Sprackland, J. (2001) 'Beyond "Daffodils": the poetry class project'. *Reading* 11(6).

Turrell, G. (1999) *Email – Punching Holes in Classroom Walls.* MAPE Focus on Communications. Birmingham: MAPE Publications, Section C, pp. 1–2.

Williams, M. (2000) 'The part which metacognition can play in raising standards in English at Key Stage 2'. *Reading* 34(1), April.

Wray, D. (1994) *Literacy and Awareness.* London: Hodder & Stoughton/UKRA.

Wray, D. and Medwell, J. (1996) 'Newspapers in education and children's writing'. *Reading,* July, 43.

Websites

Poetryclass: www.poetryclass.net
Youngwriters: www.mystworld.com/youngwriter/
BECTA: www.becta.org.uk
Literacy Trust: www.literacytrust.org.uk
National Grid for Learning: www.ngfl.gov.uk
Standards Unit DfES: www.standards.dfes.gov.uk
EMindMaps: www.emindmaps.com/

CHAPTER 7

Keeping track: assessment in writing

Deborah Jones

Writing, in the twenty-first century, continues to play a vital role in both our public and private lives. Skilful writers are empowered members of society and have the ability to influence the world around them. Therefore, the effective teaching of writing is fundamental to creating successful and confident individuals who are equipped to meet the demands of the world in which they live. Assessment must be at the heart of this and central to the process of teaching and learning. We need to identify where children are in their understanding and enable them to move forward in their development.

The current context

A depressing picture of how writing is taught in the majority of primary schools is presented. Inspection reports carried out by Ofsted (1999) describe children's writing as 'brief and fragmentary', often incomplete and 'lacking a clear sense of purpose'. Within the context of the National Literacy Strategy (DfEE 1998), teachers are described as being more confident in teaching reading (as more emphasis was placed on this initially) and as a result, spend less time teaching writing. In addition, evidence from SATs results show, 'standards of writing lagging considerably behind standards of reading'.[1] In their most recent report, Ofsted (2001:15) are more positive, stating that 'just over half the teaching of guided writing was good'.[2] In order to improve this even further, it is recommended that teachers plan a coherent and sustained approach to the teaching of writing. Children need to become familiar with different types of text, both fiction and non-fiction and also need to develop an awareness of how considerations of audience and purpose effect writing (Chapter 1).

This chapter will focus on the process approach to teaching writing. It will consider the use of writing frames as a strategy and will show how a system for assessment can be integrated into this approach by the use of assessment frames. Guidelines will be offered, concentrating on the assessment of non-fiction writing in particular, as this is the area in which many teachers lack confidence. The chapter aims to explain and build upon the approach recommended in the National Literacy Strategy (1998) and the *English National Curriculum* (1999) and in so doing, to provide structures which will enable teachers to introduce appropriate strategies into their classrooms.

The process approach to writing

At the heart of the process approach to writing is the belief that the stages children work through are as important as the final, completed text (Graves 1983). Becoming an accomplished writer involves understanding what each of these stages entails and that creating a text certainly means more than 'one shot writing'. This chapter describes the discrete stages of this approach and explains how children can be assessed and supported at each stage of their writing journey.

The process approach to writing

- Making decisions
- Planning

  Brainstorming
  Organising/grouping
  Using flow diagrams

- Drafting
- Responding
- Presenting and publishing
- Reflecting

Children may go through all of the stages shown in this box when composing a piece of writing, but as they gain more confidence, they may decide that not all of them are necessary. However, children do need to have all of the stages made explicit to them in order to give them the necessary knowledge and understanding of how writing is constructed so that they can make informed decisions later and choose which elements they need at different times. Metacognitive awareness, that is, knowing *how* they are learning, empowers children, as they become increasingly sophisticated writers.[3] This way of teaching makes writing manageable, giving children increasing control over their work as it enables them to change their writing and craft it.

Current initiatives in the teaching of literacy recognise the significance of the process approach to writing. Adopting a process approach where the different stages of 'planning, drafting, revising and proof reading' are used, is highlighted by Ofsted (1999) as an important strategy for improving standards. The National Curriculum for English states that at Key Stage 1, children should 'assemble and develop ideas on paper and screen [and] plan and review their writing, discussing the quality of what is written.' At Key Stage 2, children should 'use the planning, drafting and editing process to improve their work and to sustain their fiction and non-fiction writing'. In addition, The National Literacy Strategy acknowledges that 'through Key Stage 2, there is a progressive emphasis on the skills of planning, drafting, revising, proof reading and the presentation of writing'. Both major documents clearly identify the need for children to be taught the process approach to writing. In so doing, they are emphasising the importance of involving children in understanding their own processes of learning.

The process approach to writing assumes a particular view of how children learn, how teachers teach and of how classrooms function. It allows children to experiment with language, and to develop an understanding of how writing works within an environment where collaboration is welcomed, and independence encouraged.[4] In this context children become confident writers, secure in the knowledge that teachers will support them as they take risks and make hypotheses about the writing system.

Using writing frames

As they progress into the drafting stages of their work, writing frames, along with the support of adults and peers, can provide the scaffolds children need to enable them to develop their writing successfully. At each stage frames can support children as they experiment with many different forms of writing, both fiction and non-fiction (Chapter 1). They provide a structure and direction for children's ideas on a chosen topic and act as a scaffold to support the writer. Writing frames are designed to encourage informed dialogue between teachers and children and children and their peers. In addition, prompt sheets may provide questions which help them reflect on and develop their writing. The fundamental purpose of these frames and prompts is to encourage children to become independent writers.[5]

This approach makes the whole business of assessment transparent. Teachers can clearly see how children are tackling the task of writing, what their strengths are and where their areas for development lie. As the process is broken down into discrete stages, it is easier to pinpoint children's needs. Frames convert their thinking, at each stage, into a visible entity and enable both children and teachers, first, to reflect on the learning process, and secondly to assess achievement in writing.

In using this approach, teachers seek to promote independence in children, allowing opportunities for more focused individual and group work. It also allows the teacher to intervene effectively at critical stages in the process where drafts and completed frames provide clear evidence of children's writing development. Such frames allow teachers and children to be partners in the process of learning and assessment. Ofsted (2001) states that 'where pupils are involved in evaluating their own work in a structured way, linked to objectives, this is helpful in enabling them to understand their targets for improvement'. Effective assessment should start from the inception of a piece of writing and continue throughout the process. To leave assessment until the work is completed is to miss many important opportunities.

Breaking down the stages: what needs to be assessed?

This section will go through the various stages of the process approach, consider what they entail, and identify the assessment opportunities which each provides for the teacher. A selection of writing frames will be taken from the book *Teaching Children to Write* (Hodson, P. and Jones, D. 2001).[6] These will act as illustrations and reflect a range of Key Stages.

Decision-making

Teachers need to give children as much autonomy over the writing process as possible, by offering them opportunities to choose their own topics for writing. When pupils have control over topics this not only increases their enjoyment, but it also contributes to their sense of ownership. It is important that children are aware of the decisions that will affect the writing they are about to undertake and the appropriateness of their choices needs to be assessed. They need to have a clear sense of the following: the audience (who the writing is for); the purpose, (the reason for writing); and the form, (the type of writing that is most appropriate to this particular task). Clearly, explicit consideration of purpose and audience will affect the type of writing that children choose. Teachers can develop children's understandings by focusing on these aspects within shared reading and writing sessions. Therefore, pupils need the necessary understanding of how texts work in order to make informed decisions about their own writing.

> *Assessment focus (see Figure 7.1):*
>
> Clear linkage of purpose, audience and genre

Planning

There are many ways in which children can organise their thoughts and ideas.[7] Giving them strategies such as brainstorming, grouping and the use of flow diagrams, is a vital part of the process that will not necessarily be obvious to them.

Brainstorming

Having decided upon the topic, children need to think about the potential that it holds. Brainstorming provides children with the opportunity to record as many initial ideas as they can, whether in a written or pictorial form. At this stage, they need not be concerned with issues such as correctness of spelling, punctuation or grammar, and should be completely free from restraints of structure and organisation. A brainstorm is essentially written by the child for the child.

> *Assessment focus (see Figure 7.1):*
>
> Scope of ideas
> Relevance of ideas to main topic

Organising/grouping

Children then need to categorise the ideas from the brainstorm under relevant headings or themes. It is important to remember and emphasise to children, that not all topic areas included in the brainstorm need be used at this stage. Some may be too

	Assessment of:	Questions	Tick	Comment	Target
Decision-making	Subject matter Purpose Audience Genre	Are all elements 1. identified 2. clear 3. appropriately linked?			
Planning Brainstorming	Initial ideas	Are initial ideas 1. relevant 2. comprehensive 3. imaginative?			
Grouping	Selection Categorisation	Are ideas 1. selected/filtered appropriately 2. categorised logically?			
Using flow diagrams	Sequence of ideas	Is sequence 1. logical 2. appropriately matched to genre (e.g. simple narrative – chronology)			
Drafting 1st draft	Audience/voice style Meaning Structure Innovation Editing – (use of code)	Is work clearly edited?			
2nd draft	Spelling Punctuation Editing	Is spelling accurate? If not, does it reflect phonic/graphic awareness? Is punctuation accurate? Is working clearly edited?			
Presenting and publishing	Handwriting Use of computer Overall presentation	Is handwriting legible and at an appropriate level? (see National Curriculum) Was process of word-procesing understood and undertaken efficiently? Was type of presentation, use of graphics, etc. appropriate?			
Reflecting	Reflection Metacognitive awareness	Are both composition and transcription reflected upon? Is implicit knowledge made explicit?			
Target setting	Targets	Are strengths and areas for development highlighted? Are the main ones identified?			

Figure 7.1 Process approach: Assessment focus sheet 1

far removed from the focus of the topic and attempting to include all of them may result in a superficial piece of writing. These decisions will make for useful points of discussion between teachers and pupils and provide further opportunities for assessment.

> *Assessment focus (see Figure 7.1):*
>
> Appropriate selection of headings
> Logical categorization of ideas

Using flow diagrams

The next stage focuses on sequencing these ideas in an appropriate order that will provide the structure for the writing itself (see Figure 7.2). Teachers' interventions will be invaluable at this point as they discuss these aspects with pupils. There are key issues which children need to reflect on in order to help them structure their writing. A simple narrative or story, for example, will be structured according to time (chronological), whereas a piece of writing which focuses on a topic, such as dinosaurs, may be structured non-chronologically. The ability to maintain a structure contributes to the overall cohesion of the piece and needs to be discussed and assessed.

> *Assessment focus (see Figure 7.1):*
>
> Logical sequencing
> Matching of structure to genre

Drafting

For teachers the process is one of showing children examples of different writers' drafts, of writing for them and with them, changing, eradicating and inserting different parts of the text. It is in this way that children learn that mistakes and amendments are, in fact, legitimate, and a natural part of what it means to be a writer.[8] The success of using the process approach to writing is largely based on the idea that children are writing as real writers would and can work through successive drafts if necessary. In terms of assessment, a great deal can be learned from focusing in on the various drafts children produce.

First draft

It is important to make children aware that the purpose of the first draft is to use the ideas outlined in their flow diagram to begin composing their writing. At this stage, children should not feel the constraints of transcription issues such as spelling and punctuation. As they become more sophisticated writers, composition and greater attention to transcription may become internalised and happen simultaneously, but in the early stages, splitting the two can relieve pressure. It may be helpful therefore, for

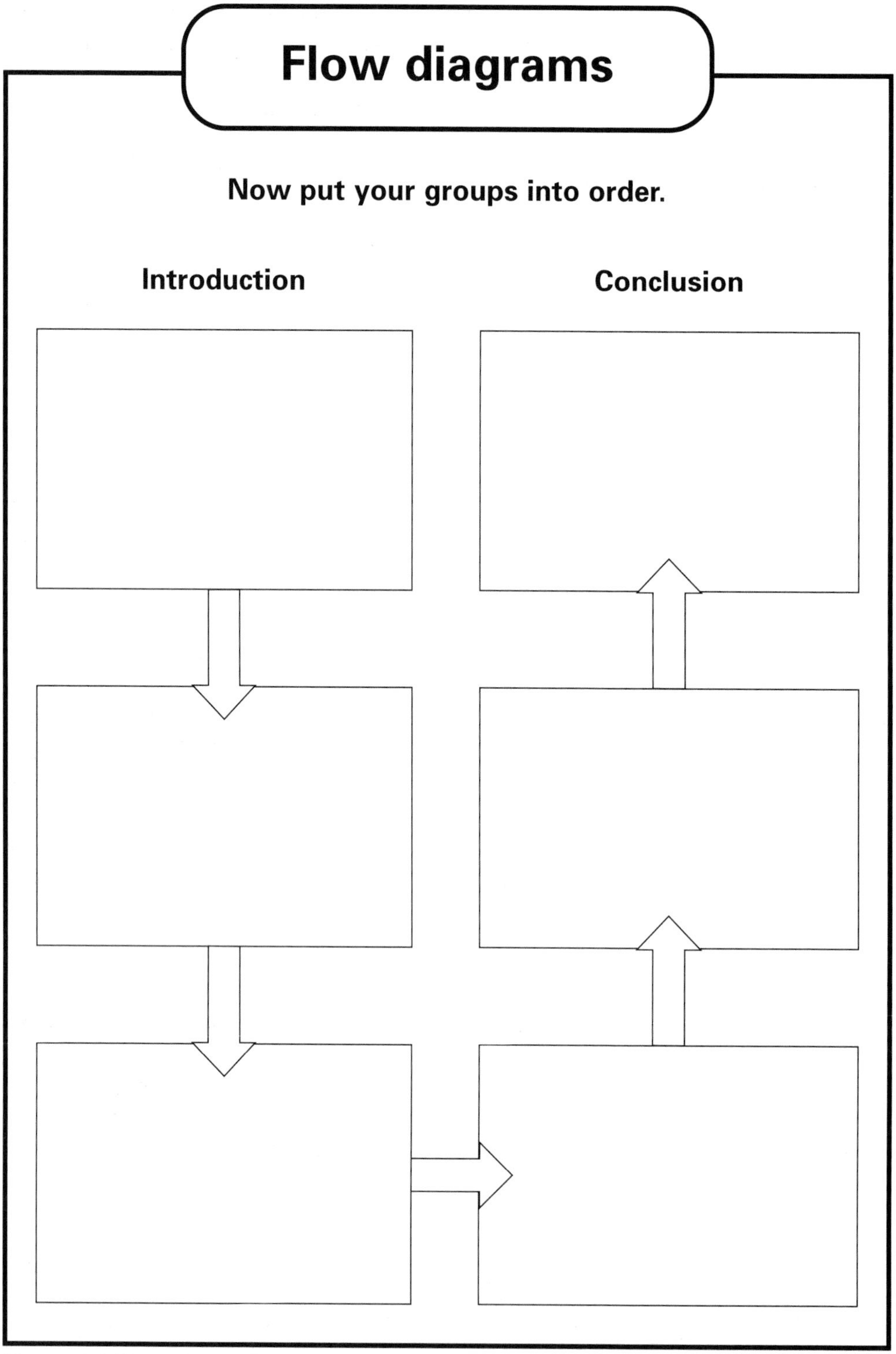

Flow diagrams

Now put your groups into order.

Introduction   **Conclusion**

Figure 7.2 Flow diagrams

children to use a drafting code focusing on reading for meaning as a prompt either during or at the end of their writing. Here symbols can be invented to denote omissions, changes needed and so on. Having a code that is shared and understood by all children is a helpful tool for collaborative writing in general.

Assessment focus (see Figure 7.1):

Clarity of meaning
Appropriateness of structure
Stylistic features
Efficiency in use of codes/editing

Second draft

Once children have reviewed their writing with a focus on meaning, transcriptional issues such as spelling and punctuation need to be addressed. Again, children can use symbols for spelling and punctuation to annotate their own text. Attention should also be drawn to the fact, that they can use a range of support structures, for example, dictionaries, computer spellchecks and response partners; and that a systematic use of these strategies can help them produce more refined texts. The aim is to give children as much autonomy as possible during the drafting process. As part of assessment, teachers should note the degree of support the child has been given.

Assessment focus (see Figure 7.1):

Accuracy of spelling
Accuracy of punctuation
Efficiency in editing

Presenting and publishing

Children can choose how they wish to present and publish their work. Readers have choices and children need to be aware of this. In discussing publication with children, a range of teaching points should be made.[9] A polished text in terms of accuracy, clarity of handwriting and general aesthetics is the reader's first point of contact (see Chapter 5). This initial encounter will result in the reader either exploring the text further, if their expectations are met, or discarding it. By sharing their writing with a wider audience, children become increasingly aware that more care needs to be taken with the finished product and this is an important part of their development as writers.

Assessment focus (see Figure 7.1):

Legibility of handwriting
Word-processing skills
Effectiveness of overall presentation

Reflecting

For all children, purposeful reflection should be an integral part of the whole writing process.[10] Reflection develops their metalinguistic awareness, that is, their knowledge of how language works. Before children embark on a new piece of writing, it is essential to look back on what they have recently completed. This reflection can serve many different purposes to:

- reflect on what they have learned;
- identify key areas for development; and
- move them forward as writers.

Reflection could take the form of a dialogue with the teacher, or it may be recorded in a private journal for the child alone. It is the child, however, who should make that decision. Children may be presented with key questions enabling them to reflect on the whole writing process and to explore perceptions of themselves as writers, for example,

'Where did you get your initial ideas from?'
'Did you reject any? If so, why?'
'Did you change your writing? If so, what for?'

Although it is probably most common for children to reflect after publication, reflection can be employed at different stages of the writing process where it could involve a specific focus on features of the text such as vocabulary and sentence construction. By analysing their experiences of the writing process, children will gain greater metacognitive awareness, will be able to exercise more control over their own learning and so gain the independence to move forward.

> *Assessment focus (see Figure 7.1):*
>
> **Ability to reflect critically on work**
> **Ability to make learning explicit**

Target setting

Targets spring from reviewing and reflecting upon work achieved and are at the centre of the learning process.[11] Setting targets consolidates and moves understanding forward, with the target conference providing an essential link between what has been learned and what the child still needs to know. This is an integral part of the reflection process that focuses on the writer's strengths and highlights areas for development. Target setting should be part of an informed dialogue between teacher and child, in which they look closely at evidence produced at different stages of the writing process. This 'target conference' also provides the opportunity for children to discuss their 'Reflection' sheets with a trusted adult who enables them to elicit strategic goals and how they can be achieved. Target cards or sheets should be used to record targets and dates set and to note when these have been achieved. The cards should be kept by the children, but teachers, parents and peers may be given access to them. As methods of recording and identifying future targets, they provide accountability and give children greater control over their own learning. They also provide clear direction and make the process of language development transparent within an atmosphere where learning is constructed jointly. Setting targets in this way, together with acknowledging achievement, provide a powerful motivator for children.

Assessment focus (see Figure 7.1):

Relevance of targets to learning needs

Teaching and assessing non-fiction texts

The explicit teaching of non-fiction, at Key Stage 1 in particular, has a comparatively short history within England and Wales and presents challenges to both teachers and pupils.[12] However, to be effective writers, children need to become proficient in using a variety of forms. The National Literacy Strategy has highlighted the need to teach explicitly the skills required to operate across a wide range of non-fiction genres. Once children have learned how to construct writing in this genre, they can transfer these skills into a range of subjects.

Collaboration should be an integral part of the writing process and one way of fostering this is by using the 'Notes' space that is included in many of the frames (see Figure 7.3). It can be used by the teacher to indicate key features of grammar or vocabulary that need attention; or to record questions for children to consider which will move their writing forward. This is a useful assessment tool that may be used throughout the process. Once an initial draft has been completed, it is useful for children to be given time for sharing their drafts with peers or response partners who may also use the box as a means of communicating suggestions for improvement. Equally, the more independent writer may use the boxes as a way of recording ideas as, and when, they emerge; these can be inserted into the text later.

In this section, the six categories adopted by the National Literacy Strategy in 'The National Literacy Strategy, Grammar for Writing 2000' provide a useful starting point (see below). For each category, examples of writing and assessment frames are offered which, when used in conjunction with the process approach, provide a coherent system for teaching and assessing non-fiction writing.

Non-fiction text types

☐ Recount
☐ Non-chronological report
☐ Instructional or procedural texts
☐ Explanation
☐ Persuasion
☐ Discussion

Recount

Children are probably most familiar with recount as it may be easily linked to their personal experience and topics of interest. The purpose of the recount is to retell events and incidents, in a way that could inform or entertain the audience. Within the recount genre there are a variety of different types of writing that children will come to recognise, such as biographies, autobiographies, diaries and newspaper reports.

As this particular type of writing is chronological, one of the most important skills involved is that of sequencing. Connectives, specific to chronological writing will be a key teaching point and the notes column draws attention to these. The recount frame (see Figure 7.3) identifies different aspects of the recount genre by using metalanguage such as 'orientation', 'events' and 're-orientation'. In order to support children's independent writing, the frame also offers key questions and appropriate connectives.

> *Assessment focus (see Figure 7.4):*
>
> Appropriateness of genre
> Clear structure –   Orientation
>   Events
>   Re-orientation
> Use of connectives

Non-chronological reports

For the purposes of this chapter, the term 'report' is used to describe or present factual information about both living and non-living things. A major challenge for children in writing these texts is that they are not structured chronologically; so providing them with writing frames offers support in understanding this particular genre (see Figure 7.5). A distinction may be made between living and non-living things in report writing, but the nature of it means that the exact sentence starters or questions will differ significantly according to the subject matter which will, in turn, drive the particular vocabulary. For example, the report frame offers sentence starters that provide a prompt for children to write their first draft.

> *Assessment focus (see Figure 7.4):*
>
> Appropriateness of genre
> Sound subject matter
> Relevant, clear description

Instructional or procedural texts

These types of texts show or describe how something can be carried out by following a series of steps and could take the form of recipes, rules for playing games, instructions for making a model, and so on. Children should be highly motivated as the outcome

Recount

First draft (b)

Title: _____

Orientation:

Who was there?

Where was it?

Why were they there?

Events:

What happened? •

Why? •

  •

  •

  •

  •

Re-orientation:
How would you sum up the event?

Notes:
Key connectives:
because, although,
so, therefore,
consequently, later,
subsequently, before,
in the beginning

Figure 7.3 Recount frame

© Pam Hodson and Deborah Jones (2001) *Teaching Children to Write*. London: David Fulton Publishers.

	Assessment of:	Questions	Tick	Comment	Target
Simple	• Appropriateness of genre	Is genre appropriately matchd to purpose?			
	• Structure Orientation – who – where – why Events – what – why Re-orientation • Summing up	Are all stages 1. identified 2. sequenced logically?			
	• Connectives	Are connectives 1. appropriate 2. varied?			
Non-chronological report	• Appropriateness of genre • Subject matter • Description	Is genre appropriately matched to purpose? Is subject matter clearly defined? Is description varied and comprehensive?			
Instructional/ procedural texts	• Appropriateness of genre • Points • Instructions • Visual images	Is genre appropriately matched to purpose? Does each point concern a single action? Are instructions 1. accurate 2. clear 3. logically sequenced? Do visual images enhance writing?			
Explanation	• Appropriateness of genre • Technical/subject-specific vocabulary • Structure General statement Sequence Summary	Is genre appropriately matched to purpose? Is technical vocabularly 1. appropriately used 2. clearly understood? – Is topic clearly introduced? – Is there a logical sequence? – Is there an effective summary and conclusion?			

Figure 7.4 Non-fiction texts: Assessment focus sheet 2

	Assessment of:	Questions	Tick	Comment	Target
Persuasion	• Appropriateness of genre • <u>Structure</u> Opening statement Key points Elaboration and development of points Summary • Voice	Is genre appropriately matched to purpose? Is topic clearly introduced? Are key points clear and logically structured? Are points developed sufficiently? Is there a clear summary? Is there a strong voice?			
Discussion	• Appropriateness of genre • <u>Structure</u> Opening issue Arguments for and evidence Recommendations Conclusion	Is genre appropriately matched to purpose? Is opening issue stated clearly? Are arguments clear, supported by evidence and logically organised? Are recommendations clear and logical? Is conclusion clear and logical?			

Figure 7.4 Non-fiction texts: Assessment focus sheet 2 *(continued)*

Report

Non-living things

The _____ is a _____
_____

Is it part of the _____ family.

The _____ has _____
_____ and _____

It can be found _____
_____

The _____ eats _____
_____

Other interesting things about _____
_____ are that _____
_____

Notes:

Figure 7.5 Report

can be both practical and immediate. Because of this, it is easy to find real reasons for writing which will be integral to classroom practice. The authors can readily assess how effective their writing has been by the group's ability to complete the task.

The instructional genre offers a range of organisational features and this frame (see Figure 7.6) makes the range of possibilities explicit. Children need to decide whether to use numbers, bullet points or separate sentences to indicate the sequence of their instructions. Whatever the decision, it is important for children to understand that each point should concern only a single action. They could, in fact, experiment with all of them and then choose the structure they feel is the most appropriate.

Another key teaching point is to highlight the sentence structure used in writing this type of text. Verbs, indicating commands (imperatives) often appear at the beginning of a sentence, for example, a recipe may begin, 'Take two large eggs...', whereas in other forms of writing, teachers would encourage children to write their sentences in different ways but within this particular genre, they should know that it is perfectly valid to repeat sentence constructions.

Assessment focus (see Figure 7.4):

Appropriateness of genre
Clear points
Logically sequenced, accurate instructions/procedures
Appropriateness of visual images

Explanation

This is a genre that children are familiar with and they will probably have seen many booklets which set out to explain how to do things or what something is. As with all genres, it is very important for children to consider who they are writing for. It can also be helpful in promoting clarity and precision of writing for them to think about the reader as a non-specialist in the chosen subject and the key questions they may want answered. This time spent discussing the chosen audience with its particular needs will help children to craft their explanations in a more focused way. In writing an explanation, children may wish to use a lot of technical vocabulary. A glossary (explicitly modelled within a shared writing session) may be used as a strategy to maintain conciseness in the children's writing, and at the same time, to ensure that the reader understands the explanation.

This particular explanation frame requires the child to write under subheadings. Children are asked to consider how diagrams or photographs would enhance their explanations and have their attention drawn to the use of relevant connectives within the 'Notes' column (see Figure 7.7). As with procedural texts, explanatory texts particularly lend themselves to being shared with a response partner. Space is given for comments to be written either by this critical friend (whether teacher or child) or by the writer after hearing the response, which may, in turn, lead to further clarification of the text within a second draft.

Instructions

How to:

In order to make a _____ you will need:

First you

Next

Then

Finally

1.

2.

3.

4.

•   •   •   •

Notes

Ask a friend to try out this explanation. Can they do it? Write the comments in the Notes box.

Figure 7.6 Instructions

Explanation

Title: How or why.................

General statement to introduce the subject:

Gives an explanation:

- how it happens/works

- why it happens/works

- when it happens/works

- where it happens/works

- what the point is/what it's used for

Summarise the main points:

Check: Do I want to use photographs/diagrams/pictures to make my explanation clearer?
Give it to someone else to read.

Notes:

Figure 7.7 Explanation

© Pam Hodson and Deborah Jones (2001) *Teaching Children to Write*. London: David Fulton Publishers.

> *Assessment focus (see Figure 7.4):*
>
> Appropriateness of genre
> Technical/subject-specific vocabulary
> Clear structure –   General statement
>   Sequence
>   Summary

Persuasion

This genre can be very manipulative, so it is important that children, from an early age, learn to read it critically. In persuasive writing, children need to know about the importance of tone and voice and, as in all texts, should consider audience and purpose. Children should be shown the importance of selecting facts and information which are relevant to their purpose so that they can persuade the reader. Here, the focus is on a specific type of persuasive writing where children are taught to argue the case for a particular point of view. In this persuasion frame (see Figure 7.8), children are encouraged to develop and elaborate by including evidence to support their opinion. It also addresses the issue that in a more sophisticated persuasion, children may also wish to consider an opposing argument which they then counter.

> *Assessment focus (see Figure 7.4):*
>
> Appropriateness of genre
> Technical/subject-specific vocabulary
> Clear structure –   Opening statement
>   Key points
>   Elaboration and development of points
> Strength of 'voice'   Summary

Discussion

This can be seen as a natural progression from persuasive writing. In developing a discussion, children will be expected to present arguments reflecting different points of view which are supported by evidence. This genre can pose many challenges to young children. An effective discussion will involve not only good ideas, but a clear and logical structure which is, in turn, backed up by evidence so that a considered conclusion can be reached. In order to fuel debate, children need to get information from a variety of sources, whether written texts, media or their own knowledge and experience.

There are basically two structures which can be used for writing a discussion. The more simple and widely used one requires children to present all of the arguments for an issue balanced by the arguments against. A more challenging and complex model requires the juxtaposition of points for and against which are presented consecutively.

Persuasion

Opening statement of point of view:

Key points/facts	Elaboration and development of points with evidence	Notes:
•		
•		
•		
•		
• It is sometimes said that		

Summary or re-statement of opening point:

Figure 7.8 Persuasion

The discussion frame (see Figure 7.9) invites children to consider each argument immediately balanced by a counter argument.

> *Assessment focus (see Figure 7.4):*
>
> Appropriateness of genre
> Clear structure –   Opening issue
>   Arguments for, and evidence
>   Arguments against, and evidence
>   Conclusions

Reflection

Children will have gained new knowledge and skills in writing these non-fiction genres and it is important that this knowledge is reflected upon and consolidated. Key questions can be presented which are relevant to any genre (see above). These will enable children to consider the whole process of text construction in which they have been engaged. The final question, 'How do you feel about the finished result?', could form the basis of a useful dialogue between teacher and child, so developing the teaching and learning process further. In this way, key features of the genre can be reinforced, appropriate targets set and metacognitive awareness developed.

Conclusion

In order to teach writing effectively, teachers need to have

- clear learning intentions;
- explicit teaching strategies;
- a logical approach; and
- a clear system.

In order to assess writing effectively teachers need to have

- clearly defined assessment opportunities;
- explicit assessment strategies;
- a logical approach; and
- a clear system.

Above all, assessment strategies should be transparent, in that they are shared and understood by the child.[13] In this way, through a process of reflection, children – with the help of the teacher – will become increasingly able to identify their learning strengths and areas for development. Through collaboration, children are enabled to make their learning explicit and the process of assessment is shared between teacher and child. This approach makes for effective assessors and powerful writers.

Discussion

I am researching:

	Media (TV/Video)	ICT (CD-ROM/ Internet)	What I know	What my friends know	Information books
Key point Evidence					
Key point Evidence					
Key point Evidence					

Figure 7.9 Discussion

© Pam Hodson and Deborah Jones (2001) *Teaching Children to Write*. London: David Fulton Publishers.

Notes

1. For full details of the evaluation of the first year of the National Literacy Strategy see Ofsted (1999) *An Evaluation of the First Year of the National Literacy Strategy.* London: HMSO.

2. Some improvement in the teaching of guided writing has been noted by Ofsted (2001). For full details see Ofsted (2001) *The National Literacy Strategy: The Third Year,* HMI 332.

3. The role of metacognition in children's learning, is explored by R. Fisher (1998) in 'Thinking about thinking: developing metacognition in children'. *Early Child Development and Care,* 141, 1–13.

4. Graham, J. and Kelly, A. (1998) emphasise the importance of the process approach which views children as authors as they think and shape meaning.

5. A comprehensive range of frames to support narrative and non-fiction writing can be found in *Teaching Children To Write: A Process Approach To Writing For Literacy* by P. Hodson and D. Jones (2001). London: David Fulton Publishers.

6. See Note 5.

7. Parker, S. (1993) notes the power of planning as it enables children to engage more effectively with the detail of composition.

8. Smith, F. (1982) clearly presents the writer as engaged in drafting and altering work in his seminal text, *Writing and the Writer.* London. Heinemann.

9. The decision to publish should come at the end of a process of collaboration and discussion between teacher and pupil. See Browne, A. (1996) *Developing Language and Literacy 3–8.* London: Paul Chapman.

10. Smith, J. and Elley, W. (1998) stress the importance of talk as part of reflection with others.

11. The importance of setting targets for literacy has been endorsed within the National Literacy Strategy documentation (QCA, 1999).

12. The view that teaching non-fiction writing is best placed at Key Stage 2 has been effectively discussed by Wray, D. and Lewis, M. (1997).

13. Clarke, S. (1998) emphasised the importance of sharing learning intentions and assessment stages with children in language which is accessible to them.

Further reading

Browne, A. (1996) *Developing Language and Literacy 3–8.* London: Paul Chapman.

Clarke, S. (1998) *Targeting Assessment in the Primary Classroom.* London: Hodder and Stoughton.

DfEE (1998) *The National Literacy Strategy: Framework for Teaching.* London: HMSO.

DfEE (1999) *English in the National Curriculum.* London: HMSO.

Graham, J. and Kelly, A. (1998) *Writing under Control: Teaching Writing in the Primary School.* London: David Fulton Publishers.

Fisher, R. (1998) 'Thinking about Thinking: Developing Metacognition in Children'. *Early Child Development and Care,* 141, 1–13.

Graves, D. (1983) *Writing: Teachers and Children at Work.* Portsmouth, NH: Heinemann.

Hodson, P. and Jones, D. (2001) *Teaching Children to Write: The Process Approach to Writing for Literacy.* London: David Fulton Publishers.

Ofsted (1999) *An Evaluation of the First Year of the National Literacy Strategy.* London: HMSO.

Ofsted (1999) *Standards in English.* London: HMSO.

Ofsted (2001) *The National Literacy Strategy: The Third Year,* HMI 332.

Parker, S. (1993) *The Craft of Writing.* London: Paul Chapman.

QCA (1999) *Target Setting and Assessment in the National Literacy Strategy.* London: QCA.

Smith, F. (1982) *Writing and the Writer.* London: Heinemann.

Smith, J. and Elley, W. (1998) *How Children Learn to Write.* London: Paul Chapman.

Wray, D. and Lewis, M. (1997) *Extending Literacy: Children Reading and Writing Non-Fiction.* London: Routledge.

CHAPTER 8

Seven keys: developing writing for EAL pupils

Martin Cortazzi and Lixian Jin

Text 1

> The Tiger got out from a zoo

One day I went to the zoo with my father, and we got to there by bus. First we buy some drink and food to eat. Then we go in the zoo.we saw many animals, we saw. Lion tiger and elephant. but one tiger was missing. Than the people saw the tiger. They all run away. And my father call the police and the police have come. They fire the gun and the tiger is die.

Text 2

It is a boy...He has scruffy hair with an almost invisible right side parting. It is black and rather long. He has a short forehead. His eyebrows are black eyebrows which are bushy. He has big eyes with short lashes and they are brown. He has a long nose. He has a big mouth with pink lips. He is wearing a Michael Jackson sweatshirt with rolled up sleeves – He has black trousers and is wearing grey trainers.

This chapter considers seven keys to help unlock the development of writing for pupils' learning or using English as an Additional Language (EAL). We suggest the keys of recognising diversity and the normality of being bilingual, using some key principles of language learning, applying keys for vocabulary development, using key visuals, developing keywords and story maps. Two further keys might be considered master keys, since they relate to all the others and override their function: these keys are metacognition and cultures of learning (see Figure 8.1).

Diversity and normality

A significant feature of schools in many countries is the diversity of the social, cultural and linguistic backgrounds of pupils. This diversity is increasing, and it is an important factor in teaching EAL and in considering the consequences for unlocking their writing in classrooms.

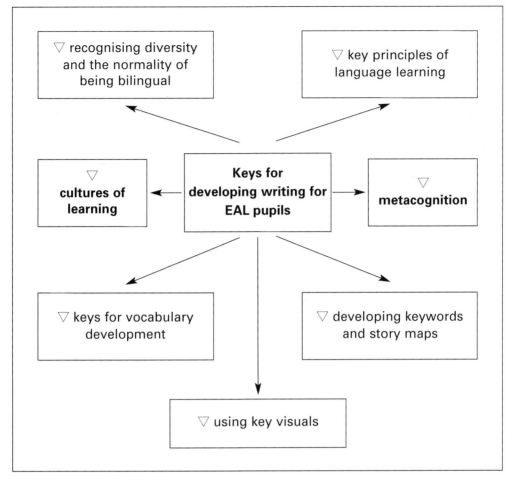

Figure 8.1 Keys for developing writing for EAL pupils

Large-scale population movements have added to existing patterns of diversity, for example, about 5 per cent of people living in Britain were not born here. Percentages of migrants received in other countries reveal how widespread this global diversity is becoming: USA 7 per cent, France 10 per cent, Canada 15 per cent, Australia 23 per cent, Ivory Coast 29 per cent, French Guiana 49 per cent, the United Arab Emirates 90 per cent.[1] The children of many of these global migrants (but not all, of course) will be learning in school through a language which is different from that spoken at home, i.e. they will be bilingual or multilingual. For teachers, it is important to understand that the situation of being bilingual is commonplace and normal – probably most of the world's children are bilingual. Recent figures in Europe suggest large percentages of national populations who can speak a language other than their mother tongue: in Luxembourg it is 97 per cent, the average across Europe is 44 per cent, in Britain it is 19 per cent.[2] This linguistic diversity, and the cultural diversity which it implies, affects schools: in London, about 30 per cent of the school pupils use English as an Additional

Language or are bilingual. In fact, pupils in London, between them, speak over 300 different languages, plus many more dialects (in New York and Melbourne they speak about 200 languages).[3] There are several implications of this global situation that are important for teachers of pupils using EAL. Language diversity in schools is increasing and becoming normal, as a consequence of population movements, continuing cultural heritages and language learning. Part of this diversity in Britain is the increasing number of pupils learning or using EAL. Since there are often several languages spoken or written in their homes, the description 'English as a Second Language' (ESL or E2L) is not necessarily accurate, and the 'additional' of the term 'EAL' recognises that these pupils are adding to existing language skills in other languages, yet they need to learn English as a core curriculum subject and as a means of learning across the curriculum since English is the language medium for learning other subjects. While the label 'EAL' applied to pupils does not necessarily imply that they need extra attention or support to develop their English skills (many are fluent writers and high achievers), the term is often used specifically to apply to those who do need support. The nature of appropriate support will vary, however, because of the diversity within EAL groups and because developing language is a continuing and normal process.[4]

Text 1 and Text 2 exemplify this diversity of needs within the group of EAL users. Both were written by pupils who are considered to use EAL by their teachers but the pupils' needs are quite different.

Text 1

The first text was written by a Year 5 Chinese-speaking pupil, after 18 months in Britain. This pupil knew very little English on arrival. In this story, written after a visit to the zoo, the sequence of the narrated events and the overall meaning are clear. To this extent the writing is successful. There are, of course, some errors and it may be worth trying to prioritise these in the light of what we might know about the learner's first language[5] (with the reservation that we would really need to know the writer as an individual learner). Those of punctuation are probably the least important in this case, although it should be noted that the writer is literate in Chinese and that in writing Chinese characters there are no equivalents to capital letters. The absence of the plural marker –s (e.g. in 'lions') in some words may be an issue, although it is worth noticing that the writer uses this marker for 'animals' and the plural 'people' correctly. Chinese has no plural marker, as such, and this is probably the source of the error, although pronunciation may also be a factor (in most Chinese dialects it is rare to have more than two consonant sounds at the end of a word, so pronouncing several consonants is difficult but this is common in English, including in many plural nouns like 'elephants'). More important for the general development of English are the tenses of verbs: some verbs are marked appropriately as past ('got', 'went', 'saw'), while others are not ('buy', 'go', 'call', 'fire'). The use of 'have come' shows awareness of different ways of expressing the past in English, but this use of the present perfect tense is not appropriate here. Again, a likely source of these errors is that in Chinese one does not add markers to the ends of words (like 'call' – 'called') or otherwise change them (like 'run' – 'ran') to signal the past.

In this example, then, a teacher may focus on helping the learner with tenses in English, and perhaps with plurals and connectives (to add linking words like 'next' or 'finally' which are relatively absent in the text). This could be done using models and examples in meaningful contexts with lots of oral interaction (Chapter 4) as preparation for further writing (see below).

Text 2

The second text was written by a Year 3 Gujerati-speaking pupil, again after 18 months in Britain. This child knew some English on arrival and has developed his English rapidly but his teacher thinks of him as an EAL learner; all other members of the class are of an Asian background and the majority clearly need support with their English. The text describes one of the writer's classmates: the writing task was that other pupils would hear this written description and then attempt to guess who was being described. In this case there are no obvious serious errors. Being bilingual, like this writer, does not necessarily mean having 'problems' with writing in English. In fact, it is worth noticing the strong points of this writing in order to encourage further normal development of them and in order to pick out features from which the rest of the class may learn. In this case, the elaborated noun phrases are worth praising and pointing out to the writer's peers. Technically, interesting features inside the noun phrases include prepositional phrases ('big eyes <u>with short lashes</u>'), relative clauses ('black eyebrows <u>which are bushy</u>'), a nice qualifying build-up before the head noun (<u>an almost invisible right side</u> parting'), and the complex phrase combining mini-versions of some of these features ('<u>a Michael Jackson</u> sweatshirt <u>with rolled up sleeves</u>'). The message here is that teachers should not necessarily think of EAL learners as having 'problems' in their writing. Rather, we should pay attention to their development as writers, noticing positive features that are worth praising and encouraging for more advanced writing.

Key principles for supporting EAL

There are a number of general principles of language development that are particularly applicable to working with EAL pupils. In themselves, each of these may appear fairly obvious but the *combination* of them provides a useful framework for developing writing. The principles may be overlooked if teachers pay too much attention to learners' errors and the structure and form of writing (which are important), rather than to meaning, expression and learning to become aware of writing processes (which are crucial). These principles will be applied to a classroom example later.

Paying attention to meaning and relevance in context

According to this principle, we would get learners to focus on the meanings of what they read and what they are trying to say in writing. This depends on the context, of course, so we should also find ways to draw their attention to the specific aims of writing tasks and how their writing is relevant to the context of such tasks (Chapter 1). For the writer of Text 1, for example, the teacher would explain the changes of meaning caused by the use of the wrong tense to raise awareness of the effect for the reader of the choice of tense.

Using modelling which combines repetition with variation

This principle emphasises that it is crucial for learners to see and hear clear examples of the kind of texts we expect them to write. The idea of modelling is that teachers draw attention to specific features of the text (Chapter 11), as target features, so the learners are quite clear about what they are aiming at. Repetition is vital for language development for EAL learners – hearing or reading a text with a key feature in it once or twice only is unlikely to be enough. However, this repetition needs to be combined with variation; this avoids boredom and mechanical repetition and shows learners how a feature of writing can be used with variety or creativity and how the same meaning can be expressed differently.

Involve learners in cognitive challenge and interaction

With EAL learners, teachers may well, with some reason, simplify language and lighten the demands of written tasks. However, simplifying the language does not necessarily mean that the thinking that accompanies it also needs to be simplified. Simplifying should not imply being patronising. This principle reminds us that language learners should also be learning to think. Since social interaction drives a large part of language development, we could also involve the pupils in verbal and written interaction with their peers. EAL learners should also be learning to work with and relate to others through English.

Helping learners to link verbalisation with visualisation

This principle draws attention to the enormously productive mutual relation between oral and written language expression (verbalisation) and the uses of visual formats for representing information and the uses of mental images and imagination (visualisation). That is, teachers can support the development of reading and writing skills by using pictures, tables or charts to represent the meanings of texts and combine this with pupils' ability to visualise. Seeing supports saying, and saying enables writing. A major way to achieve this is by using key visuals (see below).

One way to apply such principles is through a range of activities to raise awareness of writing. These activities are, strictly speaking, *pre-writing* activities in the sense that they expose pupils to chunks of text and engage them in meaningful interaction with reading and speaking before they actually write using similar words and phrases. These activities might involve pupils in copying short texts, but only after they have read, thought about and discussed the words, meanings and content. So, this further principle is:

Using pre-writing activities that involve the use of relevant words and phrases as a prelude to actually asking pupils to produce texts themselves

This principle is designed to ease EAL pupils gently into writing and give them due preparation using the kinds of activities listed below. This may solve a major problem that occurs in some classrooms with EAL pupils, where learners are asked to write something before they have had relevant opportunities to read and talk about examples and prepare to use the kind of language required by the task.

Matching: this can involve matching words on cards with phrases, sentences or pictures. Thus, pupils might match new vocabulary with sentence definitions or glosses, match names of characters in stories with actions or descriptions, or match concepts in science with pictures illustrating their application.

Sorting: this refers to sorting written cards with labels or sentences into categories. This classification activity, like matching, can relate to any curriculum area. Pupils could sort examples of different kinds of materials, or solids, liquids and gases, as a prelude to using the same words in their own writing.

Sequencing: in the classical example of this activity, pupils put sentences written on cards into the order in which they occur in a text. This is often done with stories or the chronological order of historical events, but could be done with any type of text. The point is that it gets pupils reading and thinking about the sentences, and manipulating them, before they are asked to work with them in their own writing.

Ranking: here pupils arrange cards with labels or phrases in order of importance or in some order of evaluation. This calls for judgement and, often, reasoned argument. For example, learners might put cards with pictures and verbs labelling activities into the order of how much energy the physical activity or exercise demands. Again, these words could be used in a written summary later so that the ranking activity is a preparation for the writing.

These pre-writing activities can usefully be combined into their own sequence. For example, pupils might match pictures of stages in the water cycle with keywords that label each stage. Then they could match the beginnings, middles and ends of sentences written on different coloured cards, so that the sentences make up explanations of each stage. Pupils therefore think about causes and effects. Finally, the sentences are sequenced onto a pictorial flow chart; when this is complete, pupils explain the chart to each other in pairs progressively removing the sentence cards. As preparation for writing about the water cycle, these activities engage the learners in each of the first four principles listed above, with multiple uses of relevant language in meaningful context.

Keys to developing vocabulary

A major aspect for developing writing for EAL pupils is vocabulary. While it is obvious that pupils need to extend their knowledge and ability to use words, it is less obvious that many learners (and perhaps some teachers, too) think about learning words in limited ways.[6] If teachers can help pupils to extend their metacognition regarding vocabulary this will be a key to improving writing. Such metacognition includes awareness of the multiplicity and ambiguity of word meanings; an understanding that words in combination often have a different meaning to the same words used separately; knowledge of how words enter into systematic relations of similarity, difference and classification of meanings with sets of other words.

Thus an apparently simple word like 'table' takes on multiple meanings in the contexts of 'a table of figures', 'a water table', 'a timetable', 'a league table', 'booking a table', or 'turning the tables'. We might naturally think that 'soft' is the opposite of 'hard', as in 'hard ground', but 'hard' may have rather different antonyms in collocations or combinations like 'hard work', 'hard luck', 'hard evidence' or 'hard facts'. 'Talk' might be contrasted with 'listen' or 'be quiet', but 'talking' can be classified into ways of talking with degrees of intensity, purpose, volume and emotion in 'comment', 'assert', 'mutter', 'whisper', 'argue', 'gossip' or 'order'.

Systematic discussion of such examples in relation to pupils' writing can show how different choices give different meanings and can open up a wider range of choices for learners. Fortunately, many EAL pupils have good metalinguistic awareness: as bilinguals they are often well aware of corresponding meanings and differences across languages so that the aspects mentioned above can seem normal.[7] Unfortunately, this ability is often not used as a resource in classrooms to enable bilingual pupils to share their metalinguistic awareness with their peers. Many bilingual learners are used to translating (in their heads or with their families), so they may have a curiosity about words and how they work differently in different languages. Such differences can be shared to raise a general awareness of vocabulary and how languages collocate words differently. For example, in English (and Polish, German, Greek, Swahili or Mongolian) one 'plays' a violin, but literally translated in Italian one 'sounds' it and in Spanish one 'touches' it; other speakers might 'hit' it or 'strike' it (Arabic, Urdu), 'draw' or 'pull' it (Chinese, Japanese), 'ring' it (Nepali), 'make it give music' (Xhosa), or 'steal' it (Turkish). In a multilingual class it is easy to gather such examples. These kinds of examples are seen to be important if one looks at, say, the verbs used to report investigations in English. It is not obvious that one may 'present' such things as 'results', 'evidence' 'examples', or 'arguments'. Nor it is obvious that 'come' combines with different prepositions in 'come up with a solution', 'come to a conclusion', 'come across more evidence', 'come down on one side of the argument', 'come clean about the difficulties', or 'come over as a competent writer'. Learning vocabulary is therefore as much about combining in new ways words you already know as it is about learning new words, but it is easy to neglect the former and concentrate only on the latter.

Using key visuals

A key visual is a type of visual that presents information in a particular format that, because of its layout, generally allows information to be taken in more rapidly than the same information presented in a prose text. Key visuals are accessible. At the same time, key visuals are immensely useful to support EAL pupils' language development because they can be re-expressed verbally or in writing (and vice versa).[8] They therefore complement conventional speech and written texts. The range of key visuals includes: tables, outlines and flow charts, tree and cycle diagrams, matrices, time lines, action strips and maps. Any of these can be created to help EAL pupils to understand a text or they can be used in a preliminary activity before pupils write.

An example might be the following chart that lists sinking and floating objects.

Objects which sink	*Objects which float*
A knife	A cork
A key ring	A plastic spoon
A toy train	A paper boat

The box not only represents the record of an experiment but also symbolises through its layout the idea of comparison or classification. Teachers can therefore use the chart to get pupils to re-express its information, using a variety of language. One reason why key visuals are so useful for supporting EAL pupils is that the same visual can be used at many language levels. Thus pupils may say, and later write any of the following, perhaps in a sequence of increasing complexity to express the same basic concept:

A knife sinks but a cork floats.
Whereas a knife sinks, a cork floats.
A knife sinks, so does a key ring. However, both a cork and a paper boat float.
Some objects sink. Others float. A knife is an example of the former while a cork is an example of the latter.

And the more metacognitively oriented:

We tried to predict which objects would float and which ones would sink. Then we put them in water to test our predictions. We recorded the results on a chart. The chart classifies our results. From the chart we can remember which objects sank and which ones floated. We can make other charts to classify the same objects differently. When we do this, some of the language we use to classify the objects will be the same even if the actual classification is different.

The language associated with a key visual can often be directed so that particular areas can be developed to meet learners' needs. For instance, a teacher may wish to focus on degrees of certainty and expectations in relation to floating and sinking:

We <u>would</u> expect a knife to sink but a knife with a cork handle <u>might</u> float.
A paper boat <u>should</u> float but it <u>will probably</u> sink after a short time.
I am <u>not sure</u> whether a toy train <u>will</u> sink. <u>Maybe</u> a plastic one <u>would</u> float.

Once teachers realise the power of key visuals they can use them in relation to texts. Key visuals can be used predictively as structured overviews of the main ideas or as semantic maps to pre-teach vocabulary. They can be used while reading texts as the basis for comprehension activities, say, to fill in charts of information found in the text or (with preparation and practice) to get pupils to invent their own visuals to summarise a text. Teacher-made or pupil-adapted key visuals can also be used as planning devices to prepare for writing by talking through the content and thinking through how to use suitable language. Using key visuals therefore naturally integrates pupils' oral and written skills with thinking and reflection; it also integrates visual and verbal literacies.[9]

Developing keywords and story maps

Two further keys to develop EAL pupils' writing can be added. 'Keywords' is used here to refer to the use of cards on which identified keywords from a text are written; the cards can then be distributed and sequenced for discussion activities. 'Story maps' refer to visual representations of the structure of a story using keywords in a diagram or flow chart format that pupils can use in a progressively controlled manner to recount and later write a story.

Practical application

These five keys were combined in an extended sequence of teaching with a Year 3 class. This class was in an inner-city primary school in which nearly all the pupils were of Asian background, speaking mainly Gujerati, but also Urdu, Hindi, Bengali, and Arabic. Large numbers of the pupils were identified as needing extra support for their English so an EAL teacher worked with the class two or three times a week. Additionally, a bilingual teacher helped several times a week, chiefly to help with interpreting Gujerati for newcomers to Britain, giving extra support for their English. The class teacher identified writing as the language area that needed the most improvement and asked for additional help from a local university tutor.[10] As an action research project, the following steps were progressively developed on the basis of the five keys over a number of weekly sessions.

It was decided that the most productive basis for improving the EAL pupils' writing would be extensive preparatory oral work (Chapter 11) with clear modelling and a lot of active repetition in pairs and collaborative groups to recycle the meanings of stories so that the learners would gain confidence in expressing extended meanings; later, this would be transferred to writing when the pupils had fully internalised the story for themselves. The theoretical orientation for this approach thus included the 'scaffolding' of the children's understanding through social interaction[11] until they reached a point when a gradual handing over of control would enable them to tell stories in their own way but with fluency. Initially, the class teacher doubted that this would be possible orally for many pupils, let alone in writing.

Step 1: the class heard a story in English and Gujerati, illustrated with large pictures mounted on cards. The pictures were then stuck onto the whiteboard in story order and children in pairs attempted to retell the story by looking at the pictures (many found this very difficult).

Step 2: the class heard the story again, but this time key content words were written on cards for each main stage of the story. The cards were stuck on the whiteboard and boxes were drawn with marker pens around the outlines of the keyword cards. Arrows were drawn to make a flow chart or story map. Teachers demonstrated step by step how the keywords could be used to remember the episodes. The step-by-step discussion of the story (in order to choose the keywords) and the visual mnemonic of the position of keywords on the map helped the children to retell the story. This step was repeated several times with different stories and therefore with different story maps. Each map symbolised the outline of the story.

Step 3: the keyword cards were removed from the board and distributed around the class, leaving the outline map. Children then had to decide who had which part of the story. In turns, they put their cards onto the story map and retold their part, helped if necessary by others. This step was then repeated with other stories in groups so that gradually the learners used the cards to draw the outline map themselves. Some bilingual story maps were made but the retellings were increasingly in English as children became more confident.

Step 4: using more complex stories such as the story of Rama and Sita, the learners began to write the keywords themselves. Colour coding was used for different episodes or for different locations in parts of the story. In groups children recorded their own oral versions, listened to recordings and again retold the stories while they replaced keywords on the story map. At this point a range of stories were used and retellings were much more confident and fluent.

An extract from a recording shows the children choosing keywords for the 'Town Mouse and the Country Mouse', one of *Aesop's Fables*, independently of the teacher; they are 'translating' between the note form of the keywords and the fuller story version as would be normally said and, later, written. This ability to translate and control the keywords and story map reflects a growing metacognitive awareness of the storytelling process and how to talk about it and manage it. Later this awareness would be used in improved writing.

Pupil 1: What shall we say next?
Pupil 2: 'The town mouse didn't like the country'.
Pupil 1: Well, which are the keywords?
Pupil 3: 'Don't like.'
Pupil 1: 'Don't' or 'didn't'?
Pupil 3: 'Don't'. 'Don't like country' ...
Pupil 1: 'Town mouse', 'Country mouse', 'Home'
Pupil 2: What's that?
Pupil 1: Well, that's the keywords. Write these.
Pupil 2: OK. Say it again.
Pupil 1: 'Town mouse', 'Country mouse', 'Home'
Pupil 3: (reading the keywords but expanding orally into a full sentence) 'The town mouse invites the country mouse to his home.'
Pupil 1: That's OK. Now the next bit.

While there may still be some confusion ('Don't/didn't'), the negotiation of meanings in relation to the text is becoming well established.

Another recording shows the teacher exploring the role of colour-coded cards for the first time, with the story of Snow White:

Teacher: Why is the next card pink?
Pupil 1: Because it joins the story.
Pupil 2: Because if a bit is lost you can tell which one is missing.
Pupil 3: Because all these parts are in the cottage.
Teacher: What about the yellow cards?
Pupil 4: They're all in the forest.
Pupil 3: Different colours help you to tell the story. Different bits are in different colours.

Here there is a growing metacognitive awareness of the division of stories into episodes, how episodes relate to each other, and how the colours will help tellers to remember particular episodes (at this point the children are not using the term 'episode' although they did so with confidence in later sessions).

Step 5: other activities were now included with similar stories, such as matching and sequencing sentences, so that pupils were reading the stories. Fully written versions of some stories were used with gaps for linking words, such as 'but', 'so', 'later' and 'finally'. Further story maps were made with linking words on cards added to them. Pupils were writing their versions of the stories using keywords, story maps and linking words.

Step 6: since the university tutor had been taking photos of the children, these photos were then used retrospectively to discuss with the children what they had been doing with the cards and maps and what they had been learning. This step allowed explicit metacognitive discussion of themselves at work on the storytelling and writing process. Further, the children then wrote brief explanations of what they had been doing in the photos. These explanations (examples are uncorrected below) still contain some features of EAL writing, as might be expected, but for the class teacher they represented enormous strides of progress for some pupils who a few weeks earlier had been unable to write a coherent sentence.

'I was telling Jagrati the story about Hans and Gretal my part was eksiting. It was fun with the others both of the stories were good.'
'In this photo I was stiking a card on the bord from the story about Snow White. The card said Prince. They war key words.'
'In the photo we are listening to the story of Rama and Sita. It was recorded on the tape recorder by another group of children.'
'What we were doing in this photograph is we had a pile of card with writing on them. We were in pairs. We had to ask each other questions they were about Snow White. When we asked each other the questions we had to see if that was in their story.'
'What we did is we did a story of Snow White. Mrs Smith wroite the key words that we gave her. each person in the class. had some cards. When it was there turn they had to put the card on the board. I had the poisonous comb bit.'

Noticeably, the written grammar of some of the children has improved remarkably, for instance in the complexity of foregrounding information: 'What we were doing in this photograph is ...', 'When we asked each other the questions we had to ...', 'What we did is we did a ...', and 'When it was their turn, they ...'

Metacognition

The relative success of using the keywords and story maps seems attributable to the application of the other keys: pupils engaged in lots of repetition but with variation and cognitive challenge in clear tasks. They heard and read many modelled examples, and were involved in much telling and later writing of their own versions of these. There was a lot of visual support, with clear meanings in the context. Pupils were involved in extensive social collaboration and interaction in pairs and groups and in the whole class. Oral and reading skills were developed and used in integration with writing development. An important metacognitive aspect was that the pupils became able to talk about what they were doing, to plan it, control it, and remember it, using the physical tokens of the keywords and the visual layout of the story maps. At the risk of stretching the metaphor, metacognition here might be regarded as a master key: without employing it systematically the uses of the other keys may be limited or isolated; developing the systematic awareness and discussion of their use, in contrast, relates them together and gives them more power.

Cultures of learning

The application of the keys discussed so far may be influenced by the cultural background of the learners. After closely examining literacy learning in China and in Chinese community schools in Britain and contrasting these with other contexts,[12] we conclude that there may be cultural approaches to classroom interaction and learning which differ in crucial respects around the world. Such cultures of learning are sets of expectations about how to learn which derive from culture and educational socialisation and, again, they may be master keys which open (or close) doors to learning. Chinese learners, for example, may expect to use books in certain ways and may expect certain kinds of direct instruction about reading and writing – but their British teachers may have other ideas and practices for literacy learning. This brings us back to the point about the diversity among EAL learners: if their previous learning experiences engage them in cultures of learning which are different from those which their British teachers expect, then their strengths of learning may go unrecognised and they may be puzzled by what they are asked to do here. Dissonances in cultures of learning can lead to self-doubt and can become challenges to learners' identities and frustrations for teachers. On the other hand, if the British teacher sees the advantages of ways of learning which EAL pupils bring to the classroom, then the teacher may not only enable the learners to use these effectively for learning to write in English, and learn additional British ways, but the cultures of learning brought to the classroom by

EAL pupils may become a point of learning for the teacher who, as a matter of professional development should learn about others' learning. The key here is that the teacher interacting with EAL learners should observe, enquire, and learn about the pupils' ways of learning and help them to make these explicit. Cultures of learning are thus a counterpart to metacognition.

Notes

1. See Parfit, M. (1998) Human Migration, *National Geographic*, October 4 (and map: *Population*).
2. See European Commission, Directorate-General for Education and Culture, Vocational Training and Language Policy (2000) *Promoting Language Learning with the Socrates Programme's Lingua Action 1*, Lingua Action 1 Newsletter No. 1, July 2000.
3. See Baker, P. & Eversley, J. (2000) *Multilingual Capital*. London: Battlebridge Publications.
4. See Levine Levine, J. (ed.) (1990) *Bilingual Learners and the Mainstream Curriculum: Integrated Approaches to Learning and the Teaching of English as a Second Language in Mainstream Classrooms*. London: Taylor & Francis; Edwards, V. (1995) *Writing in Multilingual Classrooms*. Reading: Reading and Language Information Centre and (1998) *The Power of Babel: Teaching and Learning in Multilingual Classrooms*. Stoke-on-Trent: Trentham Books for general considerations of supporting EAL in mainstream classes and how multilingual issues impact on teaching writing. A sampling of current 'official' thinking about EAL in relation to the British National Curriculum can be seen in SCAA (1996); DfEE (1999: 30–37); QCA (2000); and Ofsted (2001).
5. This kind of information about which errors may result from influence or interference from different languages can be found in Swan, M. and Smith, B. (1998) *Learner English, A Teacher's Guide to Interference and Other Problems* (second edn). Cambridge: Cambridge University Press.
6. There are very few books giving guidance on vocabulary development in EAL contexts, but see for one example McWilliam, N. (1998) *What's in a Word? Vocabulary development in Multilingual Classrooms*. Stoke-on-Trent: Trentham Books.
7. See Gombert, J. E. (1992) *Metalinguistic Development*, Hemel Hempstead: Harvester Wheatsheaf, for example, on the widely recognised fact that bilinguals often have greater metalinguistic awareness than their monolingual peers.
8. For classroom applications of key visuals, see Mohan Mohan, B. (1986) *Language and Content*, Reading, MA: Addison-Wesley and Dryden, A. and Mitchell, S. (2000) *Challenging Children, An Inventory of Strategies for Busy Teachers*. Hackney: Ethnic Minority Achievement Service, Nord Anglia Hackney.
9. Writers in Cope, B. and Kalantzis, M. (eds) (2000) *Multiliteracies: Literacy, Learning and the Design of Social Futures*, London: Macmillan and Unsworth, L. (2001) *Teaching Multiliteracies across the Curriculum*, Buckingham: Open University

Press elaborate the point that systematic involvement of learners in these kinds of integration is essential to develop the multiliteracies, which are necessary for multimodal and multimedia learning.

10. This meant a team approach to action research: the class teacher and the EAL support teacher carried out the teaching in their normal way, with the additional help from time to time of the bilingual teacher. The university tutor helped the teachers to plan and review the teaching, observed classes and monitored the effect of steps taken through tape recordings and photographs, but did not teach.

11. This orientation combines Vygotskian ideas (see Mercer, N. (1995) *The Guided Construction of Knowledge: Talk amongst Teachers and Learners*, Clevedon: Multilingual Matters and Wells, G. (1999) *Dialogic Enquiry: Towards a Sociocultural Practice and Theory of Education*, Cambridge: Cambridge University Press), combined with ideas about mediated literacy learning (Dixon-Krauss, L. (1966) *Vygotsky in the Classroom: Mediated Literacy Instruction and Assessment*, London: Longman and an awareness of narrative structures and functions (Cortazzi, M. (1993) *Narrative Analysis*, London: The Falmer Press).

12. See, for example, Cortazzi, M. and Jin, L. (1996) 'Cultures of learning: language classrooms in China', in H. Coleman (ed.) *Society and the Language Classroom*, Cambridge: Cambridge University Press, pp. 169–206 and Jin, L. and Cortazzi, M. (1998a) 'The culture the learner brings: a bridge or a barrier?' in Byram, M. and Fleming, M. (eds) *Language Learning in Intercultural Perspective, Approaches through Drama and Ethnography*, Cambridge: Cambridge University Press, pp. 98–118.

Further reading

Baker, P. and Eversley, J. (2000) *Multilingual Capital*. London: Battlebridge Publications.

Cope, B. and Kalantzis, M. (eds) (2000) *Multiliteracies: Literacy, Learning and the Design of Social Futures*. London: Macmillan.

Cortazzi, M. (1993) *Narrative Analysis*. London: The Falmer Press.

Cortazzi, M. and Jin, L. (1996) 'Cultures of learning: language classrooms in China', in H. Coleman (ed.) *Society and the Language Classroom*. Cambridge: Cambridge University Press, pp. 169–206.

Cortazzi, M. and Jin. L. (2002) 'Cultures of learning: the social construction of educational identities, in D.C.S. Li (ed.) *Discourses in Search of Members*. New York: American Universities Press, pp. 47–75.

DfEE (1999) *The National Curriculum Handbook for Primary/Secondary Teachers in England*. London: DfEE.

Dixon-Krauss, L. (1966) *Vygotsky in the Classroom: Mediated Literacy Instruction and Assessment*. London: Longman.

Dryden, A. and Mitchell, S. (2000) *Challenging Children, An Inventory of Strategies for Busy Teachers*. Hackney: Ethnic Minority Achievement Service, Nord Anglia Hackney.

Edwards, V. (1995) *Writing in Multilingual Classrooms*. Reading: Reading and Language Information Centre.

Edwards, V. (1998) *The Power of Babel: Teaching and Learning in Multilingual Classrooms*. Stoke-on-Trent: Trentham Books.

European Commission, Directorate-General for Education and Culture, Vocational Training and Language Policy (2000) *Promoting Language Learning with the Socrates Programme's Lingua Action 1*, Lingua Action 1 Newsletter No. 1, July.

Gombert, J. E. (1992) *Metalinguistic Development*. Hemel Hempstead: Harvester Wheatsheaf.

Gregory, E. (1996) *Making sense of a New World*. London: Paul Chapman.

Jin, L. and Cortazzi, M. (1998a) 'The culture the learner brings: a bridge or a barrier?' in M. Byram and M. Fleming (eds) *Language Learning in Intercultural Perspective, Approaches through Drama and Ethnography*. Cambridge: Cambridge University Press, pp. 98–118.

Jin, L. and Cortazzi, M. (1998b) 'Dimensions of dialogue: large classes in China'. *International Journal of Educational Research*, 29, 739–61.

Levine, J. (ed.) (1990) *Bilingual Learners and the Mainstream Curriculum: Integrated Approaches to Learning and the Teaching of English as a Second Language in Mainstream Classrooms*. London: Taylor & Francis.

McWilliam, N. (1998) *What's in a Word? Vocabulary Development in Multilingual Classrooms*. Stoke-on-Trent: Trentham Books.

Mercer, N. (1995) *The Guided Construction of Knowledge: Talk amongst Teachers and Learners*. Clevedon: Multilingual Matters.

Mohan, B. (1986) *Language and Content*. Reading, MA: Addison-Wesley.

Ofsted (2001) *Managing Support for the Attainment of Pupils from Minority Ethnic Groups*. London: Ofsted.

Parfit, M. (1998) Human Migration, *National Geographic*, October 4 (and map: *Population*).

Unsworth, L. (2001) *Teaching Multiliteracies across the Curriculum*. Buckingham: Open University Press.

QCA (2000) *A Language in Common: assessing English as an additional language*. London: QCA.

Sassoon, R. (1995) *The Acquisition of a Second Writing System*. Oxford: Intellect.

SCAA (1996) *Teaching English as an Additional Language: a framework for policy*. Hayes: SCAA.

Swan, M. and Smith, B. (1998) *Learner English, a Teacher's Guide to Interference and Other Problems* (second edn). Cambridge: Cambridge University Press.

Wells, G. (1999) *Dialogic Enquiry: Towards a Sociocultural Practice and Theory of Education*. Cambridge: Cambridge University Press.

Children's Literature

Ash, R. and Higton, B. (1990) 'The Town Mouse and the Country Mouse', *Aesop's Fables*. London: Pavilion Books.

CHAPTER 9

How to Write Really Badly: supporting children with writing difficulties

Rebecca Bunting

Introduction

The pages in Joe's workbook were clotted black and nasty. A troupe of drug-crazed centipedes in leaking ink boots had clearly held a barn dance over most of them.

How to Write Really Badly is the title of a story for children by Anne Fine (1996). Joe Gardener is befriended at school by a new boy Chester Howard, through whose eyes, we see Joe, a child with learning difficulties. Because he has no sense of time, Joe lives by the routine of the school bell, occasionally making to leave for home before the afternoon has even started. He finds organising himself very difficult and, in addition to having a very poor facility with numbers, he is also 'the Writer from Hell'. We are treated to evidence of this throughout the story: reversed letters, mess (the marauding centipedes), inability to write in a straight line, no differentiation of case, no punctuation, never more than a sentence or part of a sentence completed and, most significantly, no sense at all of having anything to say: according to Chester, this boy's work is 'ugly stuff'. Incidentally, Joe can make ingenious and intricate models from scrap materials, including a dried bread lampshade, but his teacher seems not to have discovered this.

Miss Tate has tried to help Joe by providing him with a word list for his spelling, but he has lost it somewhere in the depths of his desk (the school in the story does seem somewhat anachronistic). In any case, once located, it isn't really very much help: we learn that his words are *once knew called guess ready caught night garden school hospital break doing*, a collocation which seems to hint at an interesting narrative of Joe's nocturnal activities, but hardly the high frequency words he might need.

In fact, Chester has a better understanding of Joe's writing and learning difficulties than the teacher seems to have. He recognises and takes action to support Joe's needs, through

- enhancing his self-esteem through being able to achieve with some success the tasks he is set, and through being good at something;
- offering guided support in his written work, with structures to help him so that the chances of failure are limited, but not limiting his activity to copying;

- enabling him to undertake work in common with the rest of the class, rather than 'special' work which signals his failure to his peers; and
- helping him to manage his time on tasks, including how to use the materials he has to work with, and a range of learning strategies so that he is not over-reliant on one (his 'sound-it-outs' for spelling are driving the rest of the class crazy).

In a real classroom, in a real primary school, Chester's preternatural wisdom would not be necessary, because the teacher would know exactly how to help Joe with his writing difficulties. He would probably be on Stage 2 or above in the Special Education Needs Code of Practice (the statementing process) and would have an Individual Education Plan (IEP) that would identify his learning needs and provide for them.[1] He might have a teaching assistant allocated to him, he would have taken various national tests, ongoing diagnostic assessments would have provided some evidence of his problems for his teacher and the SENCO,[2] and he would certainly be taking part in a daily Literacy Hour (Chapter 2).

Children with writing difficulties in mainstream classes

This chapter is about children like Joe who have writing difficulties and are in mainstream classrooms but are not receiving the very specialised support arising from a Statement.[3] There are many of them and their writing is usually less well developed than their reading. Ofsted's[4] report on pupils with specific learning difficulties in mainstream schools identified that these children made more limited progress in their writing than in other language areas and that spelling and writing remained a significant difficulty for many pupils after transfer to secondary school (Ofsted 1999, para.17). This evidence is confirmed by the HMI report on the second year of the National Literacy Strategy (Ofsted 2000), which indicates that there are widespread problems with standards in writing: the statistics show that overall attainment in English has improved but that the results 'disguise an underlying weakness in standards of writing which remains a significant national issue' (Ofsted 2000, para.7). Further, 'it is worrying that almost half of pupils transfer to Key Stage 2 having achieved no better than level 2C in writing' (Ofsted 2000, para.10). Even the Additional Literacy Support initiative,[5] introduced in 1999 to provide extra help for lower attaining pupils in Years 3 and 4, has had little impact so far in terms of writing. So Joe is in good company: writing is not only problematic generally, but for children with learning difficulties it is particularly challenging.

Early identification of writing difficulties

Ofsted argues that early identification of problems is essential if strategic support is to be given: 'Better progress was made by pupils who were identified earlier in their primary schools than by those who had been given additional provision shortly before transfer to secondary school' (Ofsted 1999, para. 10).

This is not surprising: a model of support which focuses on providing a short, sharp 'remedy' cannot compensate for longer term, strategic intervention and support (as now envisaged in 'Early Literacy Support'). Children often become the subject of a statement in Year 6 because the primary school has become more overtly concerned about how they will survive in the secondary school context (para. 34), but this is too late. The need for early identification highlights the importance of teachers understanding aspects of language development and the need for them to recognise normal stages of children's development in language, as distinct from learning difficulties that impede and inhibit progress (Chapter 1). Early language development in Year R, Year 1 and Year 2 can be a stop-and-start affair but it should not be correlated with learning difficulty unless there is evidence to support such an interpretation.

Supporting children with writing difficulties during the Literacy Hour

The Literacy Hour can be very supportive for children with writing difficulties. The structure of the hour, with shared activity leading into differentiated group and individual work and followed by a plenary, enables them to experience explicit attention to the structure and organisation of words, sentences and texts in a context which is created during the hour and may extend beyond it. They can see and have explained aspects of language structure such as letter formation, syllabic structures, spelling patterns, onset and rime, punctuation, rhyme, simple syntax and verb patterns, then apply their understanding through differentiated activities which are consolidated in the plenary.

Shared writing

Shared reading and shared writing (Chapter 3) are central activities of the hour and they work reciprocally in language development. The key pedagogical concepts involved in both are modelling and explaining. In relation to writing, the teacher's role is to show how writing works through modelling and demonstrating the very process of the production of writing, and to show how language works by explicitly explaining its nature, form and function. Explicit understanding of the writing process supports the development of metacognitive awareness on the part of the child. The relationship between the production of written language and the knowledge and understanding of the language system necessary to produce that written language is complex and rather oversimplified by the Literacy Strategy's Framework. Nevertheless, the multi-sensory approach of listening to written language being read aloud, then seeing how that language is written, together with the application of aural and visual knowledge in learning to write individual words and related groups of words, create a highly structured and supportive framework for children with writing difficulties. Of particular value is the opportunity to hear language read aloud which the child might not yet be able to read independently, so that the prosody and shape of written language is available, irrespective of the child's independent reading ability.

A further strength of the Literacy Hour is the opportunity it provides for all children, but particularly those with special learning needs, to share in discussion of their own and others' writing and to talk about language in general. This is not just in order to enhance self-esteem, important though that is. It also enables children to make their implicit understanding of language more explicit, and through the development of metacognitive awareness, to articulate their own understanding and to learn from others in the class. For example, in shared writing, the child can be prompted to explain to the class where the spaces between words go, or where a full stop or capital letter is needed, or what kind of genre they are using: in other words, whatever the level of ability in writing, it is possible to take part. Whole class sessions should be inclusive: the teacher will need to plan for children with writing difficulties so that they can take part in discussion and can respond to questions. It is also very helpful for all children, but particularly those with writing difficulties, to compose orally before recording their ideas in writing: this might involve gathering and sequencing ideas, then structuring sentences from them, or taping ideas for transcription. Talk enables children who find writing difficult to be actively involved in the Literacy Hour and it contributes to children's developing metacognitive understanding of language, enabling them to think about language, not just to use it.

These principles hold for children with or without writing difficulties. As the National Foundation for Education Research discovered in its review of the literature about literacy and special education needs:

> There is no cogent evidence that, as a broad group, pupils with special educational needs which interfere with literacy acquisition require teaching approaches that are qualitatively or significantly different from those used for all pupils.
>
> (Fletcher-Campbell 2000:1)

It is therefore essential that children are not withdrawn from the Literacy Hour unless there are very good reasons to do so. There may be times when it is valuable to work in parallel with, but not to join in certain aspects of, the hour, or when the balance of the work covered in the hour might be adjusted (Chapter 2), but such an approach needs to be very carefully thought through and children should not be withdrawn for the entire period of the hour.

The Additional Guidance to the NLS Framework (DfEE 1998b) argues that for children with literacy difficulties, the aim is to teach to the year and term of the children's age. The key here, and perhaps the most challenging aspect of supporting literacy, is differentiation. This can work in a number of ways, before and during the hour. In preparation for the Literacy Hour, support can be given so that the child is able to take as full a part as possible. This might take the form of briefing the child on what the focus for the day will be and what work they will be doing, linking it with the child's personal targets; listening to the shared text on tape or reading and discussing it with support staff beforehand, so that the content of the text is known. This ensures that the child can cope with essential vocabulary in the text and that group and independent activities are understood. Using support staff in this way in whole-class teaching would go someway to resolving an issue raised by HMI:

many schools are still finding it difficult to make the best use of support staff during the first half of the literacy hour when the teacher is teaching the whole class. There were too many examples where support staff played no constructive part in the first 30 minutes, other than in detecting misbehaviour

(Ofsted 2000, para. 90).

During whole-class work, it is important to ensure that the child can see and hear, for example, by providing an individual copy of the big book where possible and organising seating appropriately so that the flipchart/whiteboard is accessible. Support staff can be primed to take an interventionist role with individual children by undertaking such activities as clarifying misunderstandings, providing additional explanation, pointing out particular aspects of the text or word/sentence level work.

Group and independent work

In the group and independent work, a range of differentiated approaches can be taken such as:

- breaking the main task down into smaller, manageable parts so that the child can work in a more structured way, which may involve non-writing activities prior to or instead of writing;
- setting modified activities by group and within groups to link with the IEP;
- where appropriate, setting work from earlier levels of the Framework;
- providing structured support within the task such as sentence starters, key vocabulary, conjunctions to help order the writing, picture prompts;
- spending more time on one particular aspect of the task;
- providing more frequent and strategic monitoring and feedback;
- the use of support staff or writing partner to work one to one;
- providing differentiated commercial and other resources to support the writing.

All of these can be linked directly to the IEP and may require separate planning and recording systems. As an example of this, Hunt and George (1999) suggest a series of five-day structured programmes, devised for children needing intensive support for basic literacy skills, planned in the context of the Literacy Hour objectives and the theme for the week. However it is done, it must sit within the broader picture of the Framework and the requirements of the Programmes of Study of the English National Curriculum.

Differentiation

One of the difficulties in setting differentiated activities is to strike a balance between practising specific word and sentence level skills and the goal of developing independent, sustained writing. Many children with writing difficulties spend much of their time with worksheets, filling in gaps or constructing limited stretches of language. Such activities are appropriate in the right context, especially where they create a sense of achievement and are genuinely consolidating a particular aspect of the child's writing, but they do not in themselves constitute a syllabus for writing development. They are support activities and as such, must lead into independent writing of a range of genres as specified in the Framework.

Developing sustained writing

Children with writing difficulties also need support to write more sustained writing, not just in terms of smaller levels of language but also in relation to whole text structures or genres. The use of writing frames can provide this support. These are outline textual structures that guide the writer in creating a specific text type and can be used for narrative and non-fiction writing. Lewis and Wray (1995) provide a taxonomy of common non-fiction types (for example, recounts and reports) and show how children can learn about generic textual features through writing within a given format. Frames show the writer typical features of genres and can be structured so that more or less independence is required of the writer. They help children to structure and organise ideas by, for example, providing connectives to link the stages of the text (such as 'then', 'next', 'in the end') and in relation to the Literacy Hour can provide a bridge between shared and independent activity: the text can be read together in shared reading, modelled in shared writing and then created independently through the use of a writing frame. The pedagogical structure for this might involve immersion in the genre, through looking at similar kinds of texts, then identification of its generic features through word and sentence level work, followed by shared writing to model and demonstrate those features, then attempts at independent construction. The final stage of the process is reflection, enabling children to explain what they have understood of how this particular type of writing is constructed and when it is used (Bunting 2000). Storyboards fulfil a similar function but emphasise narrative structures and enable children to understand the different stages of narrative.

Supporting writing across the curriculum

Although the Literacy Hour has become synonymous with the English curriculum, it must be remembered that it is not meant to be the entire English curriculum. Indeed, for children with literacy difficulties, it is essential that other time is made in the day and week for coverage of the National Curriculum and to ensure that all aspects of the IEP are met, because the hour is not enough. To consider the hour sufficient for these children would be to deny them experience of some very appropriate commercial schemes and learning approaches (for example, Reading Recovery requires a concentrated half hour and therefore does not fit the structure of the hour), and it would prevent longer time to consolidate what they have learned in the Literacy Hour. In addition, the importance of developing literacy within other curriculum areas, as advocated in the Framework for Teaching (DfEE 1998a Section 1:13),[6] would not be recognised. The Framework makes clear that children need opportunities to practise and consolidate their writing independently across the curriculum. This is because language and literacy are needed to gain access to other subjects, and also because other subjects provide real opportunities for developing literacy skills. A whole curriculum approach is essential for children with writing difficulties.

Resources and routines for children with writing difficulties

Resources

In adapting the curriculum for children with writing difficulties, a range of approaches and materials will be needed. Writing can be supported through using resources such as pictures and photographs, letter blocks and word stamps, tape recorders and headphones. In terms of ICT, word-processing can significantly help children with writing difficulties, particularly where software is used which addresses writing difficulties such as through the provision of on-screen word banks and simplified spell-check procedures. There are CD-ROMs which work alongside commercial reading schemes such as *The Oxford Reading Tree*, talking books, spelling and punctuation programs, language programs which teach aspects of language structure through a game format, graphics software which enables writing to be inserted into cartoon formats, photographs, moving images. The interactive whiteboard is relatively new in primary schools, but has enormous potential for children with special language needs because handwritten text can be immediately transformed into print, text can be highlighted and moved, notes can be stored and recovered. Individual traditional whiteboards are very useful too: children can try out spellings, give visual responses to questions (who can show me a question mark? who can find a rhyme?), but because the writing on the board is ephemeral, mistakes don't really matter.

An environment for learning

Resources such as those above are vital for children with writing difficulties, as is the language the children see in and around the classroom. Purposeful labelling (as opposed to putting the label 'sink' on the sink) which helps children to locate and organise things, displays with key words and features highlighted, advice posters about how to carry out procedures such as finding and checking a spelling or how to check your own writing, lists of high frequency words, alphabet friezes, writing tables or stationery shops supplied with a variety of models of writing such as magazines and information leaflets and different things on which to write, ranging from post-its to a computer, all contribute to a rich, supportive language environment for all children, but especially those who find writing difficult.

Routines and procedures

This environment extends to the routines, procedures and learning activities of the classroom, which can seem quite bewildering to children with learning difficulties. They need to become familiar with and feel secure in a small range of activities and procedures so that they can carry them out without anxiety, focusing on the content of the activity they are engaged in rather than worrying about how to do the task itself. This difference is not easy to distinguish, but it is important not to let confusion about what is expected of them detract from the purpose of the activity, and to ensure that children become familiar with learning activities such as sequencing, written cloze techniques, sentence completion, using writing frames, note-making, using 'look', 'cover', 'write', 'check', because they will come across them many times. In particular, familiarity with the processes of drafting is essential: many children who find writing difficult can barely commit anything to paper so it is vital that they learn that it is acceptable to make mistakes because writing can be planned, edited and proof-read. They need to learn how to carry out these processes.

Support for managing tasks is also important: children can be shown how to work with a 'things to do' list in independent work, so that they learn to manage their time; a flag can indicate 'I need help'; and techniques such as the use of highlighting (children highlight anything they are unsure of) or the 'magic line' (leaving a blank where a spelling cannot be found) will allow the children to indicate that they have a problem without bringing writing to a standstill. The use of 'have a go' spelling books serves a similar purpose and has the added advantage of revealing to the teacher the spelling strategies the child is using.

Additional adult support

The value of additional adults or support staff working alongside individuals and groups of children in the classroom is widely recognised. Teaching Assistants or Learning Support Assistants have a very important role to play in supporting children with writing and general literacy difficulties. Although the precise nature of the role may differ, they can:

- work intensively with individual children on IEP targets as a follow-on to whole-class work;
- act as scribes for children, encouraging oral contributions from them in jointly constructing the text;
- hear reading, including the children's own writing read aloud, drawing attention to word and sentence level targets;
- lead group writing activities;
- talk with children about their writing and their feelings about both the process and the product;
- reinforce writing routines and encourage use of targeted strategies; and
- prepare children for the next whole-class session.

To return to the structure of the Literacy Hour, the plenary, the crucial tying up of the Literacy Hour, is found by HMI to be 'frequently little more than a "show and tell" session(s) with groups or individuals invited to demonstrate to the rest of the class what they have done during the lesson'. Indeed, 'the plenary continues to be the weakest part of the literacy hour. The quality of this element is good in only two in five lessons and is weak in over one lesson in five' (Ofsted 2000, paras 76, 77). The plenary should not be this damp squib at the end of the hour. Well-managed, it should:

- recap what has been covered by inviting the children to review the learning objectives for the session;
- involve careful selection of children's work which will be read aloud;
- encourage the children to talk about their own work;
- consolidate what has been learned through strategic questioning and prompting;
- provide feedback to the children on what has been achieved;
- help children to review and reflect on their own and others' achievements through sharing, listening, discussion and commentary on individual and group achievement; and
- extend understanding through further teaching.

All the above are very beneficial to children with writing difficulties and help maintain the focus of the lesson.

Conclusion

In conclusion, children with writing difficulties need:

- to be included in the Literacy Hour, with differentiated activities linked to their IEP which encourage more intensive and repeated attention to basic writing skills at word and sentence level;
- a coherently structured programme of support which works across the curriculum and beyond the Literacy Hour, which recognises the inter-relation of reading and writing development and draws on what is read as a model for writing;
- a team approach between the SENCO, class teacher, support staff and parents/carers so that all are working in the same direction;
- opportunities to practise skills in real contexts and to develop sustained independent writing and a personal voice in writing;
- an approach which emphasises their positive achievements and attempts to limit their failure;
- opportunities to talk about their writing and written language in general;
- a range of strategies for spelling and sentence construction;
- knowledge of a range of genres and their characteristic features, with support to learn to write them;
- a programme for learning to write which moves from dependence to independence; and
- an approach which encourages them to think about how they are learning and to develop their understanding of their own needs and challenges in writing.

The young Chester Howard manages to achieve some of these for his friend Joe, through his project on how to write really badly, but it is essentially the teacher, in and beyond the Literacy Hour, who will make a difference for children with special needs by providing an integrated, individualised approach, thereby unlocking writing and helping them to write really well.

Notes

1. An Individual Education Plan is a formal record of a child's specific learning needs and must be taken into account in planning for learning.
2. SENCO is the acronym for a school's Special Educational Needs Coordinator.
3. A statement is the formal and legal mechanism through which provision for a child with SEN is assured and protected. It refers to the need for provision beyond that normally provided by a school. It requires the agreement of parents as well as input from them during the evidence collection phase.
4. Ofsted is the Office for Standards in Education, a government agency charged with inspecting educational provision and reporting on standards.
5. The Additional Literacy Support Initiative provides additional support for Year 3 pupils who are underachieving. Additional teaching, normally by a teaching assistant, reinforces work done in the Literacy Hour.
6. The Framework for Teaching sets out literacy teaching objectives for Reception to Year 6 pupils.

Further Reading

Bunting, R. (2000) *Teaching about Language in the Primary Years*. London: David Fulton Publishers.

DfEE (1998a) *The National Literacy Strategy Framework for Teaching*. London: HMSO.

DfEE (1998b) *Additional Guidance to the National Literacy Strategy Framework for Teaching*. London: HMSO.

Fletcher-Campbell, F. (ed.) (2000) *Literacy and Special Education Needs: A Review of the Literature*. Slough: NFER.

Hunt, M. and George, J. (1999) 'Developing your own structured programme', in Berger, A. and Gross, J. (eds) (1999) *Teaching the Literacy Hour in an Inclusive Context*. London: David Fulton Publishers.

Lewis, M. and Wray, D. (1995) *Developing Children's Non-fiction Writing*. Leamington Spa: Scholastic.

Ofsted (1999) *Pupils with Specific Learning Difficulties in Mainstream Schools*. London: HMSO.

Ofsted (2000) *The National Literacy Strategy: The Second Year*. London: HMSO.

Children's Literature

Fine, A. 1996 *How to Write Really Badly*. London: Mammoth.

CHAPTER 10

Boys into writing: raising boys' achievement in writing[1]

Robert Fisher

A teacher wanted to find out who in her Year 6 class were underachieving in writing and why. What she found was that the majority of underachievers were boys. She discovered that most of these underachieving boys did not like writing, found it difficult to identify their best piece of writing, wrote little, and rarely re-read, improved or edited their first draft. They often did not complete their work and expressed little interest in doing it. One of the boys commented: 'Writing is boring'. Another said: 'I'm no good at writing, Miss... what's the point?'. This teacher found that her underachieving boys seemed to illustrate problems shared by many teachers.

Research in the UK has consistently shown primary girls outperforming boys, especially in reading and writing. The conventional wisdom was that girls only had an initial cognitive advantage due to their reaching physical maturity at an earlier age, and that boys overtook girls in the teenage years. Until the 1980s, performance data supported these beliefs. However, since the mid-1980s in all areas of the UK the trend has reversed, boys are underachieving at all ages compared to girls;[2] that this constitutes a problem is challenged by some researchers. In their view it is not that something has gone wrong with the boys just that standards in writing have risen much faster for girls.[3] However if we wish to raise standards in writing it seems that, as the Year 6 teacher found, boys have most scope for improvement. If many boys are leaving school not well prepared to face the challenges of writing, we need to ask: 'What is the problem with boys?' and 'What can be done about it?'

Boys and motivation

Well they are boys aren't they, what can you expect? (Primary teacher)

Thirty years ago it was the problem of the academic underachievement of girls that was highlighted by researchers who investigated sex differences in the outcomes of school and higher education. This prompted much research into how females experience learning.[4] Maleness and education was not seen as a problem and many aspects of masculinity went

---

[1]   This chapter draws on research from the Boys into Writing project, part of the Brunel Research Into Literacy. See Fisher, R. and Williams, M. (eds) (2000).

unstudied.[5] Over the last ten years there has been a dramatic shift from initial concern about the attainment of girls to a growing concern about the underachievement of boys. However the 'new issue' of the '90s in Western societies including the USA, Australia and the UK became the underachievement of working-class boys. The regular monitoring of performance through end-of-key-stage assessments and exam results reveal that in all parts of the UK boys are trailing substantially behind girls in all stages of schooling. Why is this?

The perceived problem has a dual focus – many working-class boys are not, it seems, motivated to achieve academic success and neither are they motivated to become the 'new men' that women are perceived to want. Findings from brain research suggest that there may be genetic influences at work to explain the slower progress of boys, especially in relation to language acquisition. Due to slower neurological development boys are less ready for an early start in formal reading and writing than girls. As a consequence in many European countries early education includes a stronger emphasis on kinaesthetic and oral approaches to conceptual understanding and learning. We know that good spoken language skills provide the best grounding for reading and writing, and until speech is fluent and competent early formal teaching may be unrewarding and off-putting for boys.

Other factors in child-rearing may play a part in the different language capacities of girls and boys. Young girls play social games, for example with dolls, which fosters their language development. Boys' more active play, for example with toy cars, may encourage spatial learning but only language of the 'Vroom, vroom' kind. Boys' keenness for computers may only encourage low-level repetitive gaming with little use of extended, elaborate or syntactical language. In the playground girls spend more time talking than boys, and in family life may be given more responsibility for social tasks like looking after siblings. The ways children are treated at home or school may serve to reinforce natural gender differences in social behaviour. When one mother commenting on the behaviour of her 'lazy' son said: 'Boys will be boys.' Her friend replied: 'But do they have to be?'

Gender preferences in learning styles may also be a contributing factor, girls being more compliant, or as one teacher put it: 'They are just more teachable than boys'. However it is in the area of boys' attitudes to schooling that the problem seems to be most intractable. Whether due to nature or nurture, girls respond more readily to what they are asked to do, whether it is schoolwork or homework. Boys tend to be more disruptive and 'off-task' in the classroom, although disruptive behaviour is by no means gender specific. Concentration spans vary. Research in one school found 'a typical 13–14-year-old boy concentrates for only 4 or 5 minutes compared to 13 minutes for girls'.[6] Girls are not only better readers and writers at age eleven, they tend to work harder and have a greater sense of pride in their progress than boys. Levels of motivation are crucially important for boys whose learning needs to be rooted in confidence, competence and interest. Unmotivated boys, particularly at the ends of the ability spectrum, tend to fall by the wayside.

Since the mid-1990s the media have been explaining the gender gap as the result of an 'anti-school', 'anti-learning' and 'laddish' culture among boys. Researchers have, however, developed richer descriptions of the male response to schooling in postindustrial societies. A variety of styles of masculinity was found among male secondary pupils and teachers.[7] The male subcultures included not only the familiar groups of 'academic achievers' and 'macho lads', but also the 'New Enterprisers' (NE) and the 'Real Englishmen' (REM). The NE were working-class boys who wanted to be self-employed, and the REM were disaffected middle-class boys. It is possible that such groups have always existed in UK schools, but were not recognised. Male behaviour even today can be taken for granted, and summarised in unreflective generalisations such as the following from a teacher in a west London school referring to the lack of motivation for writing shown by her working-class boys: 'Well they are boys aren't they, what can you expect?'

Only the 'academic achievers' are focused on getting good grades at a full range of GCSEs and going on to do three or more A levels. The other groups rejected some, if not all, of the academic programme of schools. This suggests that one solution will not work for all groups, and that schools need to address male needs in education in a range of ways.

Subcultures of masculinity in schools

- *'academic achievers'*: focused on doing well at school
- *'macho lads'*: working-class boys who do not see the value of school and learning
- *'new enterprisers'*: ambitious working-class boys who want to be self-employed
- *'real Englishmen'*: disaffected middle-class boys

Source: Mac an Ghaill 1994

There is evidence that the behaviour of teachers can support the macho attitudes of pupils – pupils showing repulsion, for example, when boys are seen by teachers as 'effeminate' or as 'cissy'. If boys are educated in a classroom culture that rejects boys who are 'cissies' then macho attitudes will go unchallenged and be reinforced.

Another problem identified in research is the feminisation of teaching, which derives from the fact that schools have a preponderance of female teachers. The feminisation of the teaching profession has been seen as the source of the following five problems that may contribute to lack of achievement in boys:

- school and classroom regimes that favour female values and female ways of learning;
- lack of toughness in discipline;
- rejection of competition in academic and sporting matters;
- bias in favour of feminism and 'female' topics in the curriculum; and
- lack of academic/educational role models for boys.

These factors are widely seen as having an impact on boys' education but there are problems with this analysis. First it assumes that boys can be treated as a discrete stereotyped group, when as we have seen there are many subgroups in male identity. It also assumes that all female teachers follow a progressive, anti-competitive, soft, nurturing agenda; one that is rejected by male teachers. Teachers' beliefs and attitudes cannot be assumed by gender, and progressive or nurturing teachers can be of either sex. The analysis also assumes that male teachers will be automatically be better role models for boys, whereas working-class boys who reject academic achievement are often derisive about their male teachers. It also assumes women teachers automatically prefer teaching girls and value their achievements over boys, although often the reverse is true. There is no evidence to suggest that male teachers are better at motivating 'macho' boys than female teachers are. Teachers, of either sex, can be crucial to the success and motivation of boys.

It is clear that many boys lack the experience of having adult males modelling reading and writing in the early years of their lives. Many underachieving boys report little or no input from fathers or male carers at home. As one boy reported: 'My dad reads, but he doesn't read to me. He reads the *'Sun'*. At school it is possible for boys, from single parent families and experiencing only female teachers, to go through their primary years without having had any man read a story to them or undertake writing with them. Having male role models in secondary school may be too late. The crucial time for male role models may be in the early years when the development of skills and attitudes towards literacy is so important.

Another assumption is that problems with boys in school have got worse over time, when in fact the problem of hooliganism and the wayward nature of boys' attitude to education have been a cause of concern to educators in cultures widely separated by time and space. Hieroglyphic fragments from ancient Egypt bemoan the way contemporary youth was neglecting their study and causing anti-social disturbance. Teachers have failed to harness working-class boys to the academic curriculum for centuries. But what factors account for the problems persisting today?

Boys' attitudes to school, and in particular to literacy, give cause for concern. Boys tend to have less liking for English than girls and find it more difficult. Research into the attitudes of underachieving Year 8 boys in a comprehensive school confirmed findings from other studies that such boys generally:

- prefer active forms of learning like ICT, drama, PE, and puzzles and investigations in maths;
- are not keen on reading or writing, though like to read factual and hobby magazines;
- prefer 'research'-type homework if it grabs their interest;
- don't like to ask questions of a teacher in case they look stupid; and
- find it embarrassing to be praised for academic work.

One of the surprising findings from research is that underachieving boys seem to be confident and to overestimate their abilities, actually believing that they are cleverer than girls.[8] At the same time their egos are more fragile, with a great fear of failure and of peer group scorn. They also have a less realistic view of job opportunities than girls, continuing to believe that there are many job opportunities for young men leaving school with few qualifications.

Children who do not like school, whether they are boys or girls, tend not to like writing. This is of course not surprising as writing is the single most complex and challenging learning task faced by any child. It happens to be the case that most of those who do not like school and are not good at writing are boys. As one underachieving fifteen-year-old boy put it: 'Writing's hard, so why bother? Why not just say it?'

Boys and writing

The only point of a pencil is to poke someone. (Boy, aged 12)

Evidence shows the greatest gap between the achievement of boys and girls is in writing. There is a gap at the age of five and it widens over time. As one teacher researcher put it: 'They start down and they remain down.' One survey of research concludes: 'The single most important factor in "explaining" girls' superior performance in English was their control of the written language'.[9] Boys develop later than girls in writing and have more problems. The differences in achievement in social competence and literacy, particularly pre-writing skills are significant by the age of four years. By the end of Key Stage 2 substantially fewer boys reach Level 4 than girls, and the difference is greatest in writing. These differences increase by the end of Key Stage 3. Standards at all levels, including GCSE, are rising for boys and girls, but rising faster in girls. Whereas 30 per cent of boys and girls passed 5 or more 'O' levels in the mid-1970s, in 1997 these figures had risen to 48 per cent for boys and 60 per cent for girls.

Evidence from research shows that at all ages boys tend to:

- write less than girls;
- write in a narrower range of genres;
- write less well-developed ideas, plots and characters than girls;
- be less enthusiastic about or motivated by writing than girls;
- are less concerned about accuracy, presentation and less likely to proof-read than girls; but
- are often more concise than girls and more efficient and focused in choice of ideas.

Differences in attitude to writing between boys and girls show up in their writing choices. A study of GCSE coursework folders identified the patterns of choice of topic in writing, which can be summarised, and caricatured, as follows:

	Jill's assignments	*Jack's assignments*
Narrative:	Boy meets girl	Raid on bank
Discursive:	Letter to agony column on relationship with parents	Two speeches, for and against smoking
Descriptive:	My grandmother	My dream car: Porsche 925
Own choice:	About myself	Alien landing

Girls' writing tends to be extended, reflective composition, dealing with people and emotions, using more private forms. Boys writing is briefer, more episodic, characterised by action and events, more factual and using more public forms. Both boys and girls would develop as writers if they were challenged to break this mould.

Linked to boys' problems in writing is their progress in reading. Boys often have initial problems in learning to read, and more boys show continuing problems in attaining competence and fluency. Good oral skills need to be in place before children can develop well in reading and writing. Unfortunately speaking and listening have been neglected in the primary curriculum in recent years due to the emphasis of the Literacy Hour on reading and writing, and to an early start on formal teaching of these skills. However, a note of caution needs to be entered. The differences between boys and girls on measures and tests of literacy are smaller than the differences *within* groups of boys and groups of girls. What may be true at a general level may not be true at the individual level. There are many boys who write well and achieve high grades in tests, but worryingly there are large numbers who do not. Differences in academic achievement may be attributable to factors other than gender, such as class and ethnicity. It is necessary therefore to target particular groups of underperforming boys in seeking to boost levels of literacy and to look at strategies at school and classroom level to address gender imbalances in achievement. We also need to look at the tests and measures we use. As one teacher concerned about the underachievement of boys put it: 'Are we simply testing what girls are good at?'

How can we raise boys' achievement?

> Those with poor basic skills at 21 were unlikely to have been regarded as being in need of special education provision at age 5 or 10...more than half were not reported as having received or having needed additional help at school.[10]

Research into different school contexts indicates that boys' attitudes and levels of achievement in writing can vary considerably from school to school. It is important therefore for schools to make an analysis of evidence relevant to their school to see if there are problems and then to try to uncover potential explanatory factors.

Ways to gather evidence include surveying:

- statistics – is there an imbalance in achievement between boys and girls?
- pupil and teacher attitudes – what do pupils/teachers think about boys and writing?
- classroom practice – what teaching strategies appear to be effective with boys?
- samples of work – what are the strengths and weaknesses of boys' writing?
- school policy guidelines – what policy guidelines relate to boys and writing?

The widespread perception that boys are underachieving is challenged by some teacher researchers in our project. In their particular classes boys often outperform girls in writing and have positive attitudes towards it. In many classes it is the least able boys who are doing least well compared to girls, in others it may be the more able boys who are underperforming. Boys are also seen to be underperforming in particular areas, most commonly spelling and handwriting. Questions to ask include: Which boys are not doing well? In what classes/years? According to what criteria? The critical question then becomes: 'What can the school do about poor levels of achievement?'

Whole-school approaches

Improving boys' achievement in writing is a challenge for all teachers, and senior managers such as the Special Needs Coordinator or English specialist need to take the lead in identifying specific areas of concern. Schools where teachers perceive policy in this area is effective are schools where a senior teacher has an agreed responsibility, where objectives are agreed and where there is an allocation of time and resources.

The following are key aspects of effective whole-school policy in relation to boys' performance in writing:

- assessment, targeting and monitoring;
- early intervention and support; and
- a whole-school culture of literacy and language.

Many teachers complain that boys are 'lazy'; others note that boys are not so much lazy as skilled in the arts of distraction and evasion. As one underachieving eleven-year-old commented: 'If you don't want to do it you can make trouble, or pretend you've lost your pencil or say you don't know what to do. Sometimes you can sit there and do nothing and they won't notice.'

A whole-school approach needs to link improvement in writing to policies aimed at improving challenge, motivation and support across the curriculum. The following three aspects of teaching seem to be important to both teachers and pupils within the project:

- clarity of structure – writing tasks need to be clearly structured, so 'you know what to do';
- clarity of purpose – writing tasks become meaningful when there is a clearly articulated purpose, and 'it's not "just work"'; and
- clarity of support – writing tasks need teacher intervention to support the learning taking place, and 'you've got others to help you'.

Assessment, targeting and monitoring

Boys' progress in writing, like girls, needs assessment, targeting and monitoring, which means close observation followed by specific action that matches the need of the child and by some form of checking to see the action has worked. Assessment should begin when the child enters school so that underachieving children can receive early intervention and support. Baseline assessments are valuable forms of systematic observation for new groups of pupils which provide a picture of general learning ability through verbal and non-verbal tests, and assessment of early achievements in language and number. Baseline assessment provides schools with evidence of the strengths and weaknesses of class, groups, and individuals. These have helped schools to identify the needs of children, particularly boys, who are at risk and who require, in terms of their writing, intensive care. Baseline and end-of-key-stage assessments need to be augmented by careful record keeping of day-to-day assessments and by target setting including targets in writing.

Target setting is most effective when pupils themselves take shared responsibility for setting targets, such as the following target for writing set by Tom (aged 10):

I need to remember to use paragraphs, and start a new line when people are speaking.

Teachers in the project found most success when children were asked to focus on *one target at a time*. Over time they encouraged pupils to set targets not just for one main area of development but for different aspects of writing such as content, grammar and punctuation, style (sentence structure and vocabulary) and form. As one teacher said: 'You need to work in small steps. We need to be realistic, both for ourselves and our children. That means aiming for one target at a time.'

It is important in this process to monitor progress and to set time aside to review and renew targets. In this way underachieving boys will not be overlooked and are more likely to feel supported in making progress. Where progress in writing occurs it needs to be recorded as well as shared and celebrated with pupils and parents. This ethos of achievement should be part of a whole-school culture that values and celebrates success in literacy and language.

Early intervention and support

A common element in effective whole-school practice is the emphasis placed on catching problem writers early and doing something about it. One school targets handwriting, and the improvement in handwriting as a key to raising self-esteem about writing among boys. They have targeted handwriting activities for 10 minutes a day with groups of between six and eight poor writers, with a contract for practice at home. In another, a handwriting recovery programme is offered for 8 weeks in Years 3 and 4.

The box shows examples of support which seek to add value to work undertaken in the Literacy Hour to support boys' writing.

Strategies for early intervention and support

- Support in story-making, storytelling and story-response from early years.
- Small-group tuition for targeted pupils.
- Paired reading/writing partnerships – including, where possible, male models.
- Intensive withdrawal for individuals with SEN.
- Classroom assistants using specific resources.
- Experiments with single sex groupings.
- Planned work beyond time allowed for the Literacy Hour to enable extended writing.
- Behaviour modification schemes – to raise self-esteem.

A whole-school culture of literacy and language

Developing a culture of language and literacy is a whole-school issue. A 'Literate School' is characterised by certain features that include:

- a literate environment;
- quality book provision – quality books, and other reading sources, for boys and girls; and
- lively ideas to support literacy.

A literate environment promotes verbal and visual literacy through the use of display and resources. This may be evidenced in a variety of ways, for example by successful samples of writing from all pupils on display, displays of new words associated with specific topics on classroom walls, a focus on understanding and spelling new words in all subjects, support in presentation of work, agreed strategies for structured writing and opportunities for extended writing, an effective handwriting policy and valuing endeavour in writing with praise and awards. In particular teachers need to make explicit links between all kinds of literacy teaching and extended writing.

Reading experience is closely linked to writing development. Marie Clay has shown that pupils in the bottom 25 per cent of the class often read four times fewer words than those in the top quarter.[11] Quality book provision includes quality books for boys and girls. There needs to be the supply and display in tidy, attractive, accessible areas of boy-friendly books which are known and used by pupils. Strategies to involve boys in books include inviting boys to nominate and talk about their best reads and share their best reads by creating book posters or reviews on the web. One school has a web page in which boys share their best reads; other initiatives come from boys themselves sharing books they have enjoyed (www.cool-reads.co.uk).

Measures to support literacy need to go beyond the Literacy Hour, for example some Key Stage 1 classes have introduced a 'teddy goes home' policy where the class mascot is taken home each night by a different child who writes a diary of teddy's visit. Other initiatives include writing corners, making books for others, regular book weeks, the use of Curiosity Kits (UKRA), visiting males talking about their favourite reads (one school invited their local football team to visit their reading and writing display), and writing competitions. In addition specific classroom strategies are needed that reward ongoing pupil efforts in writing.

Classroom teaching strategies

Research in nursery schools shows differences in the use of language by boys and girls during play. Nursery teachers have observed that boys are less likely during play to develop stories, to speak in sentences and use a narrower range of words than girls. Boys' play tends to be active, repetitive and to involve the use of imitative noises and single words e.g. 'fight', 'bang', than girls. Teachers responded to these findings by developing teaching strategies that encouraged children to:

- Make up stories about well-known characters in picture books.
- Add more to stories being read to them.
- Use props, such as toys/puppets, to help children dramatise the re-telling of stories.
- Write the stories children tell in books to share.

- Tape record stories made up in play situations to play back later.
- Provide writing materials in indoor and outdoor play situations.
- Use a 'message' board for written messages and answers.
- Have a Question Board to write up children's questions.
- Provide parents with writing materials for children to use at home.
- Make computers available for children to use for word-processing out of school hours.

Teachers in the Boys into Writing project have been investigating gender differences in writing through observation (see Appendix 1), pupil interviews and questionnaires (Appendix 2), reflection on teaching and analysis of samples of written work. They have sought to identify and implement boy-friendly writing strategies drawn from research and from their own experience of best classroom practice. The principle underpinning this research into practice is that nothing should be done to help boys that would hinder girls' learning. Both sexes benefit from good teaching. Evidence suggests that boys are more vulnerable to poor teaching and that the kinds of tightly focused teaching that benefits boys has a similar positive effect on girls. What project researchers have sought to identify are the strategies that seem most appropriate for their children in their schools.

The following teaching strategies, derived from research and practice, have proved effective in raising boys' achievement, progress and motivation in English:

Boys need:

- Books read to them: storytelling, story-making and story-responding at all ages.
- Short-term targets and purposeful tasks, including lots of non-fiction writing.
- Teacher modelling the writing process and clear structures e.g. use of writing frames.
- A clear sense of order and discipline.
- Subject-matter relevant to their needs and interests, with real purposes and outcomes.
- Tasks supported by activity e.g. discussion, drama, ICT.
- Mentoring and support in writing, including girl/boy response partners.
- Teachers' response to content rather than length, spelling and handwriting.
- Strategies to direct attention to possible spelling and grammatical errors.
- Metacognitive review of themselves and others as writers and of the writing process.

Storytelling, story-making and story-responding

Boys need from their earliest years to be engaged in listening to, making up and discussing stories. To help sustain their focus, and to challenge and enrich their ideas they need help from adults, such as parents and teachers. In pre-school years this story-experience comes largely through assisted play and sharing books at bedtime. Boys in general are less fluent than girls in storytelling, story-making and story-responding. Throughout the school years boys therefore need to have structured and sustained opportunities to explore, discuss and create stories.[12]

Short-term targets and purposeful tasks

Teachers found that boys respond best when they are set short-term targets and practical writing tasks with a clear purpose and audience. Boys are generally less tolerant of ambiguity and long-term aims than girls. They need clear short-term targets and a structure within which to work. One way of providing structure is through the use of writing frames (below).

Teacher modelling the writing process: writing frames

Before the introduction of the Literacy Hour the writing diet offered to most children in English schools was predominantly in story form. This tended to disadvantage boys whose interests are often inclined towards factual forms of writing. However, in teaching non-fiction writing boys may still need considerable support in planning and structuring their writing. The use of writing frames has been found to be effective in helping young writers, especially boys, to be clear about the key features of the texts they are writing, such as layout, connectives and cohesive devices.[13] They have been developed as a means of supporting pupils undertaking a wide range of non-fiction tasks, but teachers in the Boys into Writing project found them equally useful in helping struggling boys to structure stories, poems and narrative texts.

Writing frames involve teachers in modelling the writing process and providing structures that can assist or scaffold the child's own writing. The objective of the frame is to help pupils gain independence in organising their writing across a range of genres so that eventually they will not need them. They help overcome the biggest problems for Simon, aged 10, which he says are: 'I never know what to write or how to begin.'

Writing frames commonly comprise a set of sentence-starters which pupils must complete that help them to shape a piece of discursive or informative writing. Completion of a writing frame may be the task, or it may be used as a planning device for notes/ideas/first drafts which a pupil will redraft as an independent piece of writing. Writing frames were developed for older Key Stage 2 pupils, but have been found by teachers to be equally useful with younger and with older pupils, particularly to involve pupils in developing the vocabulary and metacognitive aspects of writing.

Clear sense of order and discipline

One school found that the introduction of a Positive Discipline strategy with clear rewards and sanctions had a significant effect on improving time-on-task in both reading and writing activities. Another school found that giving underachieving boys responsibility and reward for exercising responsibility had positive effects on motivation and engagement in learning. Each class was given two 'executives' with clear responsibilities to assist and monitor at lunchtime and in showing visitors around school. The executives were academic underachievers, both boys and girls. Underachieving pupils also ran the library. Reward for effort included 'choosing time' on Friday, and weekly presentation of certificates.

Subject-matter relevant to their needs and interests

Levels of motivation are crucially important to boys. If teachers teach to the middle of the class, then unmotivated boys at either end of the ability spectrum are likely to lose interest in writing tasks. Underachieving boys can also be the most able. If they lack challenge, purpose and interest they may become turned off by what they see as 'easy' and routine tasks. As one able boy put it: 'English is not hard because in writing there are no right and wrong answers.'

Boys often say that they like the opportunity to, as one put it, 'write what we want to'. The problem with free choice is that they tend to repeat stock genres like aliens, ghosts, football and warfare. Clearly they need to be introduced to a range of fiction and non-fiction genres, but also be given the opportunity to respond to a topic in a genre of their choice. George, aged 9, relishes the opportunity for personal choice in writing for as he explains it gives you the chance to 'write about yourself without anybody knowing'.

Tasks supported by activity e.g. discussion, drama, drawing and ICT

A feature noted by teacher researchers is that underachieving boys prefer to *do* rather than to listen. Boys like learning activities that involve participation in discussion, and drama, and these can provide vital oral groundwork for writing activities (Chapter 4). For some boys the experience of writing is enriched by the activity of drawing and illustrating. Carl, aged 10, says he likes writing stories or 'guides' when he can illustrate them with cartoons.

Boys also like learning activities involving the use of ICT (Chapter 6) and these can have a major positive impact on pupils' motivation and confidence and improvements in literacy. This includes writing activities related to information-processing from databases, CD-ROMs and the internet, communicating through email and word-processing ideas (for example, for a newspaper report). Teachers report that a growing number of boys see spelling and handwriting as unimportant. As one eleven-year-old boy said: 'Why do I need to spell and practice handwriting when my computer can do it all for me?'

Mentoring and support in writing

Many teachers vouch for the benefit of paired reading and writing, which can not only support the writing process and provide a critical and creative audience, but can also raise self-esteem for both partners. One school found that having boy–girl partners had benefits for both boys and girls, with girls tending to offer careful attention to structure and detail, while boys often contributed more adventurous and divergent ideas.

Having male models for reading and writing was another strategy found to be effective in motivating boys. Some schools have used local policemen or fireman to read and share writing activities, others encourage visits by non-working men including fathers or grandfathers. Some female teachers seek male writing models by drawing on non-teaching male members of staff, using local retired men or by borrowing male teachers from other classes. As one teacher said: 'A good man (one who reads to children) is worth borrowing.'

Response to content and ideas

Christopher, aged 9, is typical of many boys when he reports: 'I don't like writing because I am not a very good speller.' When Jay, aged 10, is asked what writing is about he says; 'Improving your handwriting.' Many boys struggle with spelling and with handwriting. For Sean the trouble with writing 'is that you have to write a lot'. A writing lesson is better for boys when it focuses on one feature of writing, such as spelling, handwriting, sentence structure or content. Response to writing should always be first to its content and ideas. As Darren, aged 11, commented: 'I like a teacher who reads the words you wrote rather than telling you what's wrong with them.'

Strategies to direct attention to possible spelling and grammatical errors

Boys tend to be lax about proof-reading their own writing. Strategies need to be found to direct boys' attention to possible errors in their work once they have a complete draft. One strategy boys seem to prefer is to practice proof-reading and correcting a given text, on paper or computer, rather than their own writing. Using older underachieving boys to help proof-read the writing of young children has also proved an effective strategy in raising awareness of the need to check writing for mistakes. Giving them a special 'editorial pen', or pencil of a different colour, was also found effective in project schools in showing that editing writing is *a different task* to drafting or redrafting.

Metacognitive review

Boys tend to be less reflexive in their response to reading, writing and the world than girls. They need therefore opportunities to engage in metacognitive review of themselves and others as writers and of the writing process. They need to be encouraged to reflect on, discuss and develop metacognitive awareness at three levels:

- knowledge of writing task (e.g. what is the form, audience and purpose and what makes a good piece of writing?)
- knowledge of the writing process (e.g. what do you do to draft, edit, improve writing?)
- knowledge of self (e.g. what will help you become a better writer?)

Peer evaluation in writing helps develop engagement with others and metacognitive awareness of what the writing process is for other writers. After such a peer review Jason, aged 8, engages in a process of self-review when he writes: 'I need to slow down a bit, and try out different words and ideas, because my first words are not always the best.'

Feedback on writing, whether it is from teacher or from self-assessment, is most effective when it is in the form of comment on what is good and on what might be improved in terms of the content of the task. Boys in particular like to know why they are doing a task and how they are meant to do it. They prefer short-term goals, and succinct clear-cut writing tasks. Boys, and girls, who are taught to self-assess their work, have a clearer idea about how to improve their work and tend to make better progress. Time needs to be found for self-evaluation and private teacher discussion. 'I like to know', says Terry, 'what is good, if anything, about my writing and how to make it better.'

Not all boys are poor writers. Many boys, often the 'academic achievers', excel in writing and relish opportunities for writing. Some are impulsive and haphazard in their approach to writing tasks. Others are clearly failing and need intensive care to achieve their potential. What are identified here are strategies to help struggling writers whether they are boys or girls. They seek to help children like Christopher achieve his stated aim in writing: 'The words I write' he says, 'are part of me, so I want them to be the best.'

Notes

2.   Gender and Achievement website www.standards.dfes.gov.uk/ genderandachievement provides information on gender differences related to levels of achievement in school and advice on ways of raising the achievement of boys and girls.

3.   See Delamont, S. (1999) 'Gender and the discourse of derision'. *Research Papers in Education*, 14 (1) 3–21.

4.   See Paechter, C. (1998) *Educating the Other*. London: Falmer.

5.   Connell, R. W. (1989), 'Cool guys, swots and wimps: the interplay of masculinity and education'. *Oxford Review of Education*, 15(3), 291–303. Connell, R. W. (1995) *Masculinities*. Oxford: Polity Press.

6.   Bleach, K. (1996) *What Difference Does It Make? An Investigation Of Factors Influencing The Motivation Of Year 8 Boys In A West Midlands Comprehensive school.* Wolverhampton: University of Wolverhampton

7.   Mac An Ghaill, M. (1994) *The Making of Men*. Buckingham: Open University Press.

8.   See for example Murphy, P. & Elwood, J. (1998) 'Gendered experiences, choices and achievement – exploring the links'. *International Journal of Inclusive Education*, 2(2), 95–119.

9.   White, J. (1996) 'Research on English and the teaching of girls' in Murphy, P. and Gipps, C. (eds), *Equity in the Classroom: Towards Effective Pedagogy for Girls and Boys.* London: Falmer, p. 100.

10.   Frater, G. (2000) *Securing Boys' Literacy: A survey of effective practice in primary schools*. London: The Basic Skills Agency, p. 10.

11.   Clay, M. (1991) *Becoming Literate: the Construction of Inner Control*. Auckland: Heinemann, p. 209

12.   See Fisher, R. (1996) *Stories for Thinking*. Oxford: Nash Pollock; Fisher, R. (1998)

Teaching Thinking: Philosophical Enquiry in the Classroom. London: Continuum.

13. For more on the use of writing frames see Wray, D. and Lewis, M. (1997), *Extending Literacy: Developing Approaches to Non-Fiction*, London: Routledge and Hodson, P. and Jones, D. (2001) *Teaching Children to Write*. London: David Fulton Publishers.

Further reading

Arnold, R. (1997) *Raising Levels of Achievement in Boys*. Slough: NFER.

Black, P. and Williams, D. (1998) *Inside the Black Box: Raising Standards Through Classroom Assessment*. London: King's College.

Bleach, K. (1996) *What Difference Does It Make? An Investigation Of Factors Influencing The Motivation Of Year 8 Boys In A West Midlands Comprehensive School*. Wolverhampton: University of Wolverhampton.

Browne, A. (1994), 'The content of writing in the early years: issues of gender'. *Reading*, 28(3).

CCEA (1999) *School Improvement Focus on Boys: Guidance on Improving Attainment, Particularly in Literacy*. Belfast: Northern Ireland Council for Curriculum, Examination and Assessment.

Clark, A. and Millard, E. (eds) (1998) *Gender in the Secondary Curriculum: Balancing the Books*. London: Routledge.

Clarricoates, C. (1997) 'Child Culture At School' in Pollard A. (ed.) *Children And Their Primary Schools*. London: Falmer.

Clay, M. (1991) *Becoming Literate: The Construction of Inner Control*. Auckland: Heinemann.

Connell, R.W. (1989) 'Cool Guys, Swots and Wimps: The Interplay Of Masculinity And Education'. *Oxford Review of Education*, 15(3), 291–303.

Connell, R.W. (1995) *Masculinities*. Oxford: Polity Press.

Delamont, S. (1990) *Sex Roles and The School*. London: Routledge.

Delamont, S. (1999) 'Gender and the Discourse of Derision'. *Research Papers in Education*, 14(1) 3–21.

Elwood, J. (1995) 'Undermining gender stereotypes: examination and coursework performance in the UK at 16'. *Assessment in Education,* 2(3), 283–304.

Elwood, J. and Comber, C. (1996), *Gender Differences in Examinations at 18+*. Nuffield Foundation.

EOC/Ofsted (1996) *The Gender Divide*. London: HMSO.

Epstein, D., Elwood, J., Hey, V. and Maw, J. (eds) (1998) *Failing Boys? Issues in Gender and Achievement*. Buckingham: Open University Press.

Evans, A. (1996) 'Perils Of Ignoring Our Lost Boys'. *TES*, no. 4174, 28 June.

Fisher, R. (1996) *Stories for Thinking*. Oxford: Nash Pollock.

Fisher, R. (1998) *Teaching Thinking: Philosophical Enquiry in the Classroom*. London: Cassell.

Fisher, R. and Williams, M. (eds) (2000) *Unlocking Literacy*. London: David Fulton Publishers.

Frater, G. (2000) *Securing Boys' Literacy: A Survey of Effective Practice in Primary Schools*. London: The Basic Skills Agency.

Gender and Education (1997). Special issue on 'Masculinities in Education', 9(1).

Gilbert, P. and Rowe, K. (1989) *Gender: Literacy and the Classroom.* Australian Reading Association.

Gorard, S., Salisbury, J., Rees, G. and Fitz, J. (1998) *The Comparative Performance Of Boys And Girls In Wales: An Alternative View Of The Gender Gap.* School of Education, University of Wales, Cardiff.

Guardian (1998) 'Problems that arise when boys want to be lads'. 6 January, p. 6.

Head, J. (1999) *Understanding the Boys: Issues of Behaviour and Achievement.* London: Falmer.

Hodson, P. and Jones, D. (2001) *Teaching Children to Write.* London: David Fulton Publishers.

International Journal of Inclusive Education (1998) Special Issue on 'Boys' underachievement', 2(2).

Jensen, E. (1995) *Brain-based Learning and Teaching.* California: Turning Point Publishing.

Kelly, A. (ed.) (1981) *The Missing Half: Girls and Science Education.* Manchester: Manchester University Press.

Keys, W. and Fernandes, G. (1993), *What do Students Think About School?.* Slough: NFER.

Mac An Ghaill, M. (1994) *The Making of Men.* Buckingham: Open University Press.

Macdonald, A., Saunders, L. and Benefield P. (1998) *Boys' Attainment, Progress, Motivation and Participation: Issues Raised by Recent Literature.* Slough: NFER.

Malcolm, A. and Penny, V. (1999) *Raising Achievement of Boys in English.* Shropshire Educational Services, Shropshire County Council.

Mallett, M. (1997), 'Gender and genre: reading and writing choices of older juniors'. *Reading,* 31(2), 48–57.

Millard, E. (1997) *Differently Literate: Boys, Girls and the Schooling of Literacy.* London: Falmer.

Minns, H. (1991) *Language, Literacy and Gender.* London: Hodder and Stoughton.

Mulhern, F. (1996) *Girls, Boys And Exam Results: A Northern Ireland Perspective.* EOC(NI).

Murphy, P. and Elwood, J. (1998) 'Gendered experiences, choices and achievement – exploring the links'. *International Journal of Inclusive Education,* 2(2), 95–119.

Murphy, P. and Gipps, C.V. (1996) *Equity in the Classroom: Towards Effective Pedagogy for Girls and Boys.* London: Falmer.

Ofsted (1993) *Boys and English.* London: Ofsted.

Ofsted (1996) *The Gender Divide: Performance Differences Between Boys And Girls At School.* London: Ofsted.

Ofsted (1998) *Recent Research On Gender And Educational Performance.* London: Ofsted.

OHMCI (1997) *The Relative Performance of Boys and Girls.* OHMCI, Wales.

Paechter, C. (1998) *Educating the Other.* London: Falmer.

Pickering, J. (1997) *Raising Boys' Achievement.* Stafford: Network Educational Press.

Pottorff, D., Phelps-Zientarski, D. and Skovera, M. (1996) 'Gender perceptions of elementary and middle school students about literacy at school and home'. *Journal of Research and Development in Education,* 29(4), 203–11.

Powney, J. (1996) *Gender and Attainment: A Review*. Edinburgh: SCRE.

QCA (1998) *Can Do Better: Raising Boys' Achievement in English*. London: QCA.

QCA (2000) *Standards at Key Stage 2: English, Mathematics And Science*. London: QCA, www.qca.org.uk

Solsken, J.W. (1993) *Literacy, Gender and Work in Families and in School*. Norwood NJ: Ablex Publishing Corporation.

Sukhnandan, L., Lee B. and Kelleher, S. (2000) *An Investigation into Gender Differences in Education, Phase 2: school and classroom strategies*. Slough: NFER.

Swann, J. (1992) *Girls, Boys and Language*. Oxford: Blackwell.

WEST (1996) *Boys and English*. Wiltshire Education Support and Training (WEST), County Hall, Trowbridge.

White, J. (1990) 'On literacy and gender' in Carter, R. (ed.) *Knowledge about Language and the Curriculum: The LINC Reader*. London: Hodder and Stoughton.

White, J. (1996) 'Research on English and the teaching of girls' in Murphy, P. and Gipps, C. (eds) *Equity in the Classroom: Towards Effective Pedagogy for Girls and Boys*. London: Falmer.

Wray, D. and Lewis, M. (1997) *Extending Literacy: Developing Approaches to Non-Fiction*. London: Routledge.

Appendices

Appendix 1: Classroom observation

Classroom observation is valuable because it enables good practice to be observed, recorded, analysed and shared, and ineffective practice to be identified and avoided.
  Areas on which to focus include:

Patterns of grouping in the class
What methods of grouping seem most successful for pupils to perform well in writing? What do pupils think? What do teachers think?

Kinds of writing task
What kinds of writing are pupils engaged in? When do they do their best (and worst) in writing tasks? What kinds of writing do they, and their teachers, prefer?

Quality of discussion about writing
Do pupils show different strengths and weaknesses in planning, discussing or reviewing writing? How does the teacher facilitate, intervene and develop discussion? Are there patterns in pupil talk?

The amount of time spent on- or off-task
Which groups/individuals spend a greater proportion of their time engaged in writing tasks? What teacher strategies get pupils back and keep pupils on-task.

Teaching strategies used to support writing
How are pupils supported in their writing tasks? How are tasks introduced? What teaching strategies does the teacher employ to support planning, drafting, editing, sharing and responding to written work? How does the learning environment support writing?

Analysis of samples of writing
What do pupils think of their own and other people's work? What strengths and weaknesses do teachers find in samples of writing? What targets do pupils/teachers set in response to writing?

Appendix 2: Questionnaire on writing

1. *What kinds of writing do you like or not like to write?*
   Circle a number from 1–5.   (1 = like very much, 3 = quite like, 5 = do not like)

   (a) Imaginative e.g. writing stories or poems   1   2   3   4   5

   (b) Personal e.g. writing about myself, or my opinions   1   2   3   4   5

   (c) Factual e.g. writing reports or information   1   2   3   4   5

2. *The best piece of writing I have done this year is* ....
   ....
   It was a good piece of writing because ....
   ....

3. *The longest piece of writing I have done this year is:*

   (a) less than a page ...(b) more than 1 page...(c) more than 2 pages... (d) ...... pages

4. *Do you re-read your writing?*

   (a) always?   (b) sometimes?   (c) rarely?   (d) never?

5. *Do you redraft, change and improve your writing?*

   (a) always?   (b) sometimes?   (c) rarely?   (d) never?

6. *Do you edit, check or correct your writing for mistakes?*

   (a) always?   (b) sometimes?   (c) rarely?   (d) never?

7. *Do you finish your writing on time?*

   (a) always?   (b) sometimes?   (c) rarely?   (d) never?

8. *Do you like writing?*   Yes or No

   Say why. 'Writing for me is ....
   ....
   ....
   ....
   ....
   ....

CHAPTER 11

Providing a challenge: writing and the able child

Mary Williams

Introduction

Mark, at the age of six, was able to write the following, after having the story of Jack and the Beanstalk read to him:

> 'She [Jack's mother] was terrified when she saw him with the parsnips and threw them out the window so from now on he only got 4 meals a day. The next day everything was Greenesh, he rubbed his Eyes and everything was still Greenesh. He opened the window and climbed up the sunflower until he got up to the top he found himself in a house1 sign said straigt onto goldland and 1 mile later said this way to silver land and on another it said this way to bronze land, he went to gold land 1st and found a hen that laed silver eggs he nearly got caught by a monster 2nd he went to silver land and found a bag of gold and nearly got caught by some spirit and finally he went to bronze land and found a singing harp and again he nearly got caught by a spirit. The singing harp, the bag of gold and the hen that layed silver eggs was shown to Jame's mum and she was delighted to see Jack alive and with his father's things and from now on they were very rich and they were happily ever after.[1]

What does he know about the writing process? He has understanding of the main elements of the fairy-story genre and has been able to use them in his own story, knowing, for instance, that 'good' needs to overcome 'bad' and that it has to end with everyone living happily ever after. He has clearly outlined the sequence of events. His story is full of pace and he uses colourful language such as 'the singing harp' and the 'hen that laid the silver eggs' remembered from the original, as well as 'greenesh' which is an invention of his own. He is confident enough to put his own interpretation into the story with Jack/James climbing up a sunflower rather than a beanstalk. Elements of other stories creep in, such as being nearly caught by a monster and a spirit. He writes numerals and cardinals, rather than words, but this does not detract from the meaning. He uses punctuation with confidence, even getting the apostrophe right on one occasion. His spellings are either accurate or phonetically plausible. Children such as Mark deserve to have their ability cherished and enriched. One of my saddest moments as a teacher was to discover that Peter, a child who I had taught in

Key Stage 1, and who had been considered able – in part because of his prolific and imaginative writing – was writing 'safe' unimaginative pieces by the time he was in Year 5 because peer pressure and low levels of teacher expectation had made it unattractive to him to succeed.[2]

The needs of able children

It is vital that children like Mark and Peter are catered for appropriately throughout their entire education. Questions have to be raised about whether the National Literacy Strategy (1998), and the Literacy Hour itself are best placed to keep the enthusiasm and creativity of such children alive. This, as well as other issues relating to the needs of able writers, will be considered in this chapter. Before concentrating on able children's writing needs it should be recognised that the education of the whole child is important. Able children need to achieve a balance in terms of their social, emotional, physical and intellectual development. Without this any ability they possess may go to waste. All children, but particularly those who are able, have the right to an education that is stimulating and challenging. The curriculum should be differentiated to meet able children's needs appropriately and they should be taught in groupings that provide them with challenge. In addition, they deserve to be inspired by the interventions of supportive, knowledgeable adults. In other words an able child should receive an education in which 'an Optimal Match is the adjustment of an appropriately challenging curriculum to match a student's pace and level of learning'.[3]

Able pupils do not necessarily require a curriculum which is radically different from other pupils in their age group but one in which the pace is increased and level of instruction is deepened to meet their individual needs. In order to achieve this they may need an advocate in school who will act as their champion, making sure that positive attitudes – from teachers and pupils alike – are maintained towards them[4] and that they are suitably challenged and enriched.[5] Schools working within the 'Excellence in Cities' programme (1999) were required to provide an effective programme for their gifted and talented pupils and to appoint a teacher who would oversee their education. This is likely to become a requirement for all schools in the near future as Ofsted (2001:5) has highlighted a number of issues that require attention. These include:

- improving methods for identifying gifted and talented pupils;
- engaging parents and pupils;
- developing subject-specific approaches;
- giving earlier attention to the skills of independent learning;
- making the most of additional provision;
- recognising the implications for staffing;
- improving monitoring; and
- establishing a secure basis for improving mainstream school practice.

It is against such a background that the literacy needs of able pupils – with a particular emphasis on learning to write – will be considered. This chapter will consider many of the issues outlined above and, therefore, will be of use to teachers who are taking on the role of coordinator for able pupils, as well as for *all* teachers who will be sure to encounter such children in their classes.

Able children and the Literacy Hour

So far it has not always been easy to meet the needs of able children in the Literacy Hour, particularly in classrooms where a wide-ability spectrum can be found. In the early days of the National Literacy Strategy there were concerns that the Literacy Hour might fail the most able pupils. The problem centred on the texts used during 'shared reading and writing' (Chapter 2) that were supposed to challenge the whole class by being at the threshold of children's ability. Which children? Those who were able? Those who had other 'Special Educational Needs'? Those who were progressing satisfactorily but could not be said to be gifted? While coming to grips with the Literacy Hour many teachers were forced, mainly through lack of time for preparation and reflection, to match the work to the needs of the majority of the class. Unfortunately, this left the two ends of the ability spectrum without an optimal match.

In response to these concerns, in January 2000, the DfEE produced some guidance on teaching able children in the Literacy [and Numeracy] Strategies. In this, an attempt was made to identify what pupils who are able in literacy are able to do. In terms of writing they could:

- latch on quickly to the conventions of different types of writing;
- think in original ways and experiment with new styles;
- manipulate language, sentence structure and punctuation; and
- use apt terminology and varied vocabulary.

(It might be interesting to review Mark's story or that of another able child with the above in mind.)

Teachers, when questioned about how they recognised ability in writing, rated 'creativity' as the most critical distinguishing feature.[6]

In the DfEE guidance it was further suggested that *The Framework of Objectives* of the National Literacy Strategy should be wide enough to encompass the needs of the most able pupils who could be catered for by being taught,

- in greater depth (e.g. more detail and complexity);
- to a broader range (e.g. more challenging texts and tasks);
- and a faster pace (e.g. tackling objectives earlier).

This could be achieved through tasks which are given to the whole class but which require different outcomes from different ability groups, or through tasks that become more difficult as they progress,[7] such as the one shown in Figure 11.1 from a larger project on newspaper writing. (All the children in the class could probably cope with bullet points 1–3, with the more able, additionally, considering the last two).

Figure 11.1 Newspaper slants

Another strategy is to provide separate tasks linked to a common theme. For example in writing poetry the more able children adopting the form of limericks, haikus or cinquains when other children are given a less prescribed task which involves choosing their own poetic form; or the more able undertaking investigations relating to phonics, grammar and spelling, which help to consolidate rule learning, as required on an individual basis. Here are two challenges – one at Key Stage 1 and the other at Key Stage 2 – that subscribe to elements of this. The first one is a task that can be undertaken by the whole class with this particular focus being given to any able children within it. It has been successfully used with able Year 1 children but more readily aligns itself to 'termly objectives' of the NLS for children in Year 2 and Year 3.

Example of a Key Stage 1 challenge

> *'My Dad'* by Anthony Browne
>
> Read this story to the whole class (sensitivity needs to be shown towards children who come from families without traditional father figures). Ask all the children to look at the illustrations very carefully. Can they work out what inspired some of them? (For example, the visual references to 'Little Red Riding Hood' and 'Hey, Diddle, Diddle, The Cat and the Fiddle' (these were all recognised by Henrietta (see below) or the 'Three Tenors'.) Work with a group of able children to explore the use of similes and metaphors in this book:
>
> * as strong as a gorilla
> * as happy as a hippopotamus
> * as big as a house
> * as soft as a teddy.

A challenge like the one shown in the box was given to two children – Henrietta, aged 6, and her brother John, aged 8 – who were asked to consider if 'as strong as a gorilla' was a good description of their own father. They agreed that he looked like a gorilla because he was 'hairy' and thought this to be very funny! John volunteered that the opposite of this might be as 'weak as an ant'. However, when asked to describe his father for himself, he homed in on the fact that his dad is basically a happy person, so he decided that 'as happy as a crocodile' would be the more appropriate. This seemed a little odd until he explained that photographs of crocodiles nearly always show them with wide grins on their faces. After a little more prompting he opted for 'as happy as a hyena' because he knew that hyenas make a laughing noise.

Once children are familiar with such descriptive devices, they can go on to make up more for other members of their family or friends. In addition, they can be asked to think, for example, why owls are wise or brushes are daft and can be invited to write lists of other unusual combinations.

Example of a Key Stage 2 challenge that subscribes to the above

The second challenge for older able pupils would fit in with National Literacy Strategy 'termly objectives'[8] for teaching in Year 5, term 2 and term 3 (objectives 18, 19) as well as in Year 6, term 1 (objectives 15, 18) and term 2 (objectives 18, 19). (Younger able pupils could undertake such a task once their abilities and needs have been assessed and found to be up to the challenge.) This activity could be undertaken as an independent group session during the Literacy Hour (for up to six children assessed as able or exceptionally able) or it could be given to exceptionally able children as an individual task or to work on as a pair.

Writing derived from stories about the Second World War

Provide the children with several books that are set during the Second World War (see 'Children's Literature' at the end of the chapter). Before giving them access to these pose the question – 'What can you learn from these stories about what it was like to be a child during the Second World War?' Using 'higher order thinking skills' (Bloom 1956), they will be involved in analysing, interpreting, contrasting and comparing from one source to another, so opportunities should be given to them to discuss the book they are currently reading with each other. Additionally, they should have been told that they must find a way of recording what they have learnt. In other words, they must find a means of organising and classifying their thoughts. To encourage them to synthesise, pose an additional question – What would it be like to have been an English child if Germany had won the war? A written account from the viewpoint of an investigative journalist could be the required outcome from this. Finally, in the light of what they discovered, they should be ask to write 'a bill of rights' for children living in the twenty-first century. In doing this they will have to make judgements and recommendations which will involve them in selecting and rejecting proposals put forward by each other, as well as finding a compelling means of getting their message across, perhaps, using ICT to achieve this. Throughout they should ensure that there is evidence within the texts for any conclusions they reach.

Organisational considerations

To maximise the effectiveness of teaching in the Literacy Hour various organisational considerations need to be borne in mind. These include:

- *setting* – children can be 'set' across classes in schools where there is more than one class in a particular age group in order that the more able come together for literacy work. This can be very useful as it makes planning easier and less diffuse. Also, it makes the provision of challenging materials and tasks, deeper levels of questioning and swiftness in pace easier to achieve.
- *use of additional staff/adults* – extra staff can be deployed strategically to give help where it is needed. Often this tends to be given to children of lower ability but able children also benefit particularly when a teacher or helper who is an expert in a particular field can be spared to provide impetus and depth to a particular project. For example, able pupils attending a summer school at Johns Hopkins University, Baltimore were able to contact NASA astronauts by a satellite link to question them about travel in space.[9] Such an opportunity as this is likely to be rare but, on a more realistic level, visiting authors or journalists can provide similar motivation in schools.

- *use of response partner for peer review* – at the very least, able pupils should be encouraged to engage in peer review with one another in the form of a response partner (Chapter 2) which, with the growth of email and the internet, could involve able pupils from more than one school. Able writers need to be able to construct and clarify their ideas and experiences as they record them and discussion with others, as part of this process, can be very useful to them.
- *extended time for writing* – these children may want to write at more length than other children in the class. Therefore, additional time needs to be found outside the Literacy Hour for them to do this, or they need extended time within it – the Literacy Hour and a half, as many teachers are now advocating.

Thinking skills and metacognition

Thinking skills

However, getting able children to think deeply will be of critical importance to their educational development. The match and pace of the curriculum to able children's particular levels of understanding will be crucial. They must be challenged to higher levels of thinking and their ability to achieve this will depend on their teachers' ability to ask probing questions as a means of engaging them in active problem-solving.[10] The sort of higher order thinking that should be encouraged is near the top of Bloom's taxonomy (1956)[11] requiring

- analysis,
- synthesis,
- evaluation.

Teachers are required to provide such thinking within the National Literacy Strategy (1998) where they are expected to:

- probe pupils' understanding;
- cause them to reflect on and refine their work;
- expand on their ideas; and
- check and test their understanding.

They need to provide all children, particularly the more able, with cognitive challenge. This is most likely to be achieved when pupils work with others towards a specific, motivating goal. Problem-solving tasks should be set which engage them in

- information processing;
- reasoning;
- enquiry;
- creative thinking; and
- evaluation.[12]

(See Chapter 2.)

Furthermore, teachers can help children to think in this way by modelling their own thinking processes as they go about writing tasks.

Modelling and 'thinking aloud'

The modelling of strategies that successful readers and writers use is given a high profile in the Literacy Hour. Such modelling will usually be offered by the teacher but, with older pupils, it may be that able children are capable of providing this themselves. This gives them an oral challenge in the form of having to reveal their thinking processes to others. If pupils are to be involved in this way they will need to rehearse what they are going to say either with their teacher; or with each other, if they are working in a group or as a pair.

Example of teacher modelling

Maggie, a Year 3 teacher, attempted to increase metacognitive awareness of how to acquire information from reference books through modelling her thinking about how to problem-solve through information retrieval. Her problem had arisen during the course of reading a poem about *Tyrannosaurus rex* by Wes Magee. The poem was initially read aloud in unison by the whole class as part of shared reading. Maggie told the children that she had enjoyed this poem, and others about dinosaurs which had been read in previous lessons so much, that she wanted to find out more about them, particularly, *Tyrannosaurus rex*. She was particularly fascinated by a line in the poem that read – 'across the mud-flats he belts in top gear'. She asked herself, seeing that *Tyrannosaurus rex* was so enormous, why didn't he get stuck in the mud. She had several theories about this, based on what she already knew about dinosaurs, for example, the mud flats were often dried out, his bones might be very light, but needed to find out which was the most likely. She then proceeded to model approaches to finding out answers to her question by looking up '*Tyrannosaurus rex*' in a range of information books, including a 'Big Book' specially designed for this purpose, taking care to model the correct language as she went along, for example, by referring to bibliographic conventions such as the contents page and the index. Then she considered how she might find an answer to her 'new' question about how they moved. To do this she had to discover what books were available on the subject in the school library and to use these she had needed to remember what she knew about finding information from non-fiction books.[13]

Next she gave the children access to a number of books about dinosaurs, discussing with them how they should, as part of independent work, raise a question and gain information about it from a number of sources before trying to reach any conclusions. Finally she discussed various possibilities for recording what they had discovered. It was decided that a grid would be useful, so she experimented with several formats in front of them before challenging them to write up their findings for themselves.

In such a situation able children might have been able to contribute to the modelling of thinking by being set a similar project in advance of other members of the class. Then they could teach others how to go about discovering answers to their particular questions in a similar way. Part of the challenge could be the development of a suitable findings grid using ICT resources.

Example of grid

Why Tyrannosaurus rex did not sink on the mud flats

Book 1	Book 2	Book 3	Book 4	Book 5

The conclusion we reached was that:

Metacognition

As part of developing higher levels of thinking children need to gain understanding of their own cognitive processes and this can be emancipatory and empowering for them.[14] When they gain metacognitive awareness like this, they are able to make conscious decisions about how to tackle similar learning tasks in the future. Such awareness is achieved through reflection about *how* they have learned something, which enables them to understand the learning processes involved. To encourage this process, teachers should build on pupils' 'emergent' understanding of the writing process (Chapter 1) to help them learn to write in a systematic way. By asking pupils appropriately challenging questions – such as 'How do you know that is so?', or 'How did you learn that? – they can begin to acquire understanding of how they learn best in a particular situation. This can be consolidated and easily brought back to the level of consciousness through the use of aide-memoires, e.g. wall charts that remind pupils of what they have learnt, for example,

---

Remember that when you write:

Sentences begin with a capital letter
and end with a full stop.

---

or

> **What do you need to think about when you write a story?**
>
> - What is your main idea?
> - Who will be your characters?
> - Where is the story going to take place?
> - What is going to happen in it?
> - How will it all end up?

The provision of both fiction and non-fiction writing frames to help 'scaffold' or provide support for the learning of a particular genre for as long as is needed (Bruner 1960) (Chapters 1 and 7) can also be very useful.

Direct teaching of how to learn in a particular situation, is very important, for example, providing a mental framework for writing by getting the children to think of a poetry stimulus, drawn, for example, from observing a kiwi fruit, in terms of the five senses:

- What did it *look* like?
- How did it *feel*?
- What *sound* did it make?
- How did it *taste*?
- What did it *smell* of?[15]

What is being suggested here is much more complex than providing appropriate planning devices, or activating prior knowledge or experiences, but is a way of getting children to think deeply about how they have experienced something emotionally. This can be very powerful indeed when it works well, for example, in this poem by Narinder, an able Key Stage 2 child:

A Widow

A painful feeling deep inside.
A sudden cry of despair.
A shriek followed by the word 'No!'
And then you shout, 'Why did it have to happen to me?"
You look around and there in a corner your child,
mourning his father's death.
You look around seeking the young girl he married.
For the girl he left behind is now a widow.

Getting children to access an idea by discussing how would they feel about it, if it happened to them, is another very useful starting point that can be stimulated through the reading of carefully chosen stories and poems, for example:

- *Changes* – Anthony Browne for a new baby in the family.
- 'The Boy without a Name' by Alan Ahlberg about a boy who suffers from eczema or *Goggle-Eyes* by Anne Fine for children who hate having to wear glasses.

- *The Runaways* by Ruth Thomas for those who feel like running away from home.
- *Grandpa* by John Burningham and *Charlotte's Web* by E.B. White about bereavement.

The list is endless. Able children should be set challenges which captivate them on a emotional as well as intellectual level.

The oral ability of able children

The 'precocious oral ability' that so many able children possess can be used to get them to justify the language choices they make, or to suggest alternatives for other children, although care needs to be taken to ensure that they are not always given the lead, as this could have a detrimental affect on interpersonal relationships within the class. They need to be given a listening agenda, as they are often not as good at this as they are at speaking. As HMI suggests,[16] high ability pupils can act as a stimulus to other, lower attaining pupils who can benefit from hearing the extended vocabulary such pupils frequently use. Therefore, it can be beneficial to all the children in a class for able pupils to explain how they have learned something. It can help to give less able pupils metacognitive understanding while providing a challenge for the more able in terms of putting themselves across in a way that is easily understood. Such discussions can be supported by charts which outline the main points of the argument, and which offer yet another challenge to able children if they have to produce these as in the example in Figure 11.2. (This could provide an additional challenge for an able Year 4 child working to the requirements of Term 3 of the National Literacy Strategy's 'termly objectives'.) These charts could be displayed as aide-memoires to help pupils use such poetic forms in the future.

Working in groups

By implication, in much of the work suggested above, able children need to be able to collaborate with one another. This, in itself, can be quite a challenge for them, as they can be highly individualistic and easily irritated if others do not keep up with their pace of learning. Such work will only be effective if pupils know how to operate successfully as a group. This is now a requirement in the 'Speaking and Listening' Programme of Study in the *National Curriculum for England: English* (1999) and provides another element of metacognition. For example, as part of a history lesson with his Year 6 class, the teacher Alan started with an introductory discussion centred on a series of questions discussed by Greek philosophers. In addition to the subject-based, problem-setting introduction he gave equal importance to developing his pupils' understanding of how to work in a group. As a result, the first point when the class reconvened, after about 20 minutes discussion time, was not about their role as Greek philosophers but about the effectiveness of the discussion itself. In this way, he encouraged his pupils to think very carefully about how they were learning.[17] He gave them roles within the group such as chair, scribe and as 'balancer' whose role it was to report back on whether certain individuals had dominated the discussion or who took the lead. The role of scribe, or that of balancer, could easily be given to able children who tend to automatically take the lead during discussions, as this would serve to keep

Today I want to discuss what I have found out about writing *'clerihews'*.

To find out about this:

- First I asked myself what I already knew about it? *I knew they were a form of comic verse.*
- Then I asked myself what I did not know. *I knew they rhymed but did not know about their precise form. I discovered that the first line is the name of the person involved and that the verse has four lines with 1 rhyming with 2 and 3 rhyming with 4.*
- Next I sought further information from resource books in the classroom. (You could sometimes use CD-ROMs, the internet or ask a friend or the teacher.)
- Then I wrote:

> *Timothy Dale*
> *has an averson to kale.*
> *It makes him feel ill*
> *so he won't eat his fill.*

I took the name of a boy I know and related it to what we have been finding out about vegetables. *I needed to work very hard on the rhymes. I'm not entirely happy with the last line. Do you have any other suggestions for improving it?*

- The most interesting thing I found out *was that they were named after their inventor – E. Clerihew Bentley.*

Do you have any questions?

Perhaps you would like to try to write one for yourself.

Figure 11.2 Example of a discussion chart

them quiet so that others get a chance to speak, and might make them more sensitive to the needs of others in the class, while enhancing their awareness of group dynamics. Similarly, acting as the chair or balancer would involve them in analysing and evaluating the contribution of others. Before such a discussion takes place they could be asked to decide whether those who speak the most automatically make the greatest contribution to moving the task forward and to give evidence-based reasons for their conclusions. To do this effectively they might need to develop some sort of observation schedule that would provide them with another interesting writing challenge.

All these strategies help children move from understanding which is tacit or implicit to giving them explicit understanding which enables them to be more strategic and critically reflective about their learning. This will be enhanced even more when they assess for themselves what they have learned in a particular lesson or series of lessons, and are asked to provide evidence of this (Chapter 7). The keeping of a writing journal can be very useful in this respect; as will having a metalanguage with which to discuss the writing process – shared by both teachers and learners alike – as this will greatly assist in the development of such understanding. This should include:

- lexical terms which relate to phonological and graphological aspects of the process;
- morphological terms which enhance discussion of word structure and derivations;
- grammatical terminology which aids the discussion of word order, cohesive devices, the types of sentence structure and punctuation; and
- textual terms which relate to clarity and cohesion, layout and organisation.

'Directed Activities Relating to Texts' (DARTs)[18] can be very useful in getting able pupils to display their knowledge about language through group activities involving:

- sequencing (see Figure 11.3);
- predicting;
- cloze;
- underlining key points;
- finding the theme or title;
- drawing diagrams; and
- making charts

as they ensure that children demonstrate what they have understood from texts in a variety of ways, requiring them to justify the conclusions they have reached with each other.

Other tasks that might be derived from the starting point provided in Figure 11.3 are :

- If the title was removed, how does the reader know that this poem is about an eagle?
- What imagery is used in this poem?
- An evaluation of whether the punctuation helped or hindered the sequencing process.
- Could the poem be punctuated differently? How would this alter the meaning?

In addition, it could provide the stimulus for further writing. For example, children could be asked to:

- Extend the poem by another eight lines.
- Write about another bird/animal . . . in the same style.
- Justify – or disagree – with the writer's view that the eagle is male.

This sequencing task, which is a useful device for taking pupils 'inside' the mind of a writer, is suitable for able pupils in Years 5, 6 or 7 and depends on their having knowledge of poetic form and conventions. They should be required to provide reasons for choices and to record these in note form on a flipchart. They should be asked to undertake the task individually at first – for about 15 minutes. Then they should discuss their choices in groups of between four to six pupils to see if they can reach a consensus.

The Eagle by Andrew Young

And bends a narrow golden head,
Round the hill-side
Level and still
he hung down crucified.
He hangs between his wings outspread
Scanning the ground to kill,
Though as he sails and smoothly swings
He looks as though from his own wings

(The correct version can be found at the end of the chapter in the Appendix.)

Figure 11.3 Example of a sequencing activity for pupils in Key Stages 2 and 3

Conclusion

Pupils need to acquire metacognitive understanding if literacy learning is to be effective as was shown in the examples provided by Maggie and Alan earlier. This can begin from an early age. Able children can benefit from pre-school literacy experiences, home/school partnerships and by being given the opportunity to write in the course of their play. Children who showed signs of ability at the age of six knew why it was important to be literate, for example, Daniel said 'so you can read to your children when you are a daddy', and Kay who knew that it was an important part of being a teacher.[19] They had bibliographic knowledge that they used in their own stories and poems and they had the names of the 'author' and 'illustrator' suitably in place. They had insights into the writing process similar to that shown by Mark, whose story is quoted at the beginning of the chapter. Above all, they frequently used writing to plan what they were going to play, to provide props for their play or to write in role as the play got underway. Therefore, all children – not just the able – benefit from being given:

- greater exposure to the planning needed for imaginative play;
- an awareness of the power which can be gained from being literate; and
- greater metacognitive awareness of how they are learning to write.

Once they start school they will experience English as both a subject in its own right and a means of learning across the curriculum, with writing seldom being undertaken solely within the Literacy Hour but ranging across the other subjects of the primary curriculum. To meet such a variety of needs children must be able to write with an economy of words and with great precision. Opportunities may be available for this in non-fiction writing across subjects of the National Curriculum where the ability to synthesise and analyse is of paramount importance, such as in the 'Second World War' example above.

The primary school teacher is well placed to ensure that able children are challenged in their writing whatever the task in hand but this may be more difficult in secondary schools where pupils go to different teachers depending on the subject. In all schools approaches need to be consistent from one subject to another. In secondary schools, as well as in primary, all teachers should be active teachers of literacy, irrespective of their subject.[20]

Raising standards for all pupils, both in the primary or secondary sectors of education, will depend on high levels of interaction with the teacher through depth of questioning as envisaged under the National Literacy Strategy. This is of paramount importance for able children. Through using their oral abilities fully pupils must be challenged and given the opportunity to perform at higher levels than their peers. This may mean that many manage to reach higher SATs levels: much more than the required Level 4 at the end of Key Stage 2. However, there is more to it than this. They need to be motivated and challenged appropriately as their boredom thresholds are low. This is most likely to be achieved when they are encouraged to use their creativity and to solve absorbing and challenging problems where they can write with enthusiasm, across a range of genres, in response to motivating goals. Such writing is unlikely to be achieved within the Literacy Hour alone, but from exploration across most subjects of the National Curriculum.

Notes

1. Williams, M. and Rask, H. (2001) explore the relationship between play and the development of literacy in an article entitled 'Developing literacy through play' (in draft).
2. Millard, E. (1997) points out the significance of peer pressure, particularly on boys who wanted to remain as accepted members of their peer group.
3. Center for Talented Youth (CTY) (1994) *Philosophy and Program Policy*, The Johns Hopkins University, Baltimore, USA, in which the importance of the all-round development of the able child is highlighted.
4. DfEE (November 1999) *Revised Guidance on the Gifted and Talented Strand of Excellence in Cities*. SEU.
5. A theme that is explored more fully in Koshy, V. & Casey, R. (1997) *Effective Provision for Able and Exceptionally Able Children*. London: Hodder & Stoughton.
6. Brunel Research Into Literacy (BRIL) has explored aspects of the introduction of the National Literacy Strategy since its introduction in 1998.

7. From 'Bright Challenge' enrichment activities for pupils from the ages of 7 to 11. The author acted as research director for this project and was interested to see how children not normally identified as able shone by being given these problem-solving tasks.

8. Taken from *The National Literacy Strategy: Framework for Teaching* (1998). London: DfEE.

9. On a visit to Johns Hopkins 'Center for Talented Youth' in 1994 the director outlined the programme of summer schools which included this project which benefited from support from NASA.

10. Fisher, R. (2001) 'Thinking to Write: Thinking Skills in Literacy Learning'. Paper presented at the UKRA International Conference, Christ Church College, Canterbury, 7 July.

11. Bloom's taxonomy that set out six levels of thinking – knowledge, comprehension, application, analysis, synthesis and evaluation, the last three presenting the learner with the greatest cognitive challenge.

12. DfEE (1999) *The National Curriculum: Handbook for Primary teachers in England*. London: DfEE.

13. Such a framework is provided in EXIT, Extending Interaction with Texts, Wray and Lewis (1997) where a strategy for finding out information is introduced. This includes getting children to ask themselves a range of questions such as 'What do I already know about this subject?', 'What do I need to find out?', 'Where will I get this information?', 'What can I do if there are parts I cannot understand?' and 'Should I believe this information?'.

14. Williams, M. (2000) in an article entitled 'The part which metacognition can play in raising standards in English at Key Stage 2' gives a fuller description of what metacognitive awareness means.

15. An approach outlined in the 'metacognitive' article above and which was observed during the course of PhD research.

16. Ofsted (1999) *National Literacy Strategy: An Evaluation of the First Year of the National Literacy Strategy*. A Report from the Office of Her Majesty's Chief Inspector of Schools.

17. As in Williams, M. (2000) above – Note 15.

18. 'DARTs' which are directed activities relating to texts set up by Lunzer, E. and Gardner, K. (1979) to enhance pupils' understanding of texts.

19. Findings from a small-scale research project (Williams, M. and Rask, H., 2000) that looked at the ways in which able children in Year 1 extended and developed their literacy skills.

20. Taken from the DfEE standards website where the problems facing Key Stage 3 Literacy teaching were described as 'diverse and widespread'.

Further reading

Beard, R. (1993) *Teaching Literacy Balancing Perspectives*. London: Hodder & Stoughton.
Bloom, B.S. (1956) *Taxonomy of Educational Objectives*, Volume 1. London: Longman.

Bruner, J. (1990) *The Process of Education.* London: Vintage Books.

Bunting, R. (1997) *Teaching About Language in the Primary Years.* London: David Fulton Publishers.

Casey, R. and Koshy, V. (2001) *Bright Challenge.* The Elephant Centre, P.O. Box 942, South Croydon, Surrey, CR2 OBX.

Center for Talented Youth (CTY) (1994) *Philosophy and Program Policy.* The Johns Hopkins University, Baltimore, USA.

DfEE (November 1999) *Revised Guidance on the Gifted and Talented Strand of Excellence in Cities.* SEU.

DfEE (1998) *The National Literacy Strategy: Framework for Teaching.* London: HMSO.

DfEE (1999) *The National Curriculum for England: English.* London: HMSO.

DfEE (2000) *The National Curriculum: Handbook for Primary Teachers in England.* London: DfEE.

DfEE (January 2000) *National Literacy and Numeracy Strategies: Guidance on Teaching Able Children.* London: DfEE.

DfEE (2000) *Transforming Key Stage 3,* http://www.standards.dfee.gov.uk/keystage3/transforming/

Fisher, R. (2001) 'Thinking to Write: Thinking Skills in Literacy Learning'. Paper presented at the UKRA International Conference, Christ Church College, Canterbury, 7 July.

Lunzer, E. and Gardner, K. (1979) *The Effective Use of Reading.* London: Heineman.

Koshy, V. and Casey, R. (1997) *Effective Provision for Able and Exceptionally Able Children.* London: Hodder & Stoughton.

Millard, E. (1997) *Differently Literate.* London: Falmer Press.

Ofsted (1999) *National Literacy Strategy: An Evaluation of the First Year of the National Literacy Strategy.* A Report from the Office of Her Majesty's Chief Inspector of Schools.

Ofsted (2001) *Providing for Gifted and Talented Pupils: An Evaluation of Excellence in Cities and Other Grant-funded Programmes.* HMI 334.

Williams (1998) 'A Study Which Explores the Impact of the English National Curriculum (1990) on the Work of Teachers at Key Stage 2'. Unpublished PhD thesis.

Williams, M. (2000) 'The part which metacognition can play in raising standards in English at Key Stage 2. *Reading,* 34(1), April, 3–8.

Williams, M. and Rask, H. (2000) 'The identification of variables which enable able children in Year One to extend and develop their literacy skills'. *Gifted and Talented,* 4(2), November.

Williams, M. and Rask, H. (2001) 'Developing Literacy Through Play' (in draft).

Wray, D. and Lewis, M. (1997) *Extending Literacy.* London: Routledge.

Children's Literature

Ahlberg, Allan (1984) 'The Boy Without a Name', *Please, Mrs Butler.* Harmondsworth: Puffin.

Bawden, Nina (1973) *Carrie's War*. Harmondsworth: Puffin.

Browne, Anthony (1997) *Changes*. London: Walker Books.

Browne, Anthony (2000) *My Dad*. Picture Corgi.

Burningham, John (1984) *Grandpa*. Harmondsworth: Picture Puffins.

Frank, Otto and Pressler, Mirjam (eds) (1997) *Anne Frank's Diary*. Harmondsworth: Penguin.

Fine, Anne (1989) *Goggle-Eyes*. Harmondsworth: Puffin.

Ingham, A. (ed.) (1988) *The Hubbub Machine*. A Collection of Children's Writing (unpublished).

Innocenti, Roberto (1985) *Rose Blanche*. London: Jonathan Cape.

Magee, Wes (1993) *Tyrannosaurus Rex* in Foster, J. and Paul, K. *Dinosaur Poems*. Oxford: Oxford University Press.

Magorian, Michelle (1981) *Goodnight Mister Tom*. Harmondsworth: Penguin.

Serraillier, Ian (1956) *The Silver Sword*. Harmondsworth: Penguin.

Thomas, Ruth (1987) *The Runaways*. A Beaver Book.

White, E.B. (1963) *Charlotte's Web*. Harmondsworth: Puffin Modern Classics.

Young, A. (1974) 'The Eagle', *Complete Poems*. London: Secker & Warburg.

Appendix

Correct version: Eagle poem

He hangs between his wings outspread
Level and still
And bends a narrow golden head,
Scanning the ground to kill,

Though as he sails and smoothly swings,
Round the hill-side,
He looks as though from his own wings
He hung down crucified.

Index